IBSEN AND SHAW

IBSEN AND SHAW

Keith M. May

MACMILLAN

First published 1985 by
THE MACMILLAN PRESS LTD
London and Basingstoke
Companies and representatives
throughout the world

Typeset by
Wessex Typesetters Ltd
Frome, Somerset

Printed in Hong Kong

British Library Cataloguing in Publication Data
May, Keith M.
Ibsen and Shaw.
1. Shaw, Bernard—Criticism and interpretation
2. Ibsen, Henrik—Criticism and interpretation
I. Title
822'.912   PT8895
ISBN 0–333–33425–6

To Pamela and Nadine

Contents

Preface

The emotional pattern of a writer's childhood emerges in his work, even when the work lacks autobiographical detail. Beforehand no one can predict the nature of the work yet afterwards the way towards it seems to have been inescapable. Nevertheless, the writer merely followed a certain path, or rather made a path of his own, with little deliberation and just the broadest sort of social constraint. We are so determined to find causes in human as in mechanical movements that we attribute a cause where there was only an event.

Ibsen and Shaw were both deeply humiliated as children and of course the quality of each series of hurts was at once unique and representative. Then, the responses made by these children were opposed, since Ibsen chose to endure reality while Shaw decided to alter it. For Ibsen the mortifications no doubt came with his father's financial downfall and later through the belief (probably mistaken) that he was illegitimate. Shaw, on the other hand, was disregarded by his mother, wrapped up in her singing ambitions, and by his futile father. Such circumstances are common enough and never of themselves foster genius. Just the same we have no need to fall back on the implausible, indeed superstitious notion of inborn genius, for the capacity of each man lay in the peculiar complex of his childhood experiences, a complex that included both his sense of a larger historical framework and his own reactions to specific blows.

It happened that Shaw's development eventually led, in 1890, to his lecturing to the Fabian Society on Ibsen and the following year publishing *The Quintessence of Ibsenism*. This excellent yet self-serving study led in turn to Shaw's own plays which are, time and again, optimistic, argumentative variations on tragic themes of Ibsen. The facts of this literary history are established in *Shaw and Ibsen* (ed. J. L. Wisenthal):[1] here we are engaged, first, in interpretation of Ibsen's plays, secondly in discussing various works of Shaw partly in the light of his use of Ibsen, and thirdly in

considering the rival social and ethical exhortations of modern
tragedy and modern comedy of ideas.

A proper story cannot exclude strands of each writer's upbringing, or, to be more exact, his self-determining responses to the
circumstances of his youth. We begin with the ways Ibsen
fashioned himself into a zealous but imperfect stoic, trying always
to remember the natural in contrast to the social order. There is no
pretence that we may enter Ibsen's childhood mind (no amateur
psychoanalysis), but there is an assumption that we can describe
the configuration of his youthful dreams.

KEITH M. MAY

Part I
Ibsen

1   Stoic Leanings

No biographer has been able to describe the quality of Ibsen's earliest years and Ibsen himself in his sole, brief memoir written in 1881 is not much help.[1] He recalls aspects of Skien, the town of his birth: the pillory beside the church, the cells including the 'lunatic box' for crazy people beneath the town hall, the 'booming whisper' of the weirs, the shriek and moan of hundreds of sawblades at work. He remembers just two personal incidents, the first the adventure of being taken by a nursemaid to the top of the church tower and the second his loss of a silver coin, a christening present. There is nothing really subjective in this memoir, only a negligible record of his feelings. As for the town at large, it was then, in the 1820s and 1830s, 'an unusually gay and sociable town'.

All the biographers assume that in their first nine years of marriage Henrik's parents were happy enough, for they prospered and were sociable. Knud Ibsen kept an expanding general store and a schnapps distillery; his wife, Marichen, was lively, beautiful and keen on the theatre. Then in 1834 Knud Ibsen's business began to collapse. About a year later the family was obliged to withdraw to their country house at Venstøp, two miles out of Skien, and the parents at least, if not the children, stayed gloomy for the rest of their lives. Knud became sardonic and bitter, Marichen grew chronically sad.

What should be emphasised is not that the natives of Telemark in which Skien lies are proud, inflexible, pugnacious, melancholic and wryly critical (to list the epithets commonly heaped upon these people)[2] but that the Ibsen family did not especially display such traits before their financial troubles. In any event, the whole town was 'gay and sociable', scarcely composed of depressive Telemarkians. Ibsen's own prickliness was unusual rather than typical and in fact his sister, Hedvig, drew a picture of him as distinctively sullen in childhood, easily annoyed but not fearsome.[3] It seems that the young Ibsen was pompous with boys but

3

pleasant with girls. He liked dancing and clothes, but was poor at
sport and hopeless at fighting.

Only such elementary observations of the boy Ibsen have been
recorded and it is certain that no observer could have grasped
much of his inner mental world. We have readier access to that
world than the contemporaries of his youth, because the plays
embody the peculiar patterns and values that silently began to
form in Skien. If we are unfamiliar with the stuff of daily life from
which those patterns and values were made, our perspective
emphasises the larger historical threads which affected Ibsen's
development. When he was born in 1828 Europe had lately been
at war. Up to 1814 Norway was a province of Denmark; then, after
a few weeks of independence, Norway was given by Britain and
Russia to the Swedes as a reward for Swedish defiance of
Napoleon. The Norwegians were powerless, a small, scattered
population to be disposed of for political purposes. They were
likewise culturally feeble, for almost the only valuable culture
hitherto produced by them consisted of the Icelandic Sagas of the
thirteenth century. There was no painting, music or theatre to
speak of. Norwegians read Danish novels or Danish translations
of English and French novels.

Nevertheless, the prosperity of Norway had been increasing for
well over a century, chiefly as a result of exporting timber to
England, and in Ibsen's boyhood the graph of what we now call
'gross national product' was rising again after the sharp fall of the
war years. By the mid-1820s profitable and lasting developments
were in hand, entrepreneurs (such as Knud Ibsen) were striding
ahead. Even the war debt of Norway, legally the responsibility of
the Swedes but never discharged by them, was diminishing
satisfactorily.

So far as the Ibsen family was concerned these historical facts
were important chiefly because the family declined at a time of
rising expectations. Of course, there were, as always, pace-setters
and the plodding majority, but it is wretched to plod along when
you know yourself to be a natural sprinter. Knud Ibsen fell behind
when Henrik was six and he never got back in the race. According
to Michael Meyer, Knud's income in the year 1833 was the
seventeenth highest in Skien.[4] He had long made it the main
business of his life to win; all other ways were either dull or
eccentric. He was addicted to showing off, in his palmy days often
though not exclusively by spending money, throwing parties,

giving extravagant presents. He was a small-town *arriviste*, taking a pretty, rich wife from a social position higher than his own, giving her six children (the eldest died in infancy), acquiring properties, holding banquets and drinking sprees, hunting wolves in the forests. In manner he was a wag and a raconteur. At home he was lord and master; his lovely wife was rather afraid of him. When the crash came all this altered, in the direction not of docility but of malice.

This sketch of Knud Ibsen is a simplification, of course. In fact it is derived partly from the few contemporary comments and partly from three inexact literary portraits: Jon Gynt in *Peer Gynt*, Daniel Hejre in *The League of Youth* and Old Ekdal in *The Wild Duck*. However, the important facts for us are those that made up not the muddled reality of Knud Ibsen but merely the impression he made upon his son. It is the principle of Knud Ibsen that matters, the life-principle he manifested to his observant and thoughtful child. That principle, I should say, was one of thwarted vitality.

Jon Gynt seems almost an irrelevance in *Peer Gynt*: he simply enters the conversation of his widow Aase, who remembers him as first a spendthrift, then a ruined man who 'took to the road with his pedlar's pack'.[5] When Ibsen wrote *Peer Gynt* in 1867 his father was still alive and, of course, had never taken to the road. The underlying function of Jon Gynt is to help to explain his family, the bitterness of Aase and the irresponsibility of Peer. Jon had let his wife down on many occasions and is remembered only with resentment. No doubt this is a reliable version of Marichen Ibsen's feelings towards her failure of a husband (who nevertheless unnerved her).

Daniel Hejre is a striking minor character in *The League of Youth*, clearly a product of observation rather than fantasy. Here, it seems likely, are some leading features of Knud Ibsen's manner to the life. Daniel Hejre defines himself himself in Act One as an 'ex-capitalist' but, most important, 'not bankrupt'. He blames his business failures on the 'sharp practice' of others. He is a great one for litigation and once even managed to subpoena himself – 'but I didn't turn up' (Act One).[6] His oft-repeated remark is 'Enough said', by which he implies (when the phrase is more than a verbal tic) that he is restrained by the law against slander. A memorable feature of Daniel Hejre is his candid spite, the chuckling zest with which he contemplates others' misfortunes.

Old Ekdal is an older, desolated man, a completely sympathetic version of Ibsen's father, as befits the spirit of *The Wild Duck*. Gone are Hejre's idiosyncracies of speech and pugnacity to be replaced by various marks of pathos. Ekdal was once a lieutenant, then he was in the timber trade. He went to prison for cutting down timber on government ground; now he shuffles about the town in his poor clothes and dirty red-brown wig, tippling, living in the past. In scornful reference to him Haakon Werle remarks that 'Some people in this world only need to get a couple of slugs in them and they go plunging right down to the depths and they never come up again'.[7] The past is kept alive in Old Ekdal (which is to say he is kept alive) by his garret of Christmas trees where he maintains and sometimes shoots his animals.

In composing these three portraits Ibsen presented different aspects of his father, so that in each instance he made a fresh character out of features displayed or plainly suggested by Knud Ibsen. The far more substantial and interesting figure of John Gabriel Borkman may also owe something to Ibsen's father as well as to the playwright himself. None of these fictional characters can be a faithful copy. The important common quality of the real man and the literary people is of vain energies: each scrabbles to keep his foothold on a mountainside. Even as a young child Ibsen must have clumsily grasped that his father maintained his very being by the devices and gestures of social failure. This is the paradox: Knud Ibsen absolutely could not succeed, yet if he had ceased openly and savagely to regret this fact he would presumably have disintegrated, for it was not in his nature either to feign satisfaction or to surrender his will. His fate was to be a railer against fate.

Such a posture is pathetic or farcical rather than tragic, but in this instance it sowed the seeds of a tragic outlook in the next generation. No matter how crafty or how striking in personality Knud Ibsen might have been (at least until late middle age), others made more money and seemed to manage their lives quite smoothly. Yet this sardonic father was more impressive to his little son than the mother. The picture we are bound to form of Marichen manifests at best the self-effacing sort of goodness that Ibsen was never to respect. At worst she ineffectually complained. A glowing report was given by Hedvig Ibsen who spoke of her mother as 'a quiet, lovable woman, the soul of the house, everything for her husband and children. She always sacrificed

herself; bitterness and fault-finding were unknown to her.'[8]
Alternatively perhaps she did in fact criticise her husband: as
Hans Heiberg puts it in his *Ibsen, A Portrait of the Artist*, 'Some say
that she occasionally rebuked her husband, others that she was
always quiet and subdued.'[9] The common impression is of
colourless endurance and that is roughly the kind of woman whom
Ibsen in his plays never presented in a favourable light.

Once again it is the principle that matters rather than the
complex reality, and the principle of Marichen Ibsen was
reproduced in Aurelia, the gentle wife (less impressive than her
destructive rival, Furia) in *Catiline*, in the weak Aase of *Peer Gynt*,
in Beata Rosmer of *Rosmersholm*, in Thea Elvsted of *Hedda Gabler*,
in Aline Solness of *The Master Builder* and (with the 'goodness'
quite soured into bitterness) in Gunhild Borkman of *John Gabriel
Borkman*. This kind of woman is nearly always offset against a
fascinatingly 'bad' woman (Furia, Rebecca West, Hedda Gabler,
Hilda Wangel), or sometimes against a genuinely supportive
woman such as Peer Gynt's Solveig. The character ultimately
based upon Marichen Ibsen suffers and may be dejectedly 'good',
but to no fruitful purpose.

What Ibsen absorbed from his failure of a father was a restless
spirit coupled with contempt for the orthodox ways of society. The
father's contempt was, of course, sour grapes but the son's was
wholehearted. The lesson imparted was, as so often happens,
transformed by the pupil. Knud Ibsen fretted, daydreamed, made
abortive plans. He was, like the fictional Daniel Hejre, profoundly
cynical, yet he wanted to be successful in the eyes of people he
despised. Henrik turned this pattern into his own need to struggle
and his recognition of the inevitability of failure in worldly terms.
The proud little boy tended to shy away from his father, though he
did not, as an alternative, pursue social success. To make up for
Knud Ibsen's blunderings by shrewdly accommodating himself
to society came to be seen by the child as near-impossible and
anyway base. For society was the enemy, consisting as it did of the
sort of liars and hypocrites whom his father's conversation,
whatever its faults, was peculiarly apt to show up. To the child as
to the father striving of some kind was good, while society – any
society – was essentially a conspiracy. One might stand apart by
being either clownish or noble and Ibsen had no liking for vulgar
comedy. So the son spurned his father's comic pathos and opted
instead for the aristocratic spirit of tragedy.

When the family business failed Ibsen shut himself off from his contemporaries. He was rigid with anger and shame. He was better than the farm boys around Venstøp and bribed them not to walk to school with him.[10] Why did he think he was superior? It cannot have been that he knew he was cleverer than they but that he transmuted his parents' social pretensions into a higher ideal. Young Ibsen absorbed the family claims to superiority and determined to justify them in his own person. He would occupy by force of will that higher plane towards which his father and mother pathetically groped. In fact Knud Ibsen was not fastidious, Marichen was dull and Henrik's brothers and sister quickly threw in their lot with their neighbours. Henrik was isolated, the one member of the family who saw life, indeed *welcomed* life, as a rugged journey. In middle age Ibsen spoke admiringly of 'nobility' and defined this quality as follows:

> Of course I am not thinking of nobility of birth, nor of money, nor a nobility of learning, nor even of ability or talent. What I am thinking of is a nobility of character, of mind and will. That alone can liberate us.[11]

This is the developed form of the value that the little boy conjured out of his father's and mother's commonplace snobberies. He turned their base metal into gold, but we must recognize that the crude bourgeois exertion of the Ibsen parents was the indispensable first element. Further, the son performed this alchemy by choosing to esteem what his parents resentfully endured: the life-pattern of tragic peripeteia.

At what age could the young Ibsen have come to invest his daydreams with the awkwardnesses and harshnesses of real life? He was an unsociable boy though possibly his private world was a field more of observation than of escapist fantasy. Or, if you will, there entered the boy's designs a sense that one might master displeasing elements by faithfully acknowledging them, for there is a kind of liberation in facing facts. Certainly this choleric individual cannot have been a 'detached' observer but one whose sympathies had far less than the usual tendency to warp the observable realities. He must early have formed the habit of seeing with energy,[12] yet with respect for whatever was before his eyes – the real gesture and what it signified.

One especially ugly prospect for Ibsen concerned his own

legitimacy: it is possible that he either was or supposed himself to be the natural son of a certain Tormod Knudsen who was briefly and perhaps carnally acquainted with Marichen just *after* she became engaged to Knud Ibsen. Most modern commentators do not believe this tale but they acknowledge that it was widely believed in Skien when Henrik was a boy. Therefore Ibsen had to face not only his father's business failure but also this other, especially alienating rumour. Whether or not Ibsen personally supposed himself to be illegitimate he knew how it felt to be regarded as such. In a sense, then, he was in his family but not irrevocably of it. He was suspended in the little sphere of Skien and suspended in the tinier sphere of his own family.

Ibsen felt isolated in his youth: we know this not from any personal confession but as a straightforward deduction from the plays. To picture the boy outwardly is easy and useful in a small way. We naturally think of the celebrated loft at Venstøp (later to become the garret of *The Wild Duck*) where Ibsen played and discovered the book, *Harrison's History of London* with its 'horrid' cover-painting of Death carrying an hour-glass and its illustrations of churches, castles, streets and shops. He painted and read; he loved clothes and dressing up; he arranged painted wooden figures as though in a puppet theatre; he liked sometimes to involve people in *tableaux vivants*; he was a loner without one personal pal. What suggests itself from our scanty knowledge of these years is less a tendency to hide (the faint beginnings of psychosis) than a watchful, touchy pride. This does not mean that he was necessarily 'strong' in the common meaning of that word; on the contrary he might often have been apt to run away. As an adult he sometimes needed to be toughened up by his wife. Nevertheless, we can be sure that he was never 'weak' in the usual manner of readily accepting the prevailing wisdom. Already in this morose childhood there began (for such processes have precise beginnings) the rejection of the majority view. 'Democracy' in this sense, young Ibsen evidently decided, is merely another sham, a set of devices for some people to get their own way and for others to be cowards.

Clearly he was estranged from the happenings around him and often contemptuous of them, because they didn't make sense. For what other reason could he have observed so minutely, like an explorer in a strange land? People gesticulated, disguised their motives, played absurd social games and all the time (if 'innocently') exercised their wills to power. Life seemed to be intensely and pointlessly competitive. But the child Ibsen did not feel a pure moral revulsion against all this in a Christlike manner. What he admired, or what he set up against the littleness of contemporary doings, was a sort of heroism which seemed to belong to the past and was liable to be defeated. Moreover, the heroism was itself flawed, but at least it aimed high and was intolerant of the cracks in its own structure. Ibsen preferred nobility of character to what is commonly regarded as goodness and must have acquired during childhood that condition of his which Camus has described as 'bitter aristocracy'.[13]

Then at fifteen this bitter (and impoverished) aristocrat left school and went to work as an apothecary's assistant in Grimstad, a hundred miles south of Skien. Local youngsters jeered at him as he left home so that it was a typical Ibsen departure, farcical like Peer Gynt's scampering away from his Gudbrandsdal village and awful like Brand's being spurned by the townsfolk whom he has tried to lead. In fact Ibsen now left home for good, because after Grimstad he went on to become briefly a student in Christiania, then a poorly paid writer for the National Theatre in Bergen, and after 1864 a voluntary exile for a third of his life, chiefly in Germany and Italy. He kept away from Norway for long enough, but he abandoned for ever (apart from one short dutiful visit) his uncomprehending kindred. He left them, he said, because they didn't understand him.

> Do you know that I have entirely separated myself for ever from my own parents, from my whole family, because being only half understood was unendurable to me.[14]

This was written as part of a vehement letter to Bjørnstjerne Bjørnson in 1867 when Ibsen's fame was growing. No doubt the remark gives the genuine reason why Ibsen exiled himself. In the 1860s he began to communicate with other European minds by ever more discerning means, but in the early Grimstad years he was quite as isolated as he had been at home. He was an odd, full-bearded little fellow who materialised at the apothecary's, served a customer and vanished again into his hidy-hole. He was conspicuously shabby (though he had the secret tastes of a dandy) and at the outset friendless. At eighteen he conceived a child with one of the servants in the house, Else Sofie Jensdatter, whom he had to provide with paternity costs for the next fourteen years. But while humiliations of one sort or another still took place, there were also encouraging developments. He discovered various writers, Norwegian and foreign (notably Oehenschläger, Wergeland, Kierkegaard, Voltaire, Scott and Dickens) and built up a small circle of young men with whom he could discuss radical ideas.

Radicalism and literary leanings grew together in Ibsen, a familiar intertwining, but for this young writer entry into the public arena was significant and idiosyncratic. Beforehand he wrote poetry which was clever enough but undistinguished. Sometimes it was satirical, sometimes amatory, sometimes politically rebellious. Also at this time he started a novella. But then he got the idea for the verse–play, *Catiline*, which no one else could possibly have written. Various threads combined in the following way. Ibsen was trying to matriculate and for that purpose had to master (in the dead of night, after apothecary work) some Sallust and Cicero. So he encountered the deeds of Catiline as interpreted by that conspirator's enemies. He concluded first, that Catiline had almost certainly been misrepresented by the historians and secondly that he, Ibsen, an exceedingly poor worker-student, had something in common with the rebellious Roman nobleman. In the preface to the second (1875) edition of the play Ibsen explains the first notion as follows:

> As you will see when you read it, I did not at that time share the view of the two Roman authors in regard to Catiline's character and conduct, and I am still inclined to believe that there must have been something great and significant about a man whom Cicero, that indefatigable spokesman of the majority, was careful not to tackle until circumstances had so changed that there was no longer any danger in attacking him. It should also be borne in mind that there are few personages in history whose posthumous reputation has been so completely in the hands of their enemies as Catiline's has been.[15]

That is clear and interesting enough. However, what needs to be deduced from a reading of the play (for Ibsen naturally never mentioned the matter) is the yet more interesting factor of his self-identification with Catiline. No one simply reading the historians would turn Catiline's rebellion into a tragic love story,

but that is what Ibsen did. He was scarcely concerned with the
Roman politics, though he was profoundly concerned with a
certain spiritual dilemma best represented as the opposing
attractions of two women. The hero of this play (a man at odds
with the powerful of Rome as Ibsen in his republican broodings
was at odds with the grandees not only of Norway but of Europe)
is torn between two loves, as if Shakespeare's or Plutarch's Mark
Antony were to waver between his decent Octavia and the gipsy
Cleopatra.[16] Ibsen's Catiline is tempted away from Aurelia, his
loyal wife, by the vestal Furia and urged into his suicidal plot
against the senate. He is far from innocent because Furia,
libidinous, murderous and somehow admirable, does this in
revenge for the suicide of her sister who was seduced by Catiline.
Thus Ibsen began his career of making a tragical–heroic conjunction of guilt, striving, Eros and death.

This play was written late in 1849, that is in the year following
the year of European revolutions by which Ibsen had been stirred
to the writing of republican verse. Curiously though, Ibsen's play
says next to nothing about toppling the pillars of tyranny (to
adapt a phrase from his poem, 'To Hungary') but is about the
struggle for a nobleman's soul. The conspiracy as such is less
interesting by far than Brutus' and Cassius' conspiracy in *Julius
Caesar*. Things are the wrong way round, for when Ibsen writes his
supposedly introspective lyric verse he tells us little about his
thoughts, but when he writes the play his deepest preoccupations
are revealed. He is himself in the figure of a patrician before the
birth of Christ, a man whom almost everyone then supposed to
have been a desperado. Young Ibsen is essentially his own
Catiline because both are high, remarkable men seen as low by
their contemporaries, because both are divided between safety
and criminal adventure and because Ibsen too is guilty of
something or other – perhaps his illegitimate son, perhaps his own
supposed illegitimacy, possibly a complex of sinful doings for
which Catiline's seduction of the innocent sister can stand as
emblem.

For Ibsen, as distinct from Catiline, 'criminal adventure' will
come to mean soul-adventure, a series of explorations not
criminal at all yet inviting opprobrium almost as if they were.
Despite his fears he will regularly put up challenges to the
latter-day Ciceros, to social norms, to majority opinion, indeed to
opposing species of group belief, even when one of the beliefs is

revolutionary. He is naturally critical of conservatives but he is critical of liberals and radicals too, so that while he might in verse and private letters celebrate a revolt (the Magyar uprising, for example), when he writes a play, that is, a mimesis of character and action, any disturbance he depicts must have its debased components and for some of the best will end in tragedy. The last state will rarely be better than the first, but someone will have completed a destiny which, though systematically robbed of its romantic consolations, is the justification of the entire story.

But of course Ibsen's career did not advance steadily after *Catiline* and that first play was in fact a failure. For a long time neither his personal voice nor his reputation developed vigorously and it was only in the sixties that the idiosyncratically impressive *Love's Comedy* was followed by the stylistic novelties and modern characterisation of *The Pretenders* to be followed in turn by the thorough individuality and triumph of *Brand*. Before that sequence, in the fifties, the growth of Ibsen's talent was fitful because he had not found himself. Presumably he failed to appreciate the original elements in *Catiline*; certainly no one else appreciated them. What he possessed was a capacity to draw into one design accurately realised features of the external world and features which in the twentieth century everyone, following Freud, would chatter about as surface indications of the id. This second, 'deeper' category emerged first, for example in the character of Furia (quite unlike anyone Ibsen could have met in life or in books), and it was fidelity to the everyday world that would take him a long time to reproduce. That is not surprising, since apart from the rarity of Ibsen's skill as an observer, no one in Norway or even in sophisticated European centres then wanted dramatic realism.

Ibsen's later accomplishment was the combination of these two forms of awareness, the looking outwards like a representational painter and the looking inwards like a prophet. In twentieth-century language Ibsen had a highly efficient ego (perception of external reality) coupled with unusual willingness to acknowledge the symbols of the id. His father's very cynicism probably contributed to the first of these factors, since it rammed home to the acute little boy, day in day out, that if you want to understand someone's motives you interpret rather than merely assimilate his words. You look for self-interest, equivocation, ambivalence, will to power. Then, in the Ibsen household nothing

was construed moralistically without promptly being debunked
by the father. Meanwhile the mother wanly or bitterly endured
and both parents gave the impression that little mattered so much
as social success. Subject to these influences Ibsen unwittingly
'chose' to try to make his success partly out of exposing
falsehoods.

He also yearned for a sort of outlaw feminine beauty that should
accompany him – indeed lead him – in his spiritual adventures.
He wanted, in other words, a woman the opposite of his mother
and more akin, in one respect though probably not in others, to
the woman of epic inclinations, Suzannah Thoresen, whom he
married.[17] Nevertheless, the image that in different forms moves
through so many of his plays (from Furia and Lady Inger to Hilda
Wangel and Irene) is destructive, not succouring like Suzannah.
At a fairly obvious level the figure must have emboldened Ibsen as
she sometimes emboldens the hero of the play. Her own boldness
is erotic but it is more than erotic, for it offers fulfilment and death.
To give a coherent explanation of something fundamentally
irrational, we might start by saying that Ibsen saw no means of
changing the pettiness and muddle of life: these qualities help to
comprise the enemy forces against which the hero must always
fight, however vainly in a practical sense. The hero's triumph in
its completest form lies in a certain kind of death, sometimes
willed, never quite accidental. The woman leads him on to that
consummation and is right to do so. She is also right to despise
social conventions. However, she is deadly and by ordinary
standards not admirable at all. As a matter of fact she has some
commonplace faults. To add to her imperfections she is not even
sure of herself, but merely in the final analysis less given to a
standard of safety and conformity than to a fatally higher
standard.

She is plainly an image from Ibsen's mind, distinguished from
his mother because she beckons him on to his own rather than a
market-place success. She maintains his integrity whereas his
mother would have ruined it. She reminds Ibsen that transcend-
ing all this mere verisimilitude of dialogue and conduct is the
truth that man is part of nature, so that his life cannot be
controlled, and fittingly, not lamentably, must come to an end. In
short she is a figure of the true stoic outlook and a rebuff to the
mother who took the side of society rather than that of her ardent
son.

2 The Poet-Dramatist: *Catiline* to *Peer Gynt*

It is unlikely that anyone now comes to Ibsen's earliest plays 'in the expectation' – to use the words of one of their latest English editors – 'of finding unregarded masterpieces of world literature'.[1] If anything, the problem is the opposite, for many modern critics too readily dismiss the plays before *Brand*, or at least before *Love's Comedy*, as boring and unworthy. No doubt a performance today, outside Norway, of any of the works written before 1860 could scarcely smooth away Ibsen's crudities, but it would be to a minority, a curio, an oddly interesting experience. Such a minority need not be entirely made up of Ibsen enthusiasts or students of Norwegian history and culture, but might include individuals for whom Ibsen's stance, despite its gaucherie, remains more or less acceptable. For the most part, in writing these immature works Ibsen was thinking against the grain of contemporary Norwegian culture while clumsily trying to co-operate with it. Naturally he was unsure of himself, confused, sometimes even dishonest. Yet the plays remain questioning enough to satisfy a sceptic of our day, provided the sceptic has not just fallen into either a derisive or a limply 'democratic' posture. Ibsen's common procedure was to measure his own desires by the opposite standards, or at all events to set two ways of life against each other. But the conflicts are less dramatic devices than outpourings of the author's nature. More often than not, what Ibsen shows, in terms of broad methods rather than of skill and refinement, is how to anatomise human conduct without drifting towards nihilism.

Catiline, first written in 1850 then revised in 1875, is against fashionable assumptions, office-holders, venerated spokesmen, respectability itself. As we noted earlier,[2] Ibsen worked away at his matriculation studies, but was less interested in the Latin constructions than in his own antagonism towards those who seek 'reasonable formulae', who speak of 'balanced views' and 'the good of the state'. Alternatively it would be fair to say that he relished the opposition between his own seriousness and the bad faith he detected in people who give priority to harmony, power or pleasure. Of course, the relishing must itself have been a sort of pleasure, but a bitter-sweet sort.

Certainly *Catiline* contains many beginner's shortcomings. Catiline's opening soliloquy, for instance, is the kind of device which Ibsen's later, more realistic methods rendered obsolete, even for poetic dramatists. Ibsen here, at the beginning of the play, tries to make poetry out of his hero's self-division. (It is worth remarking that Catiline, no longer a young man, is compounded at this point out of young Ibsen's social perplexity, as he wonders if his 'dreams of night-time, and figments born of solitude' are necessarily less real than his spiritually squalid environment.) There are feeble pieces of dialogue: 'Behold our journey's end,' cries Ambiorix, an Allobrogian envoy, gesturing in Act One towards the backcloth of Roman grandeur. 'We have deserved his scorn', remark a group of conspirators in unison (Act Two), having feared to stab their leader Catiline, to death. Settings succeed one another in an inconvenient manner, as a 'road near Rome' gives way to a 'colonnade in Rome', to be replaced in turn by the 'temple of Vesta'. In the play as a whole there is too little colloquialism, though the opening of the second act is notably natural and fragmented. The conclusion, clearly meant to be so grand, is operatically absurd.

For all such weaknesses, the chief conception of the play and much of its detail remain stimulating enough. Catiline's insight (a representation of Ibsen's view of contemporary Norway and some central European countries) is that Rome is essentially corrupt since it offers no scope for the noble temperament. His fellow-conspirators are self-seeking and trivial, morally indistinguishable from the established figures whom they hope to bring down. Catiline knows this; he is aware of his own isolation. Lentulus, one of the gang, briefly has high hopes of the leadership, but is rejected in favour of Catiline and so sinks into impotent vengefulness. Curius, Catiline's foster-son, is tempted into treachery towards his leader, but repents and begs unavailingly to be killed.

Why is the hero superior to other characters, not excluding Aurelia, his loyal wife? After all, he is a seducer and is ready, even eager for widespread slaughter to oust a merely corrupt (not tyrannical) regime. Then, he kills his wife at the instigation of the temptress Furia. In fact Catiline is valued for his splendour of soul and complete absence of pettiness. He is nearer to Aristotle's 'magnanimous man' than to the good man of Christianity.[3] There is no one in Shakespeare much like him, though he is in some degree a mixture of Brutus and Coriolanus: ambitious in the high Roman manner, concerned for the good of the state, patrician by nature as well as birth, a hater of deceit. Catiline wants fame, even or especially of the bloody sort won by Sulla (whose unnamed phantom indeed appears in Act Three to deliver a riddling prophecy). He is killed by the shade of Furia, though his soul is destined, with Aurelia's, for Elysium. Just before his death Catiline formulates Ibsen's meaning:

> Is life then not an unabating struggle between hostile forces in the soul? And in this struggle lies the soul's true life.[4]

One of the hostile forces in Ibsen's own soul is figured in Furia. She, a vestal immured in the course of the play because the flame of Vesta is extinguished during her spell of guardianship, returns after death to kill Catiline and, so she intends, take him with her to Tartarus. Aurelia corresponds to the opposite, benign force. But Catiline's progress is a series of dilemmas. Ibsen had the tyro's nerve to allow full sway to his own confusions, not seeking to bring them to a premature or dramatically expedient equilibrium. Already in *Catiline*, despite its peaceful ending, he showed a preference for vigour over peace, and possibly a suspicion that the two will always be incompatible.

This is exactly the attitude which his second play, *The Burial Mound*, was apparently written to disavow. To be precise, Ibsen questions the value of martial vigour and finally seems to substitute for it (the sentiment is unclear) a kind of intellectual or spiritual striving. But the bulk of the play extols serenity, understood as the reward of virtue, and the substitution is made only in the concluding lines:

> The North shall also rise from out the tomb
> To purer strife on silver seas of thought![5]

In fact there are two distinct versions of *The Burial Mound*, the first written in Grimstad and Christiania in 1848–50 and the second written in Bergen, presumably late in 1853. These plays differ a great deal, but not conspicuously in their teachings. I think we should accept that for once in a career rightly celebrated for its honesty Ibsen was here either a conscious hypocrite or a self-deceiver. Because he was struggling to get a play produced and favourably noticed he affected a clear preference for benevolent Christianity over the code of the Vikings. Yet an important strand of his career can be grasped as an exploration of what he regarded as the error in that stark priority. Of course, Christian teachings and stories of the Vikings were the forms in which Ibsen first encountered a rivalry of spirit which as a rule he did not see in such specific terms. More broadly, he continued to be concerned on the one hand with a way of life that is gentle and altruistic and on the other hand a way that is proud and aspiring. Roughly speaking these are the codes between which he felt it to be intellectually and emotionally dishonest to make a clear-cut choice.

In the first form of *The Burial Mound* Gandalf, a Viking chief, arrives in Normandy with a bloodthirsty band intent on ravaging the district in which he supposes his father to have been killed. He meets and is captivated by Blanka, a Christian maiden who has been raised in piety and charity by her foster-father, Bernhard. It is true that Blanka and Bernhard love tales of icy northern lands, but their final allegiance is given to peace and southern sunlight. Bernhard, however, turns out to be Gandalf's father who survived the earlier foray and has long been reformed by Christian doctrine. In the arguments between the Saga exponents of the North (Scandinavia) and the Christians of the South (Normandy) the latter are far more persuasive. It seems certain that Ibsen, disturbed by the failure of *Catiline*, decided to write a play which should be openly about Norway (not covertly so in the manner of its predecessor) and should delight in Saga savageries while causing them to be defeated by gentle virtues. So he hoped to strike a popular chord.

Ibsen was thus engaged in a delicate balancing act: he needed to include in his play a fair amount of admiration for blue-eyed, golden-haired heroes while vanquishing a representative of the breed by the sweetness of Blanka. His heroine had to be ambivalent, appealing both to Norwegians' pride in their ancient forbears and to modern churchgoing sentiments. He succeeded moderately well, since the play was performed to decent applause on three occasions in the autumn of 1850. Ibsen had made his début, though with a play that falsified his own values.

However, some members of the audience felt the Vikings to be undervalued. Ibsen was pandering, they thought, to the decadent South. Presumably it was this criticism that Ibsen hoped to silence when he wrote the second version of the play. Now the South is Sicily instead of Normandy, and Blanka is emphatically dissatisfied with Sicilian torpor, restless for Scandinavian freshness. For all her Christianity she dreams of a Norse hero, and obtains such a one in the person of Gandalf. Perhaps this second attempt edges a little nearer than the first to recommending what the young Ibsen genuinely desired – a life of energetic, adventurous purity – though most of the signs in his early career suggest that he already believed such a way to be unattainable.

Normally we can see Ibsen's mind developing. He was the reverse of the kind of writer who starts out brilliant and complete, then either continues on a high plateau or declines as he grows older. Apart from the fitful excellencies of *Catiline*, Ibsen began rather feebly and improved (if not quite steadily) until about the early nineties, even perhaps to the very end of his career. What we can now see in the immature plays are elements of Ibsen's peculiar attitudes in the process of growing, though partly hidden by ineptitudes and by lurches towards some conventional scheme.

So far we have observed the admiring Ibsen and the solemn critic, but we have not met the satirist. Yet it is the combination of these three elements (at least) which makes up the mature playwright. Later on, a principal distinction of Ibsen will be his manner of building into a play whose impetus is aspiring, yearning, a number of realistic impediments. These naturally destroy whatever was pretentious in the forward movement; they may halt the movement itself, but they do not discredit the aspiration. Ibsen specialises not in truth and falsity, but in degrees of untruth: his favoured characters came to live, or sometimes to die, with fewer lies than they entertained at the outset.

Realistic observation begins in the early and regrettably feeble satires. *Norma, Or A Politician's Love* is the earliest and feeblest. It is an undergraduate squib which took its rise from Bellini's opera, *Norma*. Ibsen saw the opera in May 1851 when he was attending the University of Christiania and a few weeks later his *Norma* was published in the student journal, 'Andhrimner'. It was never meant to be staged and it really could not be.

What is of some interest for us is Ibsen's irreverence, not because it is typical of the student generation but for the quite different reason that he never outgrew it. Ibsen did not become 'soberly mature' in the usual misleading sense of entering into some compact of adult lies. As a boy he developed his cartoonist's eye for defects not solely out of malice but because his nature prevented him from simply joining the throng. (More often than not his adult letters are shrewd and commonsensical, distinguished by the absence not only of platitudes but also, paradoxically, of distinguishing tricks or personality.)

The target of the satire in *Norma* is the Storthing, which, Ibsen asserts in his prologue, consists merely of a talented crowd of actors. In the playlet the entire Norwegian opposition party is fused into the character of Norma, a mother past her youthful attractions, and the government is represented by Adalgisa, Norma's unreliable 'good friend' and rival. These two are both loved by Severus, to be played preferably by a 'liberal'. Ibsen's chief point, of course, is that government and opposition are more cattily friendly than seriously at odds and both are susceptible to a liberal's advances.

Norma is of no importance except as a stop along Ibsen's lonely route. It merely helps to illuminate him. He was trying to solve a number of problems, personal, dramatic and more generally cultural. Eventually Ibsen would realise that his way ahead would include a fusing of his satirical bent, his capacity for prosaic observation and his longing for tragic grandeur. Then, Ibsen's more personal difficulty was that he longed to be not only a successful but a great dramatist, yet to be great he needed to attack the very sentiments upon which success might rest.[6] His opinion of contemporary Norwegian culture was that it was largely a sham. He could not adopt what we may as well call a 'Shakespearean' procedure, in other words a way of being psychologically realistic and popularly nationalistic at the same time, because Norwegian nationalism, unlike Elizabethan, was not allied to burgeoning political power.

It might be that the most fitting approach first occurred to him in 1852, as a result of reading *Das moderne Drama* by Herman Hettner. Michael Meyer believes that this work influenced Ibsen, at least to the extent of clarifying and fortifying his own tentative notions.[7] Two of Hettner's arguments were that historical drama should be of continuing psychological relevance and that fairy-tale comedy, *Märchenlustspiel*, is at its best when it is used to expose falsehoods in the real world. Ibsen's plays down to *The Pretenders* follow one or the other of these signposts.

The second play Ibsen had produced, *St John's Night*, belongs to the kind of *Märchenlustspiel*. Indeed Ibsen's whole point is that the supernatural happenings in the play awaken the chief partici-pants to their everyday selves and genuine feelings. We can see Ibsen straining to match his talents both to Hettner's criterion and to popular taste. How he must have leaped at the chance to write a play which should be as Norwegian as the veriest patriot might wish, but at the same time include a satirical portrait of a folklore enthusiast and show up some fashionably 'patriotic' fallacies. He presumably hoped that *St John's Night* would strike the audience as both charming and shrewd, a bewitching release from common forms of bewitchment.

On her estate in Telemark lives Mrs Berg a widow, together with her step-daughter Anne, and her late husband's father Berg. Jørgen Kuist, Mrs Berg's son, is a student expected home from university along with a certain Johannes Birk to whom Juliane is discreetly and unenthusiastically engaged. When the two students arrive they bring with them a third young man called Julian Poulsen, an affected literary critic, sombre poet and founder of the Society for the Restitution of Old Norse. It should be noted here that Anne is supposed by her family to be rather odd and getting worse, though she is simply in touch with a larger, more natural reality than the conventional social world.

The attractions of St John's Night, or Midsummer Night, used to consist of a few hours of merrymaking, drinking, flirting, dancing around a bonfire; but certain superstitions enhanced the occasion by including magical encounters and transformations. What happens in this play is that a goblin who lives in Mrs Berg's loft and whom only Anne can see, mischievously drugs the festive punch with the sap of a common, wayside flower. Whoever tastes the punch, the goblin tells the audience, 'will lose his eye for outward show' (Act One, Scene 10). The four young people, Anne, Juliane, Johannes Birk and Julian Poulsen, each have a drink before proceeding up Midsummer Hill where the jollifica-tions are in progress. A scene of dancing and puzzling ceremony is

all the prosaic Poulsen and Juliane manage to observe, while the
genuinely imaginative Anne and Birk see into the hill itself, where
a great hall, 'shining like gold in the moonlight' (Act Two, Scene
5), is occupied by the mountain king with his elves and fairies. So
as a result of perceiving appropriate scenes on Midsummer Hill
each character also glimpses a true self and a suitable mate. But
the following morning no one has much grasp of the meaning of
these events. Towards the end of the third act they all stumble into
a clear, daytime recognition of what the previous night revealed
and end with congenial partners.

The play is rather cumbersome, in other words the structural
opposite of Ibsen's mature works. It was hissed by the first-night
audience, though probably for what we would regard as the
wrong reasons, and on the second night the Bergen theatre was
half empty. In later life Ibsen more or less disowned it.
Nevertheless, it is a characteristic and therefore interesting
conception. Even then, as a young man, Ibsen was fascinated by
the distinction between the natural self and the network of
mannerisms and daydreams which conceal it. Already, in a fairly
light-hearted play, he was telling his fellow-countrymen, each one
individually, to cast off any outer form borrowed from fashionable
stock.

In writing *St John's Night* Ibsen used or perhaps exploited the
genre of *Märchenlustspiel* and of course he was never interested in
fairy tales as such. Similarly, his next work *Lady Inger*, is ostensibly
a history play but is not fundamentally concerned with history.
There was a Lady Inger who lived at Østeraad on the Trondheim
Fjord in the early sixteenth century, but the nature of Ibsen's
heroine and many events of the play were unwittingly or
shamelessly invented. Since the 1880s critics have recognised the
documentary inaccuracies of the play but it is still common to
assume that Ibsen's motives were nationalistic.[8] The belief is that
Ibsen was chiefly concerned to illustrate the plight of Norway in
ths 1850s by reference to the Norway of 1528, when the Danes
were most effectively and insolently in command of the northern
country. But it is important to recognise that Ibsen, however
keenly he may have wished to right social or national wrongs,
valued tragic action above reform. The implication of his plays is
that injustice (among other factors) exists for the sake of noble
enterprise, or generally as a measure of the soul's worth.

The value of the soul stayed within his sights, more sharply defined after middle age, so that his satire (which is not particularly amusing) and his tragedy have similar purposes. The tragic in Ibsen is never the wretched; there is little lamentation. Nor is it mainly a matter of individuals falling foul of local conditions, for such conditions are only channels of constant human tendencies. That is why the contrast mentioned by George Steiner in the following remarks is misleading.

> More pliant divorce laws could not alter the fate of Agamemnon; social psychiatry is no answer to *Oedipus*. But saner economic relations or better plumbing can resolve some of the grave crises in Ibsen.[9]

The truth is that while 'better plumbing', for example, would remove the specific cause of the crisis in *An Enemy of the People*, a similar sort of crisis showing up human strengths and weaknesses constantly arises in society. To Ibsen, almost as to Aeschylus and Sophocles, tragedy was, first, the actual condition of man's life and secondly a branch of literature.

Nevertheless, it is true that Østeraad Hall exhibits the historical situation of the early sixteenth century, as Ibsen saw it: the weapons are rusting, need furbishing and even then will be fit only to hang decoratively in the Great Hall. Lady Inger herself, now a pale forty-five year old, a figure in black, 'like a ghost at midnight' (Act One, Scene 2), at fifteen made a vow that she would struggle for Norway's cause against Denmark. For ten years she did so, while more prudent women contemporaries married and began to raise families. Then she met Sten Sture, a Swedish ally of the Norwegians, by whom she had a son, but soon afterwards Sture returned to his native country, taking the baby with him. There he married, produced another son and shortly died. Later Inger married the Lord Steward, Henrik Gyldenløve, and in the course of time gave birth to three daughters. The first, Merete, grew up to marry a Danish knight and now lives prosperously though unhappily in Bergen. The second, Lucia, died of a broken heart, because her mother would not consent to her marrying a Dane by whom she had been seduced. The third daughter, Eline, is as openly nationalistic as her mother was a generation earlier. Now Lady Inger is a widow, still hostile to Denmark, but fewer and fewer Norwegians, nobles and peasants alike, any longer look to her for insurrectionary leadership. No one knows that her ardour has long been constrained by fears of what might otherwise happen to her son growing up in Sweden.

Even this rather complicated account of events antecedent to the play is a simplification. The plot itself is scarcely straightforward and, as Georg Brandes was one of the first to point out (in 1898), is even somewhat ridiculous.

> Eline Gyldenløve, for instance [he writes], is fully acquainted with the circumstances of her dead sister's [Lucia's] fate, yet has no idea of the name of the man who wrought her destruction, and is almost to the last unaware that it was Nils Lykke, the man she loves.[10]

There is much more of this kind of thing from the pen of Brandes (who managed to be both a friend and a candid critic of Ibsen), yet it seems possible that the logical absurdities to which Brandes draws attention have the strange, Ibsenist quality of receding, as it were, into the dramatic background. They are camouflaged by the vigour and suspense of the play. (A study of the discrepancies in Ibsen's better-known plays is provided by Ronald Gray in his *Ibsen: A Dissenting View*. Gray seems to assume that obtuse sycophancy has helped to prevent generations of theatregoers from noticing these matters, but in my view Ibsen was, increasingly, a master of camouflage who often calculated the dramatic value of his technical 'errors'.)[11]

Just the same, the narrative of Lady Inger is far too complex. It would have better suited Ibsen to disentangle a few simple threads from the muddle of history: Lady Inger's eldest daughter, for instance, is superfluous for the purpose of the play. Ibsen had not yet learned how to present just the degree of complexity that combines verisimilitude with something approaching the spirit of Greek tragedy. That is not surprising, since he was gradually inventing such a remarkable combination and remains to this day its only wholehearted and successful practitioner. Here as a minor feature, not very important in itself, he contrived a strict version of the unities, as in the course of a few hours Østeraad Hall is furtively visited by the three persons whose stratagems together with Lady Inger's errors complete her downfall. Olaf Skaktavl is the true patriot, an outlawed Norwegian nobleman, Nils Lykke is Lucia's seducer and Nils Stenson is Lady Inger's son by Sten Sture. She hopes that Lykke, a handsome scoundrel, will fall in love with Eline, so that Eline on learning his identity, will reject him. In fact Eline betrothes herself to Nils Lykke and is distraught when she learns who he is. Moreover, Lady Inger, assuming Nils Stenson to be Sture's second (wholly Swedish) son rather than her own illegitimate child, has him killed by Skaktavl. In the end, therefore, Lady Inger has ruined her life, because she is responsible for the murder of her son as well as the death of one of her three daughters and the utter wretchedness of the other two. Nor has she aided the Norwegian cause one jot and asks only for 'a grave beside my child' (Act Five, Scene 11).

Lady Inger was another failure, being performed only twice in 1855. What did the Bergen audience find so offensive or dreary about the play? The historical inaccuracies and the improbabilities would have meant little to them, the complications of plot are not daunting, so presumably the play failed precisely on account of its chief strength, the nature of the heroine. Like Catiline she is a 'great soul' who is scarcely virtuous in any ordinary sense. I have in mind a remark of La Rochefoucauld: 'Great souls are not those with fewer passions and more virtues than the ordinary run, but simply those with a stronger sense of purpose.'[12] This aphorism, not especially acute in itself, happens to apply to Inger Gyldenløve. Her genuine design is to raise up a free Norway; in other words, she desires this as an end in itself, not as a roundabout means to her personal happiness. The purpose is *beyond* her feelings. But she has not fewer passions than other people; she certainly has no more virtues than common souls. Indeed, her self-transcending plans are confounded at every point by the self-induced problems of her private life. That is the source of the tension which gives the play its quality and, no doubt, spoiled it in the eyes of contemporaries. Ibsen still needed to *impose* this kind of heroine (or, less commonly, hero) upon theatregoers: in the end he was so successful that the type became not merely acceptable but venerated.

Ibsen's next play, *The Feast at Solhoug* (first performed in 1856), is a weaker work by far but was favourably received, partly perhaps because conventional morality subdues what must have been the vigour of Ibsen's original conception of Margit the heroine. She is miserably married to Bengt Gauteson, Master of Solhoug, and the action takes place on the day of their third wedding anniversary (the feast in question). She is twenty-three, he an older man, weak and crass. As a teenager Margit loved her cousin, Gudmund Alfson, but he was a poor young poet and went away to better himself. The beautiful Margit was then besieged by suitors and eventually agreed to marry Bengt. On this very anniversary Gudmund returns, but he is now a fugitive on the run. He quickly falls in love with Margit's younger and simpler sister, Signe. (Ibsen refers to Signe in a letter to the actress who first played the part as 'This young woman with her childlike mind'.)[13] Margit tries to poison her husband but fails and Bengt, as it happens, is mistakenly axed to death in the dark by the King's sheriff (who himself wishes to marry Signe). Finally, Gudmund and Signe are to be married and the widow Margit resolves to take herself off to a convent.

Margit is a near-murderer, which is to say that she is a rudimentary version of Rebecca West or Hedda Gabler. The first of these two celebrated modern women drives Beata Rosmer and the second Ejlert Løvborg to suicide. Ibsen is now developing his fascination with the woman who is criminally inclined but for whom, nevertheless, he has a high regard. Margit is the embodiment of a quality in the author of which, in the 1850s, he cannot have been fully aware. Ibsen was then inching along a track of immoralism (as it should fittingly be called) and was not ready, in terms of inward realisation, to step before the public with a heroine who quite challenged age-old moral suppositions.

No doubt the medieval setting of *The Feast at Solhoug* aided its success, though, as we can now see, what Ibsen wished to say, being concerned with a loveless, sterile marriage, had nothing essentially to do with the Middle Ages. But from the time of writing *Lady Inger* a year or so earlier he had been immersed in the history and culture of the Norwegian Middle Ages, so that his studies combined with his awareness of fashionable taste to make the early fourteenth century seem the right period for the play. It is worth noting that according to Ibsen's Preface to the second edition of *The Feast at Solhoug* (1883) the characters of Margit and Signe originated in a 'splendid translation' of the Icelandic Family Sagas.[14] However, one of the Oxford editors of the *Early Plays*, James Walter McFarlane, thinks it possible that Margit owes something to the novelist, Magdalene Thoresen and Signe to Suzannah Thoresen, Magdalene's nineteen-year-old stepdaughter whom Ibsen subsequently married. That Magdalene, a passionate and darkly handsome woman, had something to do with the conception of Margit is plausible, although it is not certain that Ibsen met her or any other member of the Thoresen family until after the (wildly successful) first night of the play. Suzannah seems to have had less in common with the fictional Signe, but what we know of Ibsen's later relations with the mother and daughter vaguely resemble the stage relations of Gudmund, the married Margit and her younger, unmarried sister. In other words, it is possible either that the historical play arose from an actual nineteenth-century complication or that Ibsen weirdly anticipated his own imbroglio.

As it happens we should now consider what was, for all we know, a purely literary sort of anticipation. I mean that an uncomplicated early work by Ibsen, *The Grouse at Justedal*, foreshadows not only (as is well known) the play, *Olaf Liljekrans* but also, it seems to me, some mature works, notably *The Lady from the Sea*, *The Master Builder* and *When We Dead Awaken*. Ibsen wrote one and a half acts of *The Grouse at Justedal* in 1850, just after finishing *The Burial Mound*. In 1856 he transformed this material into *Olaf Liljekrans*, which is markedly different from the earlier fragment, though the same fundamental theme is implicit in both. It seems likely that Ibsen made successive attempts to solve a problem that first beset him as a young man, or possibly even as a child. Roughly speaking, he continued to weigh in the balance the claims of compromising social existence and a 'purer' life, which for him was somehow associated with nature. It will be apparent that what I am thinking of as 'purity' has nothing to do with flawlessness or altruism, but should rather suggest a non-human or barely human lack of sophistication.

These rival claims are clearly though clumsily expressed in *The Grouse at Justedal*. Bjørn, the son of a rich man, seems fated to marry Mereta, his father's ward. She, however, is in love with a mere yeoman called Einar. The main complication is that Bjørn himself has fallen in love with Alfhild, a strange mountain girl, en rapport with both nature and the supernatural, who belongs to the ghost village of Justedal, deserted since the Black Death struck its inhabitants.

Olaf Liljekrans has mainly fresh characters and a quite changed plot, but the important distinction lies in Ibsen's clearer understanding of his own meaning. A certain Lady Kirsten Liljekrans wants her son Olaf to marry Ingeborg, daughter of the coarse, rich Arne of Guldvick. Lady Kirsten is anxious for this union because, for all her grandeur, she is scarcely a step away from financial ruin. But Olaf is 'troll struck', infatuated with Alfhild, a simple mountain girl like her namesake in the earlier work. An interesting development from Ibsen's attitude in 1850 is that the hero, Olaf, merely imagines his naïve sweetheart to be in touch with elves and fairies. He is a dreamer and some of his dreams are absurd, but nevertheless his preference for Alfhild is justified.

Ingeborg also loves another, Arne's lowly page called Hemming, and on the evening before her wedding day these two elope by galloping off into the hills. At about the same time Alfhild, on learning that Ingeborg is supposed to be marrying Olaf the following day, frenziedly sets fire to Lady Kirsten's house. The resolution comes about when Lady Kirsten (unaccountably) tells the villagers that Alfhild will be saved from execution for her act of arson if any man offers to marry her. Olaf, of course, steps out from behind the crowd to claim Alfhild for his wife, and in similarly operatic manner Hemming is rewarded with Ingeborg's hand when he 'finds' that young woman for her father.

Olaf Liljekrans was nowhere near so successful as *The Feast at Solhoug* and Ibsen himself thought poorly of it in later life; nor, for that matter, would a modern audience like it so much as the interesting, if faulty, *Lady Inger*. Yet the dialogue often seems convincing, Arne in particular is a successful portrait and a few of the scenes (for example, the fourth scene of Act II when Olaf and Alfhild contemplate a child's funeral) are impressive. But the most notable feature for us is the character of Alfhild. As a fire-raiser and near-simpleton she is scarcely admirable, but she is meant to be a real if eccentric heroine. Perhaps she should also be recognised as an early sketch of Ibsen's last heroine, a forerunner of the pale Irene in *When We Dead Awaken*, and indeed of other women in Ibsen who, for all their peculiarities, are alike in standing outside the normal social range. Ellida Wangel in *The Lady from the Sea* and her sister Hilde, in *The Master Builder*, should also be placed in this class. Presumably this was one of Ibsen's fantasies: to be drawn away from the vicious world by a woman not amiable or Christianly good, but to a degree wild and in that sense innocent. Alfhild can be as destructive as a bitter child, and so perhaps can Hilde Wangel. But neither is remotely a dissembler and each rejects social customs.

It is sensible not to blur the distinction between Ibsen's asocial women such as Hilda Wangel and his immoral women such as Hedda Gabler, while at the same time realising that these two categories might have started out as one; might, that is to say, have originated in some youthful image of defiance and social exile. For ultimately they serve the same purpose: to challenge the beneficent notions of the nineteenth century and, as it has proved, our own humanism. A common modern prejudice is that the bad woman in Ibsen is supposed to be distasteful, though in fact any honest observer can see that even Hedda Gabler has, and was always meant to have, her high-wrought attractions.

The same should be said of Hjordis in *The Vikings at Helgeland* (1858) who, to judge by the fanciful, eerie last scene of the play is meant to be regarded as the human approximation to a Valkyrie, or indeed as a woman who in death is permitted to join the original twelve nymphs of Valhalla. In that final scene Hjordis, having thrown herself over a cliff, is glimpsed riding through the air with the man she has just slain, Sigurd, her sister's valiant and Christian husband. The implication is that the pair of them are on their way to the celestial banquet hall. Of course the audience merely hears mention of this death-flight which could be a piece of fantasy: that is Ibsen's suggestion. But what did he mean by the episode, indeed by the play as a whole?

Hjordis is more 'real' than Catiline's Furia: she is supposed to belong to the actual world, albeit the unfamiliar world of northern Norway in the tenth century. The Viking code still reigns but is weakening, while Christianity is beginning to infiltrate the region. The play is not an example of realism in the nineteenth-century sense because the language is too formal; nevertheless, the characters are developed well beyond the simplicities of Saga characterisation. It is a Viking play which in some degree imitates medieval literary language and wholeheartedly extols tenth-century ethics. At the same time, this ancient material of the play is invested with nineteenth-century psychology.

Hjordis is married to Gunnar, a rich landowner, formerly a Viking raider but now a man of peace. In any event, he was never the sort of brigand his wife admires. Hjordis' sister Dagny (Hjordis herself was adopted) is likewise a pacific, tender-hearted woman, while her husband Sigurd is, or seems to be, precisely the kind of hero Hjordis yearns for.

The pattern will be familiar to all who know Ibsen's mature plays (Rebecca West as against Beata Rosmer, Hedda Gabler as opposed to Thea Elvsted), but it is of special interest here that Ibsen has decisively moved away from the defensive attitude he

earlier took towards his 'bad' women. Far more than Catiline's
Furia, more even than Margit Gauteson, Hjordis is openly the
centre of interest of the play: it is she who counts rather than the
nice people, let alone the petty or hidebound figures by whom she
is surrounded. Ibsen has come clean; he is no longer frightened of
saying either to himself or to his fellow-Norwegians that we
should respect the type of Hjordis, not revile her according to the
usual canons.

'Happiness is his', says Hjordis at one point, 'who is strong
enough to do battle with the Fates' (Act Three). On the face of it
this remark expresses the reverse of a Nietzschean *amor fati*, but
what Ibsen, speaking through his savage heroine, meant by the
'Fates' are the circumstances one encounters as opposed to one's
intrinsic personal destiny which the individualistic Ibsen, like
Nietzsche, in effect exhorted us to love. So many of Ibsen's plays
are studies of individual destinies and thus, by a seeming paradox,
gain their resonance and universality. I am asserting about Ibsen
the exact opposite of what his friend and critic Georg Brandes,
asserted in 1867.

> We instinctively long for a stereoscope, in order to see these
> figures properly. Ibsen's propensity for the abstract and
> symbolical is due to this limitation of his talent. In the first
> place, it is the origin of the abstract figures in his dramas, which
> are merely emblematical personifications of a single quality in
> human nature.[15]

These words were written when Ibsen had progressed no
further than *Peer Gynt*, but a more fitting generalisation about
Ibsen's work as a whole world would praise his powers of minute
observation. His plays suggest that the best way to arrive at
general significance is through specific detail. Thus, Nora Helmer
illustrates women's rights because she is a distinct individual in
unrepeatable circumstances.

One should, then, love one's own fate, but not the 'Fates'. This
latter term does not embrace human destiny in the large sense:
Ibsen is not saying that we should, like Milton's Satan, rebel
against God or against our exclusion from Paradise. He refers to
purely cultural and social circumstances though these may have
lasted long enough to have the appearance of belonging to the
natural order. One such cultural attitude, for example, concerns

love and marriage. Since the Middle Ages it has been believed that we should marry for love, and only Ibsen (so far as I can reckon) and following Ibsen, Shaw, have maintained that love is absolutely the wrong basis for marriage. This argument together with the increasingly familiar argument about individual destiny forms the burden of *Love's Comedy*.

When the play was first published in 1862 Ibsen and Suzannah had been married for four years. During that period Ibsen was hard up, sometimes drunken, nervously ill for a spell and scarcely a diligent writer, for he produced very little. In one sense, therefore, it is not surprising that he should at that time write a tough-minded, unromantic comedy, but it is remarkable that he cast an aspect of himself in the figure of Falk and of Suzannah in the person of Svanhild. The point of the play is that Falk and Svanhild decide to preserve their love for each other precisely by splitting up: Svanhild chooses to marry the sensible businessman Gulstad, while Falk goes off to write his poetry. (Anyone who here senses the provenance of Shaw's *Candida* must surely be right.)[16]

Biographers are not very helpful on this point, but I do not think that Ibsen ever fundamentally regretted marrying Suzannah, though in the course of time he was drawn to at least one other woman, Emilie Bardach in the eighties. What may have happened at the time of writing *Love's Comedy* was that he composed a verse drama out of his personal creative difficulties. He made poetry out of what often seemed an inability to write poetry. In other words, he met his problems head on. He knew, or anyway was pretty sure, that his marriage was not the cause of his drying up; nevertheless, his feelings about his marriage must inevitably have been connected with an arid, bitter complex of emotions. He wrote himself out of this condition by 'pretending', as it were, with the co-operation of his wife, that it would have been better for them to have loved and parted. Thus Suzannah helped to pull him through by not subverting his fantasy – a fantasy in which she herself was both loved and respected, but placed at a distance. In this way, I guess, the fantasy might well have been laid to rest, or at least rendered dormant for a while.

But of course Ibsen's argument in this play is that love peters out for everyone, unless like Falk and Svanhild they have the foresight to preserve it *only as a memory*. Falk's remembered love will serve him poetically far better than a life of mere domestic tolerance. 'Sic transit gloria amoris,' he remarks in Act One, observing Pastor Straamand, the perfect picture of wedded dullness with his wife and eight daughters. Straamand 'was once so full of courage'; his dowdy wife used to be 'the Amazon who was to lead him into realms of undiscovered beauty' (Act One). They resembled Theseus and Hippolyta, in other words.

Falk is a falcon, a windhover whose prey is untruth. Svanhild is the name of the daughter of Sigurd and Gudrun in the *Völsungasaga*, a maiden whose own father has her trampled to death by horses. Because Falk has his share of pretensions, in which perhaps there is an element of self-satire on Ibsen's part; because Svanhild deceives herself for a while; because Gulstad is in his limited way faultless; above all because the play is a comedy, some recent critics have been too apt to detect ambiguities in Ibsen's central meaning. But he was really quite serious and straightforward. He personally wished to sail against the wind and to be buoyed up by a woman whom he could contrive to identify with Svanhild. Suzannah was such a woman, 'powerful', according to remarks made by Bergliot Ibsen.[17]

In *Love's Comedy* Ibsen took his own nature and Suzannah's, greatly simplified them to fit the needs of comedy and placed them in circumstances which form a paradigm of love and renunciation. Svanhild–Suzannah enables Falk–Ibsen to find himself, then gives him up in favour of Guldstad. Thus, he is free and for her a comfortable though unexciting life seems to lie ahead. Perhaps Ibsen sometimes wondered, privately or aloud, whether Suzannah wouldn't have done better to marry a comfortable bourgeois rather than the morose, anxiety-ridden being that he then was.

In a rare fashion Ibsen's serious theme, so far from being balanced against its setting of Christiania villa and the alternately mannered and familiar poetic style, is fused with these unlikely elements. The language is sometimes witty, sometimes rapturous, if anything over-elaborate rather than Wildeanly pithy. Nevertheless, the dialogue is usually pleasing. One of Ibsen's main achievements was to transcend rather than simply denigrate the sphere of more or less amiable romance in a summer garden.

I have suggested that the source of the quality of *Love's Comedy* might well have been a decision by Ibsen to turn his artistic difficulties to account, to capitalise on what seemed to be his own weaknesses. This is much more plainly true of *The Pretenders*, completed in 1863. In writing this play (or, to be precise, in the final re-writing of it) Ibsen must finally have learned a hard lesson, which most of us never learn, except perhaps in theory: that one can profit by one's supposed failings, instead of seeking to obliterate or disguise them. It has been recognised for long enough that the character of Skule is an aspect of Ibsen himself. Skule's problem is how to be an accomplished king of Norway if one lacks kingly qualities. In general terms, suppose a man wishes to be great yet is unsure he possesses the right capabilities. Can greatness be acquired by will-power? Is the opinion of the multitude, or even of a discerning few, a sound guide to actual (objectively existent) talents? If a man thinks himself a genius and the rest of the world derides him as a bumptious mediocrity, must he be wrong?

In the above remarks I have deliberately confused Skule's concerns with Ibsen's. To be plainer still, Skule is a pretender to the throne of Norway, while Ibsen was a pretender to the title of pre-eminent national poet. The author and his fictional character are alike in their tormenting self-doubts and Ibsen at that stage might, after all, have been what psychologists call a 'schizoid character', one who tries to compensate for his sense of total inadequacy by grandiose dreams which he knows, since he is sane, that others will never verify.[18] Now Ibsen's winning manoeuvre was to dramatise this very problem, thus to objectify and solve it. In so doing he passed at once from fitfully talented author to consistent genius.

The Pretenders is of course a history play in the obvious and shallow sense that Skule, Haakon, Bishop Nikolas and other dramatis personae are based on personages who in the thirteenth century acted very roughly along the lines indicated by Ibsen. But Ibsen saw himself in Skule and his friend Bjørnstjerne Bjørnson, the well-favoured author, in Haakon. This is widely appreciated and we therefore realise that Ibsen was wrestling with the secret of Bjørnson's success and his own failure by relating these cultural and psychological matters to King Haakon's popular reign and Skule's doomed rebellion. Haakon was sure of himself and in Ibsen's eyes a good king largely for that very reason. Ibsen was fascinated by the gift of self-assurance, which seems at once baseless and justified by events and which in extraordinary cases minimises, or even annihilates any temptation to rascally behaviour. At least to the time of *The Pretenders* Bjørnson was supposed to be a better writer than Ibsen. We now believe (or 'know') that Ibsen had vastly more insight than his rival: time has conferred this reputation or has proved this fact. As it happens Ibsen's doubts about himself were of a piece with his penetration: he needed to force the world to see with his eyes before his observations could be confirmed.

In writing *The Pretenders* Ibsen finally and comprehensively followed the recommendation of Herman Hettner in *Das moderne Drama* by converting history into psychology.[19] Indeed he went beyond Hettner's advice, since it is overwhelmingly the motives of Ibsen's characters we are interested in – both as specific studies and as general illustrations. Ibsen is now fairly launched on his career of suggesting wide-ranging laws by analysing precise and unique events. To begin with, Inga, Haakon's mother, suffers (off stage) the ordeal of grasping hot iron to establish her son's right to the throne of Norway, but it is Haakon's and Skule's reactions that we are concerned with. Who but Ibsen would have contrived a Haakon so confident that he feels no need to pray (God always favours him), yet so likeable and in important matters unfailingly right? Meanwhile Skule puts his trust in justice, or what he takes to be justice, and therefore *naturally* fails. Haakon is justified in respect of his talents and vocation; Skule has a passable case according to the normal processes of legal and logical argument. Vocation, which is a sort of luck, triumphs. In this way the opening scene is a fair example of Ibsen's technique of fusing the particular incident and the general law.

A striking feature of Haakon is his combination of naïvety and political finesse. It is artless of him to allow Skule to keep the royal seal, so giving power to Skule, but characteristically Haakon also knows that he must aim to unite the country. On the other hand, Skule is fool enough to imagine that Norway had better stay disunited. Haakon is thus a man of his time while Skule's craftiness is futilely 'unhistorical'.

All his life Skule has just missed the lucky chance or the coveted appointment. (This is Ibsen at thirty-five launching himself on the road to international triumph by dissecting his own career of failure.) Haakon, says Skule, is 'one of Fortune's children' (Act Two): people die, for instance, when he needs them to die. At this point Bishop Nikolas tells Skule that luck may be defeated by 'right', but right is nothing other than the 'lust for life' of every strong man. Here Ibsen begins to face the modern dilemma that morality might simply be the cry of overpowered people, though life without morality, or without values of some kind, seems intolerable. Nikolas goes so far as impishly to assert his own 'innocence' on the grounds that he does not know the difference between good and bad (Act Two). Once again Ibsen has twisted and simplified his own nature into a stage character, this time a Satanic and, ultimately, a powerless bishop. In the first scene of Act Three the dying Nikolas explains to Skule how his physical cowardice and sexual impotence led him to seek power through the priesthood. I doubt if this self-revelation by such an individual is plausible. But Ibsen surely knew that his own cowardice, as a boy and even now as a man, helped to spur him towards success over the boyish boys and the manly men.

Bishop Nikolas is at least potentially a notable character, a self-aware manipulator who knows that his total cynicism was produced in youth by a cowardly habit of delay between the conception and execution of every plan. At the same time, his manifestation as a ghost-monk in Act Five is a feeble piece of satire. (Hell, Nikolas reports, houses scores of popes, parsons and poets.)

Ibsen is now able to increase the proportion of figures in a play who, like Nikolas, are distinctive rather than simply functional. Even Margrete, Skule's daughter who married Haakon, manages to be more than a lay figure of divided loyalties, partly because she sickeningly knows that her husband, revered by everyone including herself, does not love her. Jatgeir, the poet, represents the author, since he possessed all Ibsen's own insight and, incidentally, Ibsen's fear of self-revelation. It is Jatgeir who tells Skule the truth that Ibsen himself is in the process of learning: that doubt is not necessarily a drawback, provided one respects one's own doubt. To adapt Jatgeir's terms in Act Four, Ibsen is now a 'sound' doubter, one who accepts his uncertainties as part of himself. We should note finally that Skule is 'completed' as it were, his humanity enhanced by the presence of an admiring teenage son who is in an obvious sense mistaken about his father, yet in a more generous sense absolutely right. At the end father and son walk hand in hand from their church-sanctuary to be killed, Skule beseeching the killers not to cut young Peter's face and then crying out, 'It is shameful to treat chieftains so.'

The Pretenders has the high qualities I have mentioned but it was only the end of the beginning for Ibsen. The dramatist we all recognise started to flourish in the mid-sixties. In 1865, after some seventeen years of trying, he cast off imitativeness completely when he wrote *Brand*. I do not think that *Brand* may be compared in an instructive way with any antecedent drama. Critics tend to discuss not the plot of this play, nor yet its characters except for the hero, but its final meaning. This is the right emphasis because *Brand* is not a work like *Ghosts* or *Rosmersholm* whose seemingly small details contribute their shades to the meaning. Until the last scene, almost until the last line (of a five-act drama) the meaning of *Brand* seems clear, then everything is qualified, some would say 'reversed'. Let us recall the chief developments.

In Act One Brand is a would-be priest trying to discover the true scope of the priest's calling. He argues with Einar, a poet, who stresses the richness of life and its joys. Brand, on the contrary, looks for suffering; he expects and indeed hopes to suffer endlessly. Brand meets Gerd, a seemingly crazy girl who raves to him about a hawk, which only she can see, and an Ice Church high in the mountains. Brand decides that he must fight against three demons: 'rashness of mind, 'dullness of mind' and 'madness of mind'.

The first part of Act Two is mainly taken up with the episode of Brand's setting off across a stormy fjord to deal with a man who has murdered his own child and now sits, a lunatic, holding the corpse in his arms. Agnes, Einar's sweetheart, leaves the poet to accompany Brand: later she will become Brand's wife. Brand meets his mother who beseeches his protection. He can do nothing for her, he says, until she utterly repents of her sins and psychologically casts off her bonds with the world. One's motto must be 'All or nothing'. Brand agrees to become priest to the desolate community in which all this is happening.

Act Three takes place after three hard but worthwhile years have passed. The sturdy vein of satire in this play now commences in Brand's first argument with the Mayor, a likeable *homme moyen sensuel*. In the same vein the Doctor exhorts Brand to be humane, to which Brand replies, 'Was God humane to Jesus Christ?' Brand's mother remains unrepentant. The Doctor warns Brand and Agnes that their child cannot survive in this inclement district, but Brand resolves to stay.

The time of Act Four is Christmas Eve. Brand's son is dead and buried. The chief feature of this act, apart from some effective mockery of the notion (even in the 1860s gaining ground) of the church as a political and social centre, is that Brand forces Agnes to give away their dead child's clothes to a gipsy.

As Act Five opens we find that Agnes too has died, worn out and broken-hearted. A grand new church has been built, to the Dean's great satisfaction. Brand turns his back on the church and leads his parishioners up the mountain, but they grow fearful and stone him. He reaches the Ice Church and for the first time bursts into tears. Gerd comes upon him, tells him he is the saviour and fires a shot at her (imaginary and emblematic) hawk, thus causing an avalanche which buries the pair of them. Lastly a voice sounds above the thunder saying 'God is love!'

From the time of the first publication of *Brand* to our own day critics and audiences have taken the final words to mean not merely that Ibsen's God is love but that Brand's entire progress is therefore an obvious, readily avoidable error. Only Georg Brandes, so far as I have been able to discover (writing as early as 1867), has properly summed up, though not explained, the ambiguity.

> . . . [The] last words of the poem carry with them no conviction; for Brand has beaten every objection out of the field, and has already admirably refuted the charge which meets him at the moment of his death, the charge of not having understood that God is love.[20]

It is true that no character and no argument in the play stands up against Brand: he towers above everyone else, even or especially from a moral point of view. Einar is a childish hedonist to begin with and later a crackpot missionary; Agnes is merely long-suffering and loyal; the Mayor, the Doctor and the Dean are all happy in Vanity Fair. Gerd may indeed be mad, though enticingly so, a variant of Alfhild in *Olaf Liljekrans* and a forerunner of Irene in *When We Dead Awaken*. Brand's mother is mediocre, one who desires a soft route to heaven.

In this play Ibsen confronts two problems at the root of Christianity. First, while God loves all men equally, it is not possible for any mortal man to do the same. We must value some people above others. Brand should be either superior in our eyes to other characters, or at worst dourly impressive. Further, Brand's so-called 'hardness' resembles the hardness of Jesus' own

teachings in the Sermon on the Mount. Brand tries to imitate
Christ and exhorts others to do the same. He says in effect, 'Take
no thought for your life, what ye shall eat; neither for your body,
what ye shall put on.' Do not ravens survive without planning
how to feed themselves? Man may do likewise. 'Do not be
doubtful', Brand says in so many words, as Christ said. 'Sell that
ye have and give alms', is Brand's precept, following Jesus. What
else is the resolve that Agnes shall give up the dead child's clothes
which she is keeping as remembrances? Brand goes across the
stormy fjord to comfort the madman with his murdered boy, as
Christ might well have done. Christ would also have given to
Brand's mother the same unyielding message, 'All or nothing'.

In short the paradox at the end of this play is a gospel paradox.
God does not necessarily show his love by granting to people what
they cravenly or even piteously desire, and Ibsen is reminding
readers about the nature of original as opposed to amended and
weakened Christianity. Yet Brand is just a mortal man, so his
imitation of Christ is flawed. It is not flawed so ignominiously that
readers should finally feel superior to him. The danger is that all
those who believe that God is love, interpreted as compassion, are
liable to condemn Brand for his intransigence. But Brand's
refusal to compromise is the original Christian refusal and is in
itself justified. The problem is that Brand in his mortality needs
iron self-discipline to accomplish even a fraction of what Jesus
accomplished naturally. So great is Brand's struggle that when
Gerd tells him that he is the Chosen One and has reached the Ice
Church he bursts into tears for the first time in his adult life. He
asks God, 'Is there no salvation for the Will of Man?' It is to this
question that the voice responds, 'God is love.' In other words
Brand's imperfect life, his mere mortality, is forgiven. Everyone
may be saved, except those who sin against the Holy Ghost, but in
human terms (the only terms we know) Brand has made a
pilgrim's progress far loftier than the vacillations of his fellows.
The Ice Church is not God's church for it excludes warmth and
fertility, yet it is the last refuge of a noble mind from God.

The vacillations which Brand condemns are, when carried to
an extreme, a fair part of the subject of *Peer Gynt*, which Ibsen
completed next, in November 1867. To put the matter so makes
Peer Gynt sound an ordinary sort of fellow, or at least an ordinary
Norwegian, and, with qualifications, that is in fact what Ibsen
intended. Peer is extraordinary in the degree to which he carries

his pretences and self-deceptions: he is a composite of human shoddinesses, an 'emperor of compromise', as one recent critic has called him.[21]

Ibsen lighted upon Peer Gynt's name and something resembling his nature in a fairy tale by Asbjørnsen. The latter's Peer is a hunter, unrivalled as a teller of tall stories, who encounters the Boyg, a slippery hobgoblin, and various trolls and saeter-girls. Ibsen intended his Peer Gynt to be the opposite of Brand (slippery as opposed to rock-hard) and a compound of Norwegian vices. But there is more to the character than that, for the fairy-story figure was based on an historical person. Then, Ibsen's hero is a caricature of Ibsen himself at his worst, and, finally, Peer is a generalised type of human rather than narrowly Norwegian contemptibility.[22]

Ibsen wrote *Peer Gynt* in confident high spirits and did not expect contemporaries, let alone posterity, to spend time solemnly analysing the hero's failings or his final awakening – if that's what it is. Nevertheless, it was impossible for Ibsen to write a purely light-hearted (in other words, an insignificant) play and *Peer Gynt* is a comic fantasy with special implications for our own age, so pleasure-loving and theoretically so keen on personal integrity.

In Act One and the first part of Act Two we find some rough resemblance to the circumstances of Ibsen's youth. The relations of Aase and Peer cannot be other than a flippant reconstruction of the relations of Marichen Ibsen and Henrik. The mother, habitually frustrated and sometimes spiteful, grumbles about her poverty and her scapegrace son. Peer brags and daydreams, and, while there is no record of the young Ibsen doing likewise, we are no doubt right to imagine the older Ibsen recalling, and presumably exaggerating, the clumsiness of his youth. Peer is awkward, transparently cunning, rather loutish, yet sometimes attractive to the local girls. He meets the newcomer Solveig, nearly has a second fight with Aslak, the smith (Aslak won easily the first time), and ends up running away with Ingrid, the bride at the Haegstad wedding.

So far this is naturalistic comedy and the manner continues through the first part of Act Two, as Peer discards Ingrid in the hills, as Aase together with Solveig and her family are searching for the runaway in the soggy moorland country and, later, as Peer dances and fools around with three rough 'herdgirls'. What emerges so far is an aspect of Ibsen's feelings about Skien, the town he left twenty-four years earlier, and his awareness of what an outsider he had been on his home ground. 'The whole parish is out in a mob to get me', says Peer in Act Two, exulting in his unpopularity. The sentiment is so odd that it seems possible that Ibsen found it piquant either to image himself persecuted, or within limits, to suffer persecution. It is also true that Ibsen here shows enough detachment to see himself as his childhood detractors saw him. There had been understandable reasons for his unpopularity.

Now the fantasies begin. Peer's affinity with the Woman in Green encourages her father, the Dovre-Master, to treat him as an aspirant troll. Peer has only to abandon the human maxim, 'To thine own self be true' and live instead by troll wisdom which declares 'To thine own self be – all-sufficient.' These alternatives form the central meaning of the play without grasping which so many features – especially Peer's desertion of Solveig, his wanderings and money-making, his relation with the soulless Anitra, the lunatic asylum at Cairo, the satanic Thin Man, the peeling of the onion and the encounters with the Buttonmoulder – cannot themselves be understood.

Ibsen is preaching individualism while making it abundantly clear that this doctrine is the antithesis of what Peer Gynt and millions of others think it is. The unnamed youth in the play who cuts off his finger to avoid military service is an individualist and his action astounds Peer Gynt. On the other hand, another sort of individualist might welcome even life in the army: there is no rule except that of being true to oneself. Peer would wed Solveig instead of fleeing to America to make money, if he were true to himself. As it is, becoming a millionaire is for him (not necessarily for everyone) a troll-like achievement: he grows rich because it is the thing to do, and yields fleeting pleasures.

Being oneself is not necessarily or even normally pleasurable, secure or selfish. On the contrary, we run away from ourselves towards vices. The trolls tempt Peer Gynt into infinite adaptability: he may be whatever it pleases or comforts him to be at any moment. That is easy, not hard and it is also commonplace. Most of us, naturally including those who (with or without knowledge of *Peer Gynt*) preach anti-Gyntian sentiments, are nevertheless Gyntians in some degree. The great Boyg advises Peer to 'go round and about', to be devious and politic. Many people follow the Boyg's advice as a matter of course.

In Morocco, Anitra is attractive to Peer Gynt because she hasn't a soul: she is just a vacuously appealing concubine. The lunatic asylum at Cairo houses not individuals stoutly maintaining their eccentric selves but abnormally frightened people who have retreated into false selves. How accurate Ibsen was about this! In a sense lunacy is a result of excessive malleability not of rigid selfhood. It is not the inevitable result, for one can resemble Peer Gynt in being a sane but onion-like creature with no organic core.

The image of the onion is not exact because its core is absolutely missing, while Peer, so the implication runs, might still acquire a 'core' of selfhood. But as the play draws to a close it seems too late for him to change. In Act Five, Scene 6 the Threadballs, the Withered Leaves, a Sighing in the Air, the Dewdrops and the Broken Straws in turn announce themselves as representing different though related sorts of grave omission from Peer Gynt's life. He has lacked too many natural human qualities. (No one ever expected him to be faultless.)

In contrast the youth who hacked off his own finger became thereby a criminal, a public sinner, but, according to the priest at his graveside a lifetime later, (Act Five, Scene 3), he was rightly regarded as a 'great man' around his hearth and home because he was immovably himself. Such a person is obviously not a saint, not necessarily even a good man, but will be rescued from the Devil. The analogy used by the Thin Man (Satan or some emissary) is that of photograph and negative. Good people resemble the first, bad people the second, but Peer Gynt is useless even to the Thin Man because his negative has been hopelessly smudged. Since Peer has been neither good nor purposively bad, neither positive nor negative, the Buttonmoulder confidently waits to melt him down. At the end of the play the Buttonmoulder is still waiting, because Solveig's faith, hope and love are, at this stage, merely a stay of execution. Peer might yet be reprieved, but only if he maintains his true being, with or without the help of the blind and aged Solveig.

So Peer Gynt ends more pitiable than comic, cradled by a woman who has waited for him (in the fantasy manner of much of this play) since the time of her first communion. There is little that is conventionally flattering in Ibsen's self-portraits. Though we may respect the first in the gallery, Catiline, his character has been divested of the qualities a comfortably popular writer would

manage to detect in his own make-up. In the 1860s Ibsen mad
disinterested use of his own personality. Falk in *Love's Comedy* i
sometimes absurd, King Skule of *The Pretenders* is wrong-headed
destructive, and even Jatgeir, Skule's court poet, does no
represent an appealing strand of Ibsen's tangled web. None c
these characters was just a dramatic expedient, for Ibsen wa
engaged in finding himself, as a main objective. Brand and Pee
Gynt were by 1870 the most important 'discoveries', in the sens
of uncovered selves, and Stensgaard in *The League of Youth* (1869
was yet another unflattering self-projection. Ibsen remarked in
letter,

> Brand is myself in my best moments just as I have also, b
> self-dissection brought out many features in both Peer Gyn
> and Steensgaard (sic)[23]

'Myself in my best moments': Brand is the tyrannously spotles
model whose standards Ibsen sometimes achieved. Brand'
beckoning finger led Ibsen on. Peer Gynt, on the contrary, is
condensed version of Ibsen's moments of vaingloriousness. Sinc
Brand and Peer Gynt are opposites, it is remarkable what Ibse
could get out of himself. But for all their opposition these tw
figures have something in common: each sets himself above th
common man. Ibsen always wished to stand apart, for h
possessed, or sought, that nobility 'of mind and will' which h
regarded as the only source of moral distinction.[24] Brand is th
achievement of such nobility, Peer Gynt a travesty of it. Ibse
wanted to hold aloof from the great majority who take attitude
from one another and resent the hero whose life, he thought, alon
makes sense of theirs.

3   *The League of Youth* to *The Wild Duck*

n 1869 Ibsen completed the first of the kind of plays we most readily associate with his name. Thus when there is a reference to 'Ibsenism' people think first, not of *Brand* or *Peer Gynt* but of *Ghosts* or *The Wild Duck* – of prose and realism as opposed to verse and fantasy. Yet this pioneer work, *The League of Youth*, might be said to be excessively unpoetic, lacking the sort of pattern of anticipations, echoes, settings, and phrases colloquial in style though pregnant in context which in a manner 'poetically' enriches Ibsen's plays from *Pillars of Society* onwards. Further, *The League of Youth* is not a tragedy but a cynical comedy whose theme is connected with the absence of tragic possibilities. It is satire on the disappearance from Norwegian politics of the degree of commitment that invites nemesis. In the way of all Ibsen's mature works, except *Emperor and Galilean*, everything is thoroughly Norwegian and *therefore*, as it has proved, universal.

Ibsen did not suddenly realise in the late sixties that his extraordinary mimetic powers might be used not merely to support but in part to replace dramatic poetry of the obvious sort. He fiercely wrote a prose drama because the critics had poured scorn on his poetry, for example, Clemens Petersen had belittled *Peer Gynt*. Now he would be prosaically accurate and 'low' as a form of revenge.[1] As it happens Ibsen's exact observations have a range of reference far wider than Norway in the mid-nineteenth century. The subject of *The League of Youth* is small-town politics, which Ibsen saw as *essentially* untruthful, and the interesting fact is that his imitation of a Norwegian example stands for a general pattern of democratic procedures. In such a play it is not the idea of falsehood, for instance, that matters so much as specific pieces of falsehood, for which Ibsen's eye was peculiarly keen. (And in all kinds of imaginative literature the signs of particulars may survive through the years, but not the signs of abstract ideas.)

43

The leap from the different types of marvel in *Brand* and *Peer Gynt* to the near-marvellous ordinariness of *The League of Youth* was not explained by Ibsen in letters. At this stage he could not have realised that great precision may pass paradoxically beyond its utilitarian purposes towards the less definable connotations of poetry. In the past he had been at home with the somehow admirable errors of his Catiline and Lady Inger, and with the grandly savage ways of his Hjordis, but if we have to distinguish one mark of the older Ibsen it could well be his manner of making a commonplace milieu an arena for grandeur. His people are normally bourgeois yet the cast of mind by which they are judged and which as heroes they exhibit is anciently aristocratic or 'pre-moral'. The best people sooner or later make choices which are suggested not at all by moral suppositions, let alone by frivolous desires, but by iron facts. These figures first recognise the facts (a hard enough task in itself) and then embrace them. Sometimes the want of this cast of mind is Ibsen's implicit subject, as it is in *The League of Youth*. His cynicism about politicians is not quite of the common sort ('they're only out for what they can get') but to the effect that political objectives are pared down more or less unwittingly in the interests of ambition, security and ordinary social accommodation. Ibsen's chief target in this play is the spirit of Stensgaard, the leading character, who refers, for example, to 'the miserable satisfaction of being consistent'[2] (Act Two). The pace of alliances formed and broken, of plots conceived, changed, discarded, accelerates until in the fourth and fifth acts the play has at times almost the speed, but not the emphasis, of farce. Though Stensgaard doesn't always dictate the pace, he is happy with it, for it is his *métier*. He is not just the type of any wily politician, ancient or modern, but a kind of man thrown up by democracy who has 'the gift of carrying the crowd with him' (Act Five). Lundestad, a still shrewder politician, makes that judgement, but it can pass for Ibsen's own.

Stensgaard is thirty, a comparative newcomer to the district (based on Skien) anxious to make his way. To begin with we trust him or at least withhold judgement. At the Independence Day fête he makes an unrehearsed speech proclaiming the birth of a new political party to be called 'The League of Youth'. Later he conveniently discloses (indeed, decides) that he is in love with Ragna Monsen, daughter of a local landowner who is himself politically energetic and hostile to the controlling interest, led by

Chamberlain Brattsberg, an ironmaster, and Lundestad, a farmer and member of parliament.

Stensgaard's speech is a series of vacuous pronouncements about individual liberties and the need for those currently frustrated, namely the young people of the district, to 'demand opportunities for initiative, for drive, for vigour' (Act One). Admittedly the fête is no occasion for anyone to put forward specific proposals, but Stensgaard's very vagueness is part of his nature and appealing to those of his audience who feel themselves in some way hard done by. Stensgaard's world, as we come to learn, is composed of noise and gusts of feeling, unallied or expediently allied to external facts. Nevertheless, he still seems if not a fine fellow at least pleasanter than Brattsberg and Lundestad. Whatever weaknesses come to light (for example, an earlier attempt, now disowned, to make friends with the Brattsberg family) may be excusable: he is only young.

It happens that Chamberlain Brattsberg assumes that Stensgaard's speech was an attack, not upon him but upon Monsen. In Act Two Lundestad takes advantage of Stensgaard by suggesting that he might stand for parliament with the backing of the local rich men. By now Stensgaard has grown friendlier with the Brattsberg family. He explains to Fjeldbo, the works' doctor, that in his Independence Day speech he was assaulting principles not personalities. This is true but it ignores the fact that he and a great many other people naturally link the personalities of Brattsberg and Lundestad with the principles in question. These two men are rightly associated with repressive staleness.

Stensgaard now begins to ally himself to Brattsberg and accordingly – for such is his perfectly sincere way – to grow enamoured of Thora, Brattsberg's daughter. 'It's strength of will that counts in this world,' he cries in Act Two, a sentiment that Ibsen would not have despised, but Stensgaard's will is variable in everything but self-seeking. Towards the end of Act Two Stensgaard has concluded that the Brattsberg family are agreeably, dignifiedly rich, in contrast to the nouveau riche ways of the Monsens. He apologises to Brattsberg for the speech at the fête, so enlightening and enraging the ironmaster.

In Act Three it turns out that Eric, Brattsberg's son, has forged his father's signature on a bill for 2000 dollars. By now Stensgaard is openly against the Brattsbergs and feels that he can no longer take an interest in Thora, since the whole family must share Eric's disgrace. Love as well as ambition is subject to such calculations; no veering about is too absurd or shameful. Nevertheless, it is necessary to insist that Stensgaard is an honest chameleon who would take another person's constancy to be a pose or a folly. Two comic touches in the fourth act support that estimate. First, Stensgaard comes to feel that too much contact with the people, half-educated numbskulls and nitwits that they are, will sully his love for them. Secondly, he finds that Monsen's son, Bastian, makes himself ridiculous by nicely aping the Stensgaard style of rhetoric. In both instances Stensgaard is, as usual, without irony.

The progress of this exemplary careerist continues helter-skelter to the end. Forsaking Thora, he tries to regain Ragna Monsen, but she will have nothing to do with him. So he announces that he is engaged to Mrs Rundholmen, a rich and mildly vulgar widow, but she is by then betrothed to Bastian Monsen. Stensgaard ends bereft of women and political advantage. But he will prosper, Lundestad ways in Act Five, because 'he's lucky enough not to be hampered either by character or conviction or social status [so] he can very easily be liberal-minded about things'.

That remark ought to ring down the years. Ibsen already knew that the liberal attitude, because of its very virtue, attracts people who simply cannot make up their minds. Since there is no action, however atrocious or stupid, for which no one can produce a rational defence, the facile sort of liberal concludes that 'there is something to be said' for everything except shameless tyranny. But that is the way to retreat from values, not pursue them. In the end nothing is left but a vague feeling that the will itself (which early Christians, for example, acting out as they supposed the will of God, exercised to prodigious lengths) is the only source of wickedness.

Early Christianity is a good part of the subject of *Emperor and Galilean*, on which Ibsen worked in one way or another from 1865 to 1873, intensively after 1871. To be more exact, the subject, focused through the career of Julian the Apostate, is related to Ibsen's topic in his youthful work *The Burial Mound*, and in *The Vikings at Helgeland*, namely the rival claims of Christianity and paganism. But by now Ibsen had left the Viking lands behind him and had lived in Italy, with the result that paganism means not so much the heroic – martial code in its unrepressed simplicity as the entire Graeco-Roman ethos of many gods and earthbound, sensuous experience. To such affirmation of life is opposed the denial of life which Ibsen, like Nietszche, saw as the basis of Christianity. In the fourth century this life-denial proved too strong for even a Roman emperor to check. And the emperor, anyway, was sure of nothing but his doubts.

There is no point in trying seriously to modify the usual adverse judgement of this play as a play. Both parts, *Caesar's Apostasy* and *The Emperor Julian*, are unsatisfactory on purely dramatic grounds, but there are effective features. To take examples, Act Four of *Caesar's Apostasy* includes some neat comedy at the expense of the courtier mentality followed by the striking scene of Helena's derangement before her death. Helena, Julian's beautiful wife, has been poisoned on the orders of the Emperor Constantius and now she raves at Julian to the effect that he is dirty, sexually loathsome, and further that she is with child by Christ Himself who has impregnated her through the medium of a priest. Then, Act Five of this same part, in which Julian finally opts for 'life' as the Emperor of Rome rather than for the 'lie' of Christianity, is exciting throughout. It is not difficult, I think, to make a (non-exclusive) selection of similar grounds from *The Emperor Julian*. This should include the antiphony of the utterances of the Procession of Apollo and the Procession of (Christian) Prisoners in Act Two; the cruel episode of Cyrillus' torture in Act Three and, more generally, the almost Shakespearean movement towards Julian's downfall and death in Acts Four and Five.

Nevertheless, the two parts are generally weak, often unexciting in terms of plot and much below Ibsen's usual level of characterisation. The historical material itself was promising in several ways: turbulent episodes, characters vigorous yet still capable of subtle fictional development (like those Shakespeare found in North's Plutarch) and the fact that Julian's reign was a key phase in the growth of modern values. In the histories Julian is a fascinating figure: stocky, soldierly with darting 'clever' eyes and intellectual passion, for he valued philosophic enquiry above everything else – warfare, religion, domestic bliss. He fought hard and in the end desperately against the tide of enthusiasm; against the priests, the rival sects, the joyful martyrs, the plebeians infectiously sensing a route to equality, aristocrats 'lapsing' one by one into the faith. In fact, despite the shortcomings of Ibsen's play, it is from him more than anyone else except Gibbon that a

modern reader gets an impression of how and why Christianity
took hold throughout the empire.

It did so, according to Ibsen, partly because the Emperor
Julian, persecuted the Christians. At least the persecutions gave
fresh impetus to fragmented and sometimes languishing doctrines, all of which we now designated 'Christian'. So by his
actions Julian joined Cain and Judas Iscariot to become the third
of the 'great helpers in denial' (*Caesar's Apostasy*, Act Three).[3] The
early faith was peculiarly strengthened by the enmity it aroused.
Cain is the legendary figure whose story established the pattern:
kill the good man (Abel or any successor in righteousness) and
you aid the survival of goodness as an ideal. Culturally speaking,
the bad man must lose or reform himself. (Does this not mean that
the brutally self-assertive ways of a Cain-figure must always be
vanquished or, less commonly, 'justified' in a cultural setting, but
in daily life disguised?)

In rough outline the story of Ibsen's Julian is as follows. When
we first meet him he is a prince, not yet Caesar (which then meant
heir-presumptive to the Emperor), and full of 'evil thoughts'. His
apostasy thus begins as an acknowledgement that many of his
natural thoughts are not merely unchristian but positively hostile
to Christianity. The night before he was born his mother dreamed
that she was giving birth to Achilles, and Julian tends to admire
the Homeric spirit. At this stage Julian's half-brother Gallus, is
sent to join the army in Asia, while Julian himself manages to
journey to Athens, his spiritual home as he thinks. There he takes
to logic-chopping but also, intermittently, to asking valuable
questions such as 'Why was pagan sin so beautiful?' (Part I, Act
Two). He learns in Athens that 'The old beauty is no longer
beautiful and the new truth is no longer true' (Part I, Act Two). In
other words, the beauty of paganism has faded and the truth of
Christianity does not hold up. In the third act Julian comes to
believe that while Adam himself displayed perfect balance
between spirit and flesh (indeed the two categories could not then
be distinguished), great men have since been unbalanced: Moses
stammered, Alexander was a drinker, Jesus a physical weakling.
Julian is attracted to the teachings of Maximus, a mystic, who
proclaims 'Logos in Pan', the spirit or understanding fused with
the natural universe. A mysterious voice announces to Julian that
freedom and necessity are one and the same. Maximus later

explains that first there was an empire founded upon the tree of knowledge (Greek learning) and next an empire founded upon the tree of the cross (life as willed Christian suffering, or joy-in-suffering). A third empire is at hand founded upon both earlier trees 'because it hates and loves them both' (Part I, Act Three). Maximus never explains what he means by this, but he may have in mind (and it is Ibsen's own message) an encompassing attitude which delights in learning but does not suppose that knowledge will ever sweep away the tragic ground of life. It is a message of never-ending richness – and suffering.

But Julian's novitiate phase is over when he learns that his brother Gallus has been murdered (presumably on the orders of the Emperor Constantius) and that the emperor's sister Helena, is to be his bride. He must choose either to be emperor himself or to join the ranks of 'Galileans'. He zestfully opts for power.

At the outset of *The Emperor Julian* we learn that Constantius is dead and the Julian is indeed his successor who wishes in true philosophic fashion to 'root out error' (Act One). His model is Marcus Aurelius, his emphasis is upon Dionysus and his maxim is 'Life, life, life in beauty!' (Act One). The new emperor is so eccentric as to dress as Dionysus, but he soon becomes disgusted with Dionysian revels when he sees that these are merely squalid and insolent. Is it for this sort of thing that he is urging a great revolution? In the second act he is confronted by the formidable Christian stubbornness and falls into the trap of issuing decrees against the faith, contrary to his earlier pluralistic or lenient assumptions. He embarks on a career of torture and persecution of the Christians. He is now facing the monumental irrationality of the Galileans: these people are mad and out of control. Julian interestingly remarks in Act Four that Socrates loved the world while Jesus hated it. However, by now the Emperor is spiritually declining. In Act Five he finds himself losing the war with the Persians and feels as his end draws near that Christ has won: 'Thou has conquered, Galilean!' Julian's is an ironic death, for he knows that he has proved to be only a 'rod of correction' to the religion he set out to destroy.

Whatever either theologians or historians say about Julian's rule, Ibsen saw him (or, less likely, for dramatic purposes affected to see him) as a great reviver of the foundering faith. That was his historical significance. So, according to Ibsen, the triumph of Christianity depended upon a concatenation of events and personalities which few could have predicted. If it was inevitable it was so after the manner of all historical sequences: since it took place, nothing else in practice could have happened.

Ibsen was not predominantly concerned with history, for all his research, but with a kind of tragic inevitability, which he seems to have thought recurred in every generation. *Emperor and Galilean* is a 'World-Historic Drama' not only because it represents a far-reaching series of events but also because it summarises what Ibsen felt to be the normal pattern of historical change, specifically a dialectical pattern in which at least some of the participants aid the antithesis of the movement they favour. It seems clear when we think of Ibsen's ventures into history that for him tragedy was the ground upon which history must be played. Tragedy was primary to him and religion an historical, secondary manifestation.

Julian's apostasy, we should note, begins reasonably and naturally. He is not cruel or envious of the faithful, but he detects in Christianity a loss as well as a gain. A Philosopher (so designated) tells the young Julian in Athens (Part I, Act One) that there is a 'whole world of splendour which you Galileans are blind to'. The world of splendour consists partly of song and roses and foaming goblets, but also of the 'blows of fate' which the Philosophers' students can bear, because they find truth congenial. The truth is not Christ, nor yet the Christian godhead but the universe of never ending creation. It is a Heraclitean universe, of which Christianity, though it pretends to justify the whole, is an infinitesimal part.

In Ibsen's presentation of early Christianity the emphasis is not upon morality but upon the fundamental belief that, in Luke's words, 'the kingdom of God is within you'. Ibsen portrays the overcoming by Christianity of non-Christian political power as a result of this root attitude of the believers: they ignored political power along with other mundane realities. The Christian conquered because he barely acknowledged the real world, except as a terrain to be traversed. He regarded his soul as essentially apart from reality.

Ibsen's own soul, on the contrary, was inextricably bound up with his day-to-day awareness of the external world, including, of course, his awareness of his personal past and of history. These innumerable externals were primary in his vision: it was not that they were somehow 'greater', more consequential than he, but that his own possibilities as a man and artist were enhanced the more faithfully he acknowledged them. He valued the 'truth' of phenomena far above the 'truth' of ideas, explanations or wishes. An early Christian had the chance to strengthen his soul to the extent that he could disregard his environment or treat it solely as a testing-ground. But to Ibsen the test lay in his capacity to see the differentiating details of every unique situation, not knowing in advance what they might portend. For instance, the details of *The League of Youth* suggests some sort of right-wing political analysis, while those of *Pillars of Society* are anti-conservative, or at any rate anti-bourgeois. Similarly *A Doll's House* concerns one marriage and the final decision by one woman to leave home. No other woman is in Nora Helmer's situation. If we think generally of 'doll's house' *ménages* we are slipping into the kind of categorisation that Ibsen distrusted.

On the evidence of the plays he believed that truth should be sought in percepts, not concepts. His are the reverse of plays of ideas. He treated any schematic utterance less as an explanation or summary of many signs than as yet another sign: everything depended on how, when and by whom the utterance was given. I think that to Ibsen (who was no philosopher and a severely practical psychologist) observing, thinking and judging were nearly the same activity.

And when we go to an Ibsen play our preconceptions are soon pushed aside. To be more exact, if we arrive with a cluster of images in mind, then the play is calculated to bring us back to concrete situations. For instance, images of women's liberation fade before a production of *A Doll's House*: they are not contradicted so much as replaced by the 'reality' of Nora and Torvald. At the end of each of Ibsen's modern plays from *Pillars of Society* onwards there is no lesson the audience can carry away, except that in each situation of a lifetime the only valid deduction it is possible to make must be highly specific. To generalise is to be an idiot and the habit of energetic observation is the one habit Ibsen might be said to recommend.

An excellent illustration of Ibsen's particularity is in fact his next play, *Pillars of Society*, which manages mildly to assail its leading character, a somewhat unscrupulous merchant, and the scandalous practice of sending overweighted ships to sea while not making a general or political attack on mercantilism. The play is, as I earlier remarked, anti-bourgeois, but not in the familiar nineteenth-century manner of Flaubert or Maupassant. Georg Brandes was right when in the eighties he wrote, with seeming ambiguity, that in *Pillars of Society* Ibsen had 'aimed a blow at the leading classes in his country', though 'the play had no social–political tendency whatever'.[4] Brandes' remarks should remind us of Ibsen's general tendency (still sometimes misunderstood) to attack a form of behaviour associated with a social group without in the least suggesting a change in the social system.

Ibsen laboured over *Pillars of Society* from 1875 to 1877, the longest period he had devoted to any play except *Emperor and Galilean*, but despite the notes and drafts kept in Oslo University Library[5] we can only guess that he was detained in part by his advance towards what the Germans felicitously came to call 'Realpoesie'. *Pillars of Society* is the first of Ibsen's plays to display much *Realpoesie*, an unorthodox term which denotes the sort of density and radiance Ibsen became so skilled at bestowing upon ordinary language, people and events. The point is that his progress towards this quality subterraneously accelerated between 1875 and 1877, for it is not conspicuous in the drafts.

Nor are the notes and drafts illuminating about Ibsen's characters. Each is so much an individual by now, so composed of idiosyncracies, memories, special ways of looking at the world. Did any of these dramatis personae just 'come into his head' or could he generally have pointed to the provenance of the traits he had given them? In particular, how often were even the shoddier people based upon aspects of himself? Is it possible, for instance, that Karsten Bernick, the shady and rather self-deceiving businessman of *Pillars of Society*, has anything in common with the supposedly uncompromising artist who created him? Perhaps it is not much to the point that fifteen years before the action of the play Bernick conducted a liaison with a married actress, Madam Dorf, and that when both she and her husband a little later died, Bernick took their daughter, Dina, into his own home. So far this may be at most romanticisation of Ibsen's 'guilty' past at Grimstad, the illegitimate son by Else the maid, for whom he had to provide paternity costs for fourteen years.[6] For it is generally appreciated that *Pillars of Society* is a 'Grimstad play' loaded with memories of that small coastal town. What is far more important, though, is that Bernick at one youthful stage was attracted to Lona Hessel, but then married her younger step-sister Betty, with whom he was not at all in love, in order to get money for his mother's ailing business. He proceeded to pull the business round and has never since looked back.

The details of Ibsen's own marriage are not amply known; the biographers scrupulously confine themselves to the few recorded facts. But the plays encourage a particular conjecture. These, whether written before or after marriage, regularly include two women, rivals in some fashion or other, one more spectacular or fiercer than the other. Often the women are related by blood or marriage and the older is the audacious one. So it is, for all the variations, in many plays from *Lady Inger* (if not from *Catiline*) to *John Gabriel Borkman*. Perhaps Irene and Maia of *When We Dead Awaken* are connected with the same fundamental theme. The pairs differ greatly, of course, and each member or each pair is an individual, but still a pattern is there.

What I think possible is that when Ibsen met Magdalene and Suzannah Thoresen he made precisely the prudent choice which his plays, before and after his marriage, call into question. Perhaps he was ever afterwards liable to be tormented by the thought that he of all men, such an enemy of safe settlements, had run away from the blazing woman he could have won. For Magdalene was bold where her daughter was steadfast. Most likely he did the 'right' thing, since Suzannah seems to have been the sort to help Ibsen in the ways he wanted or essentially needed, rather than according to her own, necessarily uncomprehending ideas: an excellent wife for an artist. On the other hand, Magdalene was self-willed and an artist herself, a novelist. Further, she was on the verge of middle age when Ibsen met her. Just the same, it seems possible that Karsten Bernick's choice of Betty rather than Lona, and Lona's blunt questioning of his motives as the play proceeds reflect the subtler situation in Ibsen's own life.

Pillars of Society is certainly not the first of Ibsen's plays in which the logical weight of the past falls upon the present lives of the main characters, but from this play onwards such a structure is conspicuous as the foundation of his work. As Hans Heiberg remarks in his *Ibsen: A Portrait of the Artist*, Ibsen replaced the morally irrelevant nemesis of classical tragedy by 'a curse from their own past and character'[7] for his tragic figures. He persuades us that everyone reaps what he sows, and that most if not all sow some measure of the malign. In this play, then, we learn that Bernick made a profitable marriage and took the child Dina Dorf into his house. As he began to revive the family business, Lona Hessel followed Johan Tonnesen her step-brother, to America. By emigrating Johan was taking upon his shoulders the scandal of adultery with Madame Dorf. Moreover, Bernick failed to halt the rumour that Johan had taken money belonging to Mrs Bernick's business, and this enabled Bernick to keep creditors at bay for long enough to refashion the shaky foundations of the firm. This is the dramatically fertile part of Bernick's past which put him on the road to becoming a pillar of society and for which, according to Ibsen's tragic scheme, he must sooner or later pay the price. 'Look into any man's heart you like,' Bernick characteristically says in Act Three, 'and in every single case you will find some black spot he had to keep covered up.' This is no doubt true, but it is a half-truth, for Bernick fails to add, or even discern, that the spot cannot be circumscribed but must spread into a stain, unless it is exposed. At any rate that is what Ibsen seems to have believed.

Consul Bernick is treated sympathetically rather than the reverse: we have here neither the blank hostility of a Flaubert towards his bourgeois nor that superior kind of sympathy on the further side of condemnation which Ibsen later managed for such compromisers as Solness and Rubek. Yet Bernick is an intelligent scoundrel, intelligent in practical ways though as a rule spiritually stupid. His remarks are often irritating but may be delivered with a certain charm. (It depends on the actor and producer.) 'My dear Betty,' he says to his wife in the first act, 'it's not a thing [the railway scheme] for the ladies to worry about.' So far as he is concerned men transact business, women do 'social work' and 'the family is the nucleus of society' (Act One). This last sentiment may be valid but Bernick himself requires a family that is a refuge from the hurly-burly of society rather than a nucleus of it.

However, these are minor matters. Far more important are the past evasions about Johan and the family business. Now he orders Aune, the shipyard foreman, to get the *Indian Girl* ready for sea in an impossibly short time to comply with the instructions of the American owners. He knows that this will be dangerous, but pretends to himself and the world at large that any objection to his orders must be solely (instead of partly) due to Aune's distrust of the new manpower-saving equipment. (How good Ibsen was at suggesting the proper complexity of many practical coniderations, without losing sight of the moral thread.) In the end he *Indian Girl* is scarcely repaired and Bernick knows it. Olaf, Bernick's thirteen-year-old son, stows away on that leaky ship and Bernick is aghast until he learns that Olaf has been taken off and the sailing postponed. All this happens as Bernick is being fêted by the town. In his speech of thanks he makes various confessions (an episode which falls short of the plausible by a hairsbreadth, I think) and seems to be reformed and enlightened. So his suffering, which may not be severe enough for poetic justice, is over. Is the play, after all, a tragedy manqué? Bernick remains misguided enough to exclaim, 'That's something else I've learnt these last few days: it's you women who are the pillars of society.' How is he supposed to look as Lona puts him right: foolish, modestly grateful, bewildered? Perhaps Ibsen, who often held his hand against the most obvious targets, did not wish to stress Bernick's defeat. And there was a little of himself even in that fraudulent businessman.

On the other hand, Ibsen's next play, *A Doll's House*, lacks not only targets for his contempt but also any form of self-projection on the author's part. He is 'outside' the play, observing the Helmer's marriage with unaccustomed – and largely unrecognised – leniency. His sympathy towards Nora does not lead him to disgust with Torvald, or with Krogstad, who is the only exonerated blackmailer I can think of in fiction. It is well known that the fate of the authoress Laura Kieler helped to launch Ibsen on this play, though the earlier creations of Selma Brattsberg in *The League of Youth* and Dina Dorf in *Pillars of Society* are precursors of Nora. In other words, Ibsen had been concerned with the figure of the wife owned and cossetted like a doll since at least 1869, so Laura Kieler's troubles, which reached a climax in 1878, must have merely, though vigorously, focused his attention. Fru Kieler had once written a novel called *Brand's Daughters*, which arose from her enthusiasm for Ibsen's play, and had subsequently made his acquaintance. In the mid-seventies she secretly borrowed money to get her tubercular husband away on holiday to Italy. Ibsen advised her in a letter to unburden herself to her husband, but she forged a cheque instead. A bank refused payment and she then confessed everything to Kieler. He was outraged beyond reason or compassion and stormed at her until she had a breakdown. So Kieler had her committed to a lunatic asylum (for a month as it turned out) after which he took her back into their home, but only on principle, not out of affection. This is a ghastly story while Ibsen's play, on the contrary, is exhilarating, and indeed a faithful representation of Laura's tale, including the asylum, would have received even warmer execrations than those later directed at *Ghosts*. In fact *A Doll's House* might well be said to have made a stronger impression than any other work in the history of the theatre. For however excited people might be by a production of the *Oresteia* or *King Lear*, they see those dramas chiefly as theatrical events, while *A Doll's House*, whatever its comparative merits, is widely received as a reflection of personal experience. Further, Michael Meyer says of it ,'What other play has achieved as much?'[8] meaning that Ibsen caused people to see marriage as a human rather than divine institution, hence reformable.

However, Ibsen had no such radical intentions and was not particularly interested in the position of women in society. As always, he was concerned to show the poisonous effects of falsehood, though he recognised that truth, likewise, can be destructive. In other words, he did not regard the blurting out of truth as an eighth cardinal virtue but he nevertheless wished to foster a society which should be minimally bogus. I believe he thought the cultivation of such a fresh-air psychology should take priority over the pursuit of either happiness or justice, since the psychology must be the groundwork (not the perfect instrument) of a happier and fairer people.

What makes the Helmers' partnership universal, despite its unique characteristics and for all the legal advances since Ibsen's day, is that marriages commonly include a measure of deception. Nora's attitude towards her married life might be expressed as follows:

> I necessarily and rather nobly borrowed twelve hundred dollars from Mr Krogstad by forging my dying father's signature on an I.O.U. as a means of taking my dangerously overworked husband to Italy for a vacation. So, while everyone thinks of me as a childlike, incompetent creature who must be spared adult worries, I have somewhat impoverished myself for Torvald's sake: it was a brave, decent and creditably secret manoeuvre. For Torvald, a kind and worthy man who cherishes me, cannot be allowed to know, at least for the time being, that I saved his life.

Helmer's assumptions about his marriage are that he is blessed with a sweet, essentially subservient wife whom he will continue to make happy so far as humanly possible. Nora must be spared pain because she could not stand it, so he is her bulwark against the world. He should try to get on in life but not do anything so unmanly as to burden his wife with the laborious details of work, professional competition and the like. He sees himself, not Nora, as the guardian of virtue, for she is too innocent, too uninformed to be a judge in ethical matters.

Thus there are two distinct, unobtrusively opposed fields of vision in the Helmer household, each of which happens to be spurious in some respects. That this is a widespread condition in our supposedly candid period as much as in the 1870s may be an underestimated element in the continuing popularity of the play. For the Helmers' deficiencies are familiar but not quite familiar enough in their specific forms to be painful. And almost everyone rejoices when Nora chooses to cut loose and start again. (However, not everyone realises that her action is dangerous and might lead either to felicity or to any sort of degradation.)

Up to the time of that celebrated final scene Nora is pleased with her acts of self-sacrifice and ingenuity, since, apart from the help given to Torvald, these prove – not to others but to herself – that she is no flibbertigibbet. 'I too have something to be proud and happy about,' she confides to a sceptical Mrs Linde in the first act.

But for long enough she has assumed the role of doll-wife: indeed the role *is* her, or would be but for her one assertive and, as it happens, criminal act. Nora's relation with her father was rather like the relation with Helmer. Yet obviously her character is also a sham: she is what she has sensed others have willed her to be. It has seemed natural for her never to object to Torvald's addressing her as his 'little sky-lark' or 'little squirrel', though it has merely been comfortable. Her life has normally been such a masquerade and she scarcely knows of any alternative. She realises that she is a bundle of charms, including her delectable little vices – the macaroons, the urge to say 'Damn', the recently acquired skill at the tarantella. Nora accepts Helmer's estimate of her because of her upbringing, because it accords with a widespread view of woman and because to contest it would entail the anguishing, possibly vain, frequently selfish pursuit of an individual self. Nor is that self lurking about 'within' her, waiting

to be discovered. On the contrary, it will have to be more or les
created, moment by moment. In Act Three Torvald admonishe
her by saying, 'First and foremost you are a wife and mother
Nora replies, 'That I don't believe any more. I believe that firs
and foremost I am an individual, just as you are – or at least I'r
going to try to be.'

This is not an open and shut matter, settled at the end of th
nineteenth century. Most people think they are human being
first, then male or female beings, natives of a race or countr
members of a social class, perhaps even members of an occup
tional group: all these categories take precedence, they suppos
over individuality. Individuality is the part remaining when suc
categories are subtracted and it is somehow inessential. Nora'
attitude is commonly held to be selfish. Women, especially if the
are liberated, quite often think of themselves first and foremost a
women, which is no liberation at all. The antithetical view (t
which Nora is possibly groping) is most clearly expressed by D. H
Lawrence and consists of seeing individuality as co-present wit
life itself. Even insects are individuals so that the lowliest creatur
is unique.[9] A good deal of philosophic confusion can occur whe
people fail to make their positions clear on this point.

So Nora passes with convincing suddenness in the third ac
from 'inauthenticity', not indeed to its complete existentialis
opposite but to the search for that opposite. Torvald remain
stuck in his condition of being-for-others. He is baffled at the en
because he equates the good with the socially acceptable an
cannot comprehend any other view. To be against society or even
as it were, to 'irritate' society by one's individualistic assertions i
by definition evil. Thus, Helmer's is a morality of custom, fa
older than Christianity yet as modern as Marxism.

This principal theme of *A Doll's House* is unobtrusivel
supported, not diffused, by the three lesser characters, Kristin
Linde, Dr Rank and Krogstad. (There are also six very mino
characters whom we forget though they add substance to th
Helmers' household – the maid, the nursemaid, the porter and th
three children.) Krogstad's role is plainly necessary, for b
sending his letter to Torvald (the letter which languishes in th
locked box in the hall and which Torvald is detained from readin
by Nora's desperate tarantella) he precipitates the final dis
closures and Nora's metamorphosis. But apart from that Krogs
tad is an interesting and indeed necessary figure of frustration an

mbitterment, the perfect though surprising partner for Mrs Linde. In addition to aiding the mechanics of the plot these two enrich the theme, for they have both suffered in humiliating ways, as the relatively comfortable Helmers have not. At the end there is an appropriate kind of ripening for them both. Mrs Linde's lot has been unenviable, a loveless marriage in order to support her mother and brothers, a series of exhausting jobs. The townspeople know Krogstad to be an unprosecuted forger, so of course he has stayed near the bottom of the ladder. In Act Three Mrs Linde says to him, 'Nils, what about us two castaways joining forces?' She means it; it's not just a device to stop him betraying Nora's secret, though that is also the desired effect. There is a touch of seediness about both of them: the self-sacrificing, mildly resentful Mrs Linde, plain as well as spirited; Krogstad hitherto steeped in malice. And they come together *tragically*, which is to say with no higher hopes for a happy future than their pasts will allow.

But what of Dr Rank? He is not irrelevant to the plot and how much the play would lose without his resignation and clear, harsh view of society. Knowing himself to be physically sick (tuberculosis of the spine), he says of Kristine Linde's belief that the morally sick need to be protected, 'It's that attitude that's turning society into a clinic' (Act One). The remark is not crabbed, merely stern. When Rank sends his visiting card marked with a black cross to indicate that he has withdrawn from society to die, his action, one must assume, later helps Nora to steel herself for her departure. Once she childishly refused to acknowledge Rank's love for her: in the end she shares his knowledge of a sterner dimension. For *A Doll's House*, though it ends in a manner 'happily', has the temper of tragedy: it is cast in a tragic mould and is therefore enlivening in the ancient, ambivalent fasion.

The same sort of ambivalence is yet more marked in *Ghosts*, which was published in 1881 and first staged in Chicago in 1882. I refer, of course, to the melancholy beauty with which Ibsen has invested the topic of spiritual and physical degeneracy. This logical contradiction should detain us for a while. To begin with, everyone knows about the gibberings which greeted the 1891 production at the Royalty Theatre in London: 'a lazar house with all its doors and windows open', for instance. (Was it better for lazars if they were denied fresh air?)[10] Just the same the source of our pleasure in the story of Oswald and Mrs Alving is far from obvious, for this play lacks various alluring tragic attributes: the

splendour of the classical heroes and heroines, the rich languag
of Renaissance dramatists, and even, apart from Regine Eng
strand's attractions, the sensuality which is a seldom acknow
ledged part of the fascination of many tragedies, ancient an
modern. The very question seems ridiculous, but what is there t
rival these traditional qualities in Oswald's hereditary syphilis
or schizophrenia, if that's what it is?[11] And Mrs Alving, thoug
undoubtedly a heroine, is a heroine in some more obscure sor
than, say, Antigone or Cleopatra.

Ibsen referred to Mrs Alving as if she were forced upon him
'after Nora, Mrs Alving of necessity had to come'.[12] Surely h
meant that criticisms of Nora's departure impelled him to Mr
Alving. For Ibsen's mind regularly worked in a controversial an
logical fashion: one play grew out of his defiance of the hostil
responses to its predecessor. He was forever arguing with som
section of the public. For example, people said that a woman mus
place her marriage vows before her so-called 'happiness' o
'self-fulfilment'. Very well, remarked Ibsen in effect, suppose th
husband is a chronic debauchee. Then the wife is likely to b
wretched, came the response, but she must bear it as best she can
Ibsen knew that people who argue thus deaden their imagination
whenever they might picture consequences incompatible witl
their wishes. Note that Ibsen is still not recommending a form c
behaviour, but pointing out that whatever one does bears fruit
Helene Alving's way is neither better nor worse than Nor;
Helmer's: each way simply produces its characteristic conse
quences.

As usual everything is precise, distinct, localised. After a year o
her marriage to Lieutenant Alving, young Helene felt she couldn'
stand his profligacy any longer and ran way to the house of Pasto
Manders whom she greatly respected and, for that matter
desired. Being an ass, Manders told her that marital duties cam
first: what right had people to happiness? She returned to Alving
and endured years of his drinking and lewdness. Now Captair
Alving (as he became in the course of time) has been dead for ter
years and in Act One Mrs Alving tells an astonished Manders
that her husband continued his career of debauchery. She sen
Oswald, their child, away from home at the early age of seven, no
out of selfishness as Manders has always typically supposed, bu
to remove him from his father's influence. Now with a sum o
money exactly equalling the amount Alving brought as a young

man to their married life together (he was quite a 'good catch'),
Mrs Alving has had an orphanage built on her estate. It will be
known as the 'Captain Alving Memorial Home'.

Here we should consider the point of the play. This is summed
up in the title which has two distinct messages: first, that past
deeds commonly 'haunt' or influence the present, and secondly
that each generation inherits ideas which are no longer appropriate – ghost ideas, neither living nor dead. Captain Alving left
behind him in addition to his long-suffering, still handsome
widow (descended, I think, from Lady Inger of Ibsen's youthful
play), a natural daughter Regine, and a son Oswald, now on the
verge of disintegration as the consequence of his father's venereal
disease.

I mention these well-known matters not for the sake of doing so
but to emphasise Ibsen's meaning. He was well aware of luck,
pure contingency, but was not especially interested in it. On the
contrary he wanted to show by startling means that behaviour
makes the future as a flame runs along a fuse. In so far as one's
actions have been influenced by the doings of one's parents, the
only way to modify the pattern is presumably to become fully
aware of the influence. Early in *Ghosts* we learn that when he was a
young man Alving copulated with the maid Johanna, who was
prudently married off to the carpenter Jacob Engstrand, her value
being enhanced by a bribe of three hundred dollars. Alving's child
by Johanna was name Regine and raised as Engstrand's daughter. Now Regine is herself maid to Mrs Alving and at the close of
Act One is fondled by Oswald in the conservatory. Her expostula-
tion is much the same as Johanna's a generation earlier.

(One reason to doubt, by the way, that Oswald is himself in an
advanced stage of syphilis is that he, a decent enough young man,
would then be unlikely to embrace Regine. All the more reason to
suppose that it is imminent madness which tires him out so easily,
gives him headaches, fills him with irrational dread. Oswald says
in Act Two, 'Mother, it's my mind that's given way ...
destroyed'.)

However, what can be done to lay this type of 'ghost'? In this
instance Oswald and Regine are both better off when Mrs Alving
recounts the facts, in Act Three. Similarly it is beneficial for
Mrs Alving to tell Pastor Manders (in the first act) that Alving
never reformed and that his, Manders's, advice led to her
miserable married life. These are debilitating mysteries and the

people concerned are able to bear the truth, indeed to profit from
it.

In a sense, too, it is part of Captain Alving's legacy that the
orphanage should be named after him, for Mrs Alving has
naturally never corrected the favourable impression he managed
to make. His name really ought not to live on in this pious fashion,
as Ibsen implies by causing the orphanage to burn down,
uninsured on Manders's advice, since the building is God's and
He will provide.

This last item brings us to the other form of haunting, the
tenacity of old beliefs. Scarcely anyone would now fail to insure
one of God's buildings, yet that older attitude is perfectly
reasonable for a devout Christian. To what extent can believers
take providence into their own hands before, psychologically
speaking, they no longer need divine providence? Of course, it is
Manders himself who carelessly throws an unextinguished candle
among some wood shavings and so starts the fire. What does
Ibsen mean? Is he linking everything together: degeneracy, the
Church, hypocritical secrets?

One critic has argued that that is indeed what Ibsen set out to
do: Daniel Dervin in his *Bernard Shaw, A Psychological Study*
contends that Ibsen 'has willed the highest (the Church) to the
lowest (V.D.) with an invisible time fuse.' The movement, Dervin
says, is from Manders's morality to Oswald's disease.[13] That is
certainly so, but the connection made by Ibsen should be seen as
part of an all-embracing conviction. He thought that our culture
as a whole, including Christianity, had *unavoidably* led us astray.
Madness lies in devising a culture which demeans the link
between man and nature: the instincts, the flesh, the infinitely
slow processes of evolution. Among Ibsen's jottings at the time of
Ghosts we find the following comment:

> The fault lies in the fact that the whole of mankind is a failure. If
> a man demands to live and develop as a man should, then that
> is megalomania. The whole of mankind, and especially Christ-
> ians, suffer from megalomania.[14]

It is a man's nature to aspire, but in doing so he is guilty of
hubris. As a sort of aspiration, Manders, for instance, wants a
mankind which is minimally, decorously, 'economically' sexual.
So did the Church generally; Manders is orthodox. Therefore the

sins of such as Alving become doubly wicked, for lying is added to lechery. Manders and his like wish to distance man from nature, but there is nothing eccentric about that ambition. I think Ibsen realised that it is not God but the pagan gods who punish hubris, yet God Himself is the most colossal expression of our hubris, the means by which we try to convince ourselves that we are out of place on earth. That God should be man's supreme tragic error – what a notion!

I do not know if it was ever Ibsen's conscious notion. Certainly Pastor Manders is God's representative: let us not be so foolish as to assert that he speaks only for the narrow northern Church. Manders's victims are, of course, Oswald and Mrs Alving. As has too often been remarked, they are sufferers from a convention, but the convention is itself an expression of God and the Church, since it is set forth on the words, 'Those whom God hath joined together let no man put asunder.' Because no one sundered the union of Alving and Helene, Oswald was born with the germs of a slow-ravaging disease. As for Mrs Alving, she is a figure of fortitude, intelligence and, in the end, complete if horrified understanding. If she had not, as a young woman, returned to the lustful (and life-loving) Alving, Oswald would not have been born and the sequence would never have taken place. Now in the knowledge that she shares the responsibility for all this pain, Mrs Alving is faced with Oswald's assumption that, as a loving mother, she will give him poison tablets. They shake hands on the agreement, she assuring herself that things will never reach such a pass. As Oswald sinks into a stupor she is bereft and terrified. All her stoical years have come to this: she must murder her son or, if she hasn't the nerve, watch him mumbling and drooling for the rest of his days. Mrs Alving is a heroine because she is the proud and sensitive focus of every point of wretchedness in the play.

It is necessary to add that daybreak comes while this ordeal is taking place, not solely to signify the closing of a chapter of misery, but to place these human doings in their natural as opposed to religious, context. So Oswald is right to mutter contentedly and we are right to feel elated as the sun clears the fjord mists.

If anyone suggests that there is a gulf between the Ibsen of *Ghosts* and the earlier, fiercer Ibsen of *Brand*, who seemed actually to welcome suffering, the response must be that he has not gone over to the ranks of comfort-lovers and happiness-seekers. No doubt Brand, like Manders, would tell Mrs Alving to return to her husband, but would do so fully aware of the rigours of her life, with or without Alving. Manders, for all his pastoral functions, is a worldly wiseman and Brand a pilgrim ('myself', as Ibsen said, 'in my best moments').[15]

Ibsen's distaste for some features of conventional religion did not mean that he preferred secularism in its easy guise. Just before writing *Ghosts* he had started *An Enemy of the People* and while the storm was raging over *Ghosts* he completed the other, less disturbing play. It is well known that the finished version of *An Enemy of the People* (1882) is informed with Ibsen's feeling over the reception given to *Ghosts*. He probably alternated between fury with the critics and a calmer disdain for them. He no longer expected sensible comments from the general run of critics and, further, he was growing sure that society must by its very nature be hostile to 'truth'.

This attitude of Ibsen is quite the reverse of the Marxian belief that it is possible to rid society of its alienating elements, so that each individual may express himself in his work and thus become a 'species-being', recognising his own forces, in Marx's phrase, 'as social forces'.[16] To Ibsen, on the contrary, while a man is normally and obviously a member of some social group, while his forces are certainly of a social nature, new truths constantly replace existing customs and the proclaimers of the new must inevitably be persecuted. The dynamic of society is therefore a struggle not between classes but between the tiny vanguard and the multitude. I do not think that Ibsen saw any end to this process. We might note, too, that in his view truths were not ancient and unalterable – though they rested on a constant tragic base – but forever evolving. Nor were these truths objectively true at all, but merely ways in which people temporarily found it convenient to organise and explain the world.

This manner of thinking is implicit in *An Enemy of the People*, which is not simply a play about one honest man and his false community but about the usual relation of the pioneer to the compact majority. In this instance, however, the pioneer is scientifically correct, so his enemies are unambiguously wrong. Once again Ibsen did not project himself into a fictional character but this time took some traits of Bjørnstjerne Bjørnson, in particular Bjørnson's generous, artless ways, and incorporated them into a plot suggested by two actual incidents.[17] Thus Ibsen distanced his outer personality from a drama whose well-springs, nevertheless, were his own anti-democratic feelings. He really believed by now that the majority is always wrong and the minority always right. He can only have meant, as a sensible proposition, that a minority makes the future and so is proved 'right'. It is hard to say how far Ibsen welcomed progress: he seems to have believed in pressing forward as a vigorous way of life and because there are always wrongs to be righted, but not on the grounds that the future must generally be better than the past. The play is really about leaders and led, both of which as psychological types may be found in any social class. The business in *An Enemy of the People* of the contaminated water is only the occasion of Dr Stockmann's or Ibsen's general conclusions.

Stockmann is in part made up of Bjørnson's ways and Ibsen's opinions. To be precise the conclusions to which he stumbles are Ibsen's. As a complete character Stockmann is meant to be somewhat irritating, or rather, from the point of view of the audience, a palatable copy of an irritating man. He has the shortcomings as well as the strengths of one who is only dimly aware of the usual social manoeuvres. He has spent years working in an ill-paid capacity up north and has returned to town breezily confident and politically innocent. He is noisy, cheerful, heedless and insensitive. He doesn't notice nuances; for example, when his brother, the Mayor, remarks disapprovingly of the diners at Stockmann's house, 'It's incredible the amount of food they manage to put away,' Stockman replies, 'Yes, isn't it good to see young people eating well' (Act One). Later when every important citizen is against him he relishes the prospect of sweeping these 'dodderers' aside (Act Three). He is contemptuous enough to make a modern social democrat blench. To his wife, when she exasperates him, he shouts like a very Torvald Helmer, 'Go home and look to your house and let me look to society' (Act Three). In Act Five he wants his servant to clear up the mess but typically cannot remember her name, so uses a periphrasis: 'that girl who's always got a dirty nose!'

Stockmann's progress is from ebullient innocence to scarcely less ebullient experience. He learns in Act One that analysis of the water samples shows the new baths to be a 'whited poisoned sepulchre' and therefore looks forward to a rumpus with the authorities. At this stage he assumes that all decent townspeople will be with him against any corrupt official who tries to hush things up. Morton Kiil, Mrs Stockmann's foster-father, does indeed side with him out of malice, but later buys shares in the baths on his assumption that the whole business must be a Stockmann-inspired confidence trick. The local journalists are excited by this discovery of bacteria, because it gives them an excellent opportunity to lambast the Mayor and his cronies. When, in Act Three, the Mayor points out that to rectify the water system will put up the rates, these same journalists change sides on the spot. Aslaksen, the printer, feels all along that the facts about the bacteria can somehow be 'moderated' into an unexciting technicality. Above all, the Mayor, almost a replica of the Mayor in *Brand*, is just such a one who will find a way to moderate the question. He sincerely believes his brother to be eccentric, vulnerable and vile.

What Ibsen demonstrates through the sincerity of the Mayor is that rogues in politics usually do not know they are rogues. Nor do they belong to an exclusive category, for sooner or later very many people are liable to join them. It is the Mayor's unexceptional opinion that to act on behalf of one's community is to be a good fellow whatever the lies it entails. Ibsen, as always, regards the community as Vanity Fair, redeemed only by the few who see it rightly. The ethic he demands surpasses the community in order to confer value upon the community. The immediate issue of this play is straightforward: if the authorities ignore Stockmann's findings people will catch cholera or typhus. But it is clear from Stockmann's speech, which takes up a good deal of Act Four, that we are supposed to see the pollution of the water as a symptom of spiritual disease.

The subject of the public meeting called by Stockmann is, of course, the water supply, so when he starts discoursing on metaphysics Aslaksen and the Mayor point out his irrelevancy. Stockmann explains the connection to his brother as follows:

> You must be mad, Peter. I'm sticking as close to the subject as I can. For that's what I'm trying to say: that the masses, this damned compact majority – *this* is the thing that's polluting the sources of our spiritual life and infecting the very ground we stand on' (Act Four).

Stockmann thus goes beyond the immediate issues to what he regards as their groundwork. It was Ibsen's own nature to do this in his letters and notes, while in the plays he increasingly preferred to demonstrate rather than argue. After *An Enemy of the People* ideas seem to be quite replaced by natural behaviour. Nevertheless, we shall be right to trace an unobtrusive philosophic pattern in the details of the plays from *The Wild Duck* onwards. And of course the stance of such a man as Dr Stockmann is bound to be unpopular, because it subordinates both the personal and the collective will to a transcendent criterion.

Ibsen was certainly right to stress Stockmann's unacceptability in the eyes of the majority. Throughout the play only two people consistently stand by him: his daughter Petra, and Captain Horster, a seaman who holds cheerfully aloof from the rest of the town. Finally Stockmann together with Petra and his wife Katherine, whose attitude has wavered for much of the play, resolves to start a school for the local 'guttersnipes'. Ibsen's own message, cracker-motto in form though not in content, is Stockmann's closing remark: 'The thing is, you see, that the strongest man in the world is the man who stands alone.' At least for the time being Ibsen unqualifiedly meant what he had Stockmann say. Perhaps he continued to mean it, for he never wrote a play warning people about the perils or the wickedness of standing alone. (I think that *John Gabriel Borkman* should no more be considered in that light than *Brand*.) Just the same, he seems generally to have believed that ready formulas are ill-suited to human situations, and Stockmann's is the last formulated message in the canon.

Was 'truth' itself so sacred to Ibsen as turn-of-the-century critics sometimes suggested? Down the years Ibsenites have rightly supposed that the next play, *The Wild Duck* (1884), is a deliberate repudiation of the view, already in the 1880s attributed to Ibsen, that truth-tellers are necessarily beneficial. In other words, so the assertion runs, Ibsen is here either clearing up a misconception about himself, or more likely, having second thoughts. The pernicious Gregers Werle is one who puts truth before everything else: that is the priority to be imposed willy-nilly upon others as well as zestfully accepted by himself. F. L. Lucas writes that Werle is a 'muddling idiot of an idealist . . . a sort of Rabbi Zeal-of-the-land Busy'.[18] M. C. Bradbrook remarks that Gregers, 'is the man who has found the entire solution to life in a creed, whether that of Marx or Freud, the Oxford Group or Yoga'.[19] The chapter of Professor Bradbrook's book in which she makes this comment is entitled 'The Humanist', summarising her belief that Ibsen's attitudes from *The Wild Duck* to *Hedda Gabler* were predominantly humanistic. A man of that persuasion would dislike the ways of a Brand and revile the ways of a Hjordis: he might well regard a few illusions as a small price to pay for happiness.

I suggest, however, that Ibsen's actual development at this point in his career was from social lawgiver to student of individual psychology. He had always been both in some degree but from now on the emphasis would be overwhelmingly upon the latter. Nor would his psychological observations generally obliterate distinctions of value among persons in the way that humanism encourages and science demands. But it is true that *The Wild Duck* itself, the transitional play, does take that lenient or morally uncertain form. He wrote in a letter of 1884 that 'long daily association with the persons in this play has endeared them to me, despite their manifold failings.'[20] Nevertheless, his notes and jottings at this time often display the same old contempt for the bulk of mankind.[21] The great thing now was to realise oneself. In 1884, while working on *The Wild Duck*, he wrote to Frederick Hegel, 'I believe that none of us can do anything other or anything better than realise ourselves in truth and in spirit.'[22] Ibsen's increased tolerance probably amounted to a belief, first, that no one, not Christ Himself or Saga hero, should be the universal model, and secondly, that even self-realisation was beyond the reach of most people. Just the same, to resist or cast off a false self was an achievement, possibly a kind of heroism. *The Wild Duck* is a tragedy which faintly foreshadows the late twentieth-century mode of piteous comedy, about a group of people most of whom cannot breach a structure of ego-defences. But to rid oneself of such a structure was to Ibsen, as to Freud, a proper goal. In future plays the person who manages this stands forth as hero, admirable despite failings, and more often than not, the discovery of self necessarily coincides with death. That is not modern humanism but more nearly ancient tragedy.

Now *The Wild Duck* is a play without a hero. Gregers Werle is an ersatz truth-teller, for he resembles an incompetent psychoanalyst who blurts outs his discoveries to a patient before the patient is ready for them. He constitutes an attack less upon Ibsen's earlier attitudes than upon critics' assumptions about those attitudes. That is not to say that Hjalmar Ekdal and even the poor child Hedvig, if we imagine her spared Gregers' clumsy disclosures, would not be better for sooner or later learning the truth. And of what sort is the truth? It is neither a philosophic concept nor an article of religious faith: it is more nearly the psycho-analytic facts, the route an individual's thoughts and feelings have followed, or that which is left high and dry when rationalisations and fantasies have fallen away.

More needs to be said about the flaw in Gregers Werle, for in Act Five Dr Relling tells him, 'Take away the life-lie from the average man and straight away you take away his happiness.' This is rightly regarded as the sort of sentiment Ibsen might personally have uttered, but he did not therefore rate life-lies and reality-perceptions equally. He lacked enthusiasm both for average men and for ordinary happiness. According to the critic Harold Clurman, people who seize on the word 'average', as I do now, are 'rationalising', yet Relling uses it to mean 'unexceptional', while Ibsen himself always preferred exceptional individuals.[23] He was no democrat, but – to adapt Camus' excellent phrase – a 'bitter aristocrat'.[24]

We must appreciate, too, that Gregers's desire to enlighten Hjalmar Ekdal is not quite disinterested, for he surely takes pleasure in hurting Haakon Werle. The older Werle says to Gregers towards the end of the first act, 'I don't think there's any man in the world you hate as much as me.' A few moments later Gregers realises that he has found a goal in life, 'an objective I can live for'. He means that he will expose falsehoods and begin by letting the Ekdal family know how they have been exploited. It is at worst a simplification to regard Gregers as one who favoured his mother and is now punishing his hated father. Of course, he thinks he is doing so by irreproachable means. He sees himself as a crusader and is thus the subtlest self-deceiver in the play, if not the most grotesque.

As a child and youth Gregers's sympathies flowed towards his mother, while he found his father distasteful. Nevertheless, he insists to Haakon Werle, 'I am not neurotic' (Act One), and he is certainly intact, impregnable. To escape from home Gregers arranged for himself to be employed in the family works at Hoidal, up north. Subsequently Haakon Werle started an affair with Gina Hansen, the housekeeper, but owing to Fru Werle's understandable (and alcholic) jealousy, Gina was forced to quit. Fru Werle died and fairly soon Haakon took up with Gina again. He probably made her pregnant (Ibsen is not explicit), but for an

unexplained reason Gina married Hjalmar Ekdal, and the
daughter Hedvig, has rightly or wrongly always seemed to be
Hjalmar's. At that time Haakon Werle provided the money to set
Hjalmar up in business as a photographer. Old Werle's manipulations of the Ekdal family may not have ended there, since it is
likely that he was privy to the scheme for cutting down timber on
government land, for which crime Old Ekdal went to gaol. The
latter is now a pathetic drunk, while Werle is still prosperous,
tricky and even libidinous, for he plans to marry the attractive
widow Mrs Sorby.

Ibsen does not provide the facts about either Hedvig's paren-
tage or the felling of government timber, and this restraint keeps
sympathy for Gregers Werle completely at bay, for if we knew
what we only suspect, if at some point Haakon Werle's rascally
ways were revealed to the audience, then we too might wish that
Gregers would somehow reveal them to Haakon's victims. Werle
fades into the background, so that neither his villainy nor for that
matter his promise as a complex character is ever realised.

Consequently we are disposed exclusively to blame Gregers
Werle and the ridiculous Hjalmar Ekdal. Hjalmar, the finest
dramatic character of them all, is a familiar enough type in
everyday life, though not in fiction. His being is saturated in
sentimentality: his love for Gina and Hedvig, his occupation as a
photographer, his recollections of the past, his present modest
means, all these elements are filtered through delectably self-
pitying phrases. Hjalmar turns miseries into pallid joys by the
gestures with which he expresses them. Even Hedvig's suicide will
soon be the occasion of a pose – bowed head and lowered voice
'Give him nine months,' says Dr Relling, 'and little Hedvig will be
nothing more than the theme of a pretty little party piece' (Act
Five). Hjalmar Ekdal is probably the best illustration in the world
of art of how to transform wretchedness into pleasure by the
processes of eye-piping, brow-wiping, hand-wringing, shoulder-
hunching *charm*. And, of course, he is farcically married to his
opposite, the decently non-moralistic Gina, who seems to have no
shell of make believe. Gina will live as best she can and scarcely
ever suppose that even an inward drama, let alone an exhibition
might help to console her for the loss of Hedvig.

In writing this first of his truly distinguished plays (a work not
faultless but quite undimmed by time and socio-culture change)
Ibsen, as is widely recognised, found objective correlatives for his

emotions about childhood at Venstøp. Old Ekdal embodies the pathos though not the sardonic energy of Knud Ibsen, the derelict old man worsted by the sort of shrewdness he continued to admire. As for Gregers Werle, whether or not he owes something to a man Ibsen observed, he is probably a figure of the temptation which Ibsen usually resisted, the impulse to show up a malpractice, an insincerity, no matter if some simple souls are incidentally hurt. And little Hedvig, at a guess, represents not so much the real and rounded sister of Ibsen, but his feeling that his sister was an innocent victim of family failings and misfortunes. It is Hedvig Ekdal who dreams in the loft and reads *Harrison's History of London* – the solitary practices of Ibsen's own childhood.

To these local but representative matters Ibsen adds his universal wild duck. The hunter's tale has it that a duck goes down to the bottom of the lake when it is wounded: the creature's trauma is such that it hides in the depths from man and nature. That is the nicest conceivable image of the wounded psyche held fast in fantasy or madness.

Of course, the duck is more than that, for it represents and amalgamates a number of strictly disparate features of the play – as James Walter McFarlane, the Oxford editor, has demonstrated.[25] And in a much larger sense it suggests the quality of wildness, now 'Freudianly' confined in mock-arboreal gloom. Indeed the Ekdal's partitioned studio houses a miniature forest, complete with animals as well as trees, so that in the fantasies of the two men of the house nature itself is pent in an urban attic. From now on Ibsen will copy behaviour with an accuracy unprecedented in world theatre and then, on that mimetic foundation, reintroduce the proper forms of nature as part of an exceedingly ambitious, perhaps scarcely conscious attempt to transvalue all values.

4 *Rosmersholm* to *When We Dead Awaken*

The unprecedented problem that finally forced itself upon man's attention at the end of the nineteenth century was how to retain morality when the divine author of morality had slipped away. To be sure, there were optimistic thinkers who believed that religion had merely illuminated an inborn moral sense or, alternatively, had fastened a knowledge of right and wrong into man's make-up for evermore. But others could not share those sanguine expectations. In England Thomas Hardy, for example, treated the Church as itself purely a culture within the vastness of a soulless universe. Consequently Hardy's characters are to a greater or lesser degree responsive to natural rather than moral urgencies and are sometimes torn between the two. There are no commandments, not even the Comtean psychological laws with which George Eliot had recently tried to replace the gospels.

Now the idea that solicited Ibsen at the time of writing *Rosmersholm* must have been this: the best of those who forsake the faith (such as Rosmer and Rebecca West) must nevertheless have some conviction for which they are ready to sacrifice themselves. For otherwise no distinctions of value will survive and there will be an endless night of factional, if rational argument and ghastly but insignificant crime.

We can guess how this idea grew out of *The Wild Duck* and possibly some early, Scandinavian reactions to that play. In 1885, between the first production of *The Wild Duck* and the planning of *Rosmersholm*, Ibsen went back to Norway for the first time in eleven years. At Trondheim he made a speech to a workers' procession, the following sentences from which are often quoted:

> An element of nobility must find its way into our public life, into our government, among our representatives and into our press. Of course I am not thinking of nobility of birth, nor of money,

not a nobility of learning, nor even of ability or talent. What I am thinking of is a nobility of character, of mind and will. That alone can liberate us.[1]

This quality, he added, would come not from all ranks of the citizenry but from women and workers. A year before the speech Ibsen had patently excluded nobility in any sense from *The Wild Duck* which may be one of the reasons why it is so highly regarded in our mock-plebeian period. But we ought now to be able to see that *The Wild Duck* was a transitional play, in the composition of which Ibsen widened his hitherto rather narrow sympathies. Afterwards he embarked on his final, most confident and subtle search for a scheme of right and wrong – or better, high and low – which should replace what he regarded as the faded Christian scheme. Let us approach *Rosmersholm* as the first part of that search, or in other words contemplate it to begin with as a play of ideas, even though the ideas in question are thoroughly woven into the characters and their relations with one another.

For all the people of the play (except Mrs Helseth, the housekeeper) are creatures of their time, historical figures in an unusual sense of the word, since each responds in the quick of his or her being to certain contemporary arguments. They embody the arguments without thereby relinquishing their humanity. Thus Johannes Rosmer is a former clergyman (so designated) for the very reasons that only a generation earlier would have impelled him to the cloth. He wants to do people good, but in the modern way of 'liberating their minds' as well as the traditional way of 'purging their wills' (Act One). The two processes are no longer antithetical but now dependent on each other.

More than that, Rosmer wishes, he says, 'to make all my countrymen noble' (Act One). How should we apprehend this notion of nobility with which Ibsen was once again preoccupied? Here he seems to have been thinking of Christian or 'post-Christian' ethics, compounded of love, altruism and disinterestedness. Yet the term 'noble' etymologically belongs to 'master morality' rather than 'slave morality', to borrow Nietzsche's distinction and in an Ibsenist context is usually reminiscent of Aristotle's account in the *Nichomachean Ethics* of the 'magnanimous man' (who can only be an aristocrat).[2] The essential features of magnanimity are freedom of behaviour and generosity of mind. Such a person is motivated from within by his own spontaneous choices rather than from without by social pressures or private persuasions. He uninhibitedly does what he wishes, but what he wishes is never resentful or fainthearted. He is truthful, disdainful of consequences, a keeper of promises. He is jealous of his honour and correspondingly susceptible to shame, though not, it seems, to moral guilt. In a special sense (and this in fact applies to the transformed Rosmer and Rebecca at the end of the play) he is also fatalistic.

Aristotle and Nietzsche both commonsensically ascribe such characteristics to a minority, but Rosmer in the manner of a late nineteenth-century idealist wishes to work for a 'noble' Norwegian population, according to his understanding of the term. Why then do we not forget about the ancient, aristocratic scale of values? The answer is that a creative confusion of the two codes lies at the heart of the play, alongside or beneath the superficial struggle between them.

Rosmer wants a noble democracy, in his sense, because he himself is effortlessly virtuous. He lacks the old Adam; both his aggressive and his sensual impulses are weak. Years earlier Rosmer's father, a Major, horsewhipped Ulric Brendel, the boy's radical tutor, out of the house and, it seems, Johannes grew up disliking authority but too sweet-natured to rebel, or even to feel resentment. His Christianity presumably used to be of an endlessly merciful sort and he is now a secular, visionary philanthropist. After he married Beata he found she had 'wild fits of sensual passion' which 'appalled' him (Act Two) and she in turn was appalled by her husband's religious doubts. Beata did not understand the extent to which Rosmer was susceptible to reasonable argument, especially when the reasoning was steeped in the spirit of benevolence. In this way the personal qualities that once drew him into the ministry later drove him out of it – towards the ranks of the young and unconventional.

Rebecca West, for her part, came to the district with her foster-father Dr West, in her mid-twenties. (At the time of the play she is thirty to Rosmer's forty-three.) She and Dr West formerly lived in Finmark and she, though not he, was bred in that far province of snow and darkness and legendary enchantments. But the doctor was a free thinker and he passed his attitudes on to Rebecca who thus developed her extraordinary combination of ancient allure and modern rationality. (Ibsen so often achieved his effects by using qualities which our categorising minds keep firmly apart.)

At this point the contribution of psychoanalysis is inescapable. According to Freud, who famously diagnosed Rebecca's condition almost as though she were one of his patients, Dr West was not only her natural father (a fact Kroll discloses to her in Act Three) but must also have been her lover.[3] So in the course of the play Rebecca discovers she is guilty of incest and is therefore drawn to suicide.

Freud's deduction is persuasive (though contrary to a canon of literary criticism) if only because it explains as nothing else could Rebecca's distress when, in Act Three, Kroll convinces her that Dr West was her father. Thus Freud clarified the psychology of the play, but not what we might properly call its 'philosophy'.

At the end Rosmer's aspirations are in ruins: 'You know,' he says to Rebecca, 'people can't be ennobled from the outside' (Act Four). Since nothing valuable of his personality has ever exceeded or evaded those aspirations, his only recourse is suicide. This ex-Christian, like many ex-Christians, must have faith in something: a purely empirical, let alone a merely fashionable way of life will not do. He could potentially have faith in Rebecca's love, but that love itself is suspect unless she is willing to die with him. So the couple reach a perfect tragic impasse.

It happens, moreover, that Rebecca is now spiritually lacklustre. She killed Beata in effect and, so we are inclined to believe, she was her father's mistress. But leaving aside such courtroom categories of guilt, Rosmersholm has sapped her vitality. She says to Rosmer: 'It is the Rosmer philosophy of life . . . or in any case *your* philosophy that has infected my will . . . And made it sick. Made it a slave to laws that had meant nothing to me before. You . . . being together with you . . . has given me some nobility of mind . . .' (Act Four).

By now Ibsen ought somehow to be making it clear that 'nobility' in Rosmer's and Rebecca's etymologically perverse sense is pretty well the opposite of the historical nobility of, say, Germanicus or Brutus. It is not simply different or a natural development from the ancient code; it is a denial of exactly that will, that pride in self-determination which was of a piece with the vitality of a warrior or statesman of the old world. Rebecca's own will, bold yet honourable in its way, has succumbed to the contagion of virtue which infests the very air of Rosmersholm.

Ibsen himself was baffled by the dilemma, yet he knew it to be the modern dilemma that sooner or later must be resolved. To put it bluntly, as Ibsen already suspected in 1850 at the stage of *The Burial Mound*, and as he asserted at length in *Emperor and Galilean*, vigour and virtue of the Rosmer variety are positively opposed. From now on all Ibsen's heroes and heroines who go voluntarily to their deaths do so because they would rather be dead than wanly alive. Hedda Gabler will not be a cowed victim of Judge Brack; Solness will not continue to build humdrum dwellings; Borkman will no longer entertain his grand illusion, and Rubeck no more fashion petty sculptures.

Here, however, Rosmer and Rebecca have reached the end of their resources, each for a different, indeed opposed reason. Rosmer presumes that the social ideal with which he has replaced the Christian ministry is flatly impossible: he cannot make others 'noble'. As a result his life is unalterably futile and he ought simply to die. He wants only Rebecca's love and brief companion- ship. Rebecca, on the other hand, has worshipped pagan gods but finds these gods worsted by the pallid spirits of benevolence and guilt.

She dies for Rosmer's sake, it is true, but also because her life-force has almost perished along with her paganism. To live philanthropically (the commonest course for repentant sinners) would falsify her very being and, further, the one kindness she alone is qualified to do is to kill herself along with Rosmer. That might be said to be a romantic sort of kindness, absurd from a utilitarian point of view. Yet even from so unpromising a perspective these two fictional characters should be seen to contribute in no trifling manner to the quest for values that we fitfully pursue a hundred years on, suspecting ourselves to be units in a universe of valueless energies.

It is a philosopher's task of course, but it was also Ibsen's after his artist's unsystematic fashion, to ask how human beings can properly distinguish themselves from the wanton forces of which they are composed. His unformulated question was not: How do people differ from structures of energy pure and simple? On the contrary, he was modern enough to ask in effect: In what way are we pure structures of energy differentiated from others? To judge from the mature plays and other utterances of the same period his answer might have taken the following form.

All conscious beings make meanings of their environments, but man first, has an unlimited environment to render meaningful and secondly, confers values upon human activities as part of the process of interpretation. Man is the measure of all things, though he is also bound up with all the things he measures. He is not an independent measuring creature situated in measurable contexts. The only distinction we can discern is that man, unlike other beings, is able to know things, to know that he knows them and thus to make conscious choices. In other words, his energies can in part be directed towards apprehending, or at least interpreting their own origins and functions. Man is free to choose, obviously not in the sense that he is without unconscious motivations, but because he can grow progressively aware of his motivations. In this way he is potentially able to reject persuasions that do not meet his fundamental requirements. (In contrast, a wild animal has the advantage, so to speak, that it is not distracted from its proper self by culture, but such unconscious 'integrity' is part and parcel of an inability, beyond severe limits, to modify the environment.)

The foregoing remarks indicate the sort of attitude that lies behind later plays. Ellida Wangel, the heroine of *The Lady from the Sea*, has an excess of Rebecca West's affinity with nature, but quite lacks Rebecca's sophisticated intellect. Thus, although she is a less powerful figure than Rebecca, she is a more extreme 'case', and that, I suspect, is one of the reasons why Ibsen conceived her. She is non-rational (rather than irrational) and in a manner without will. Ellida's signal feature is that, as her husband Dr Wangel puts it, she is 'one of the sea people' whose 'thoughts and feelings ebb and flow like the tide' (Act Four).[4] She, whose father is or was a lighthouse-keeper and whose mother went mad, has difficulty in distinguishing herself clearly and firmly from the sea. She is convinced that the sea is her natural element and her mind, beneath the surface, is barely accessible to others or even to herself except through sea-imagery. The assertion, 'Her thoughts and feelings ebb and flow like the sea', is rather more exact than most similies.

Her name is a ship's name and she conjectures that 'if only man had learnt to live in the sea from the very first' he would have developed more successfully (Act Three). Ibsen wondered in his

preliminary notes to the play if human evolution had 'taken the
wrong path'.[5] Why do we not belong to the sea – or to the air? 'The
great secret,' he commented a little later, 'is the dependence of the
human will on "the will-less".'[6] What he meant was that man
cannot control his being which is irredeemably part of nature, and
that is ancient Stoicism, specifically the doctrine of Zeno. The
implication of the plays is that each individual can at best
faithfully acknowledge his own being and so, I suppose, reach
what is, after all, the unpretentious goal of psychoanalysis: love of
fate. Ellida thinks constantly in images, not words. Wangel tells
her in Act Five, 'Your mind works in visual terms.' Indeed she is
presented with pictures that threaten to overwhelm her. Society
doesn't adequately set off such magnetic private symbols and,
until the end of the play, neither does Ellida's family life. I have
emphasised that she herself is 'will-less' and so in the ordinary
sense she is. Just the same her very lack of normal will is a
negation of the community, her husband, her stepdaughters
Bolette and Hilde, and almost all the rest of humankind.
Consequently this lack has the *force* of will; it acts as a barrier or,
since 'barrier' wrongly suggest solidity, as the blackest ocean
depths.

Ibsen had been interested in figures of roughly the same sort
since his youth when he created Anne of *St John's Night* and Alfhild
of *The Grouse at Justedal*. The relevant aspect of his vision (which
concludes, in public terms at least, only at the end of *When We Dead
Awaken* when Irene and Rubek are engulfed by an avalanche) is
connected with an awareness that modern man is estranged from
his biological roots. Ellida is a rare individual in that she retains
something of the patterns of feeling and response of our remote
ancestors. Those forefathers did not differentiate themselves from
their environment. The trees housed spirits, the mountains spoke,
a storm was a god's wrath; everything was alive in a human
fashion and concomitantly the human fashion was of a piece with
the non-human. Nor did our ancestors think in anything resembling our manner, by which I mean the manner of the last three
thousand years. They were *entirely* responsive to their surroundings and paramountly 'will-less' in Ibsen's meaning of the term.
Therefore they were not 'alienated' and their varieties of anthro-
pomorphic culture reflected their mad intensity and vulnera-
bility amid the varieties of natural magic. Now, Ellida is a gentle
savage who in the course of the play is emancipated from

savagery: that is, she is transported from anthropomorphism to modern self-responsibility in a few dramatic moments.

To see the play in such a light is of course to divert attention from the domestic tensions and psychopathological interrelations with which it is certainly concerned. However, the matters I have so far mentioned form the foundation for the psychological drama. And all matters, cosmic and local, tend to one end, which is the propriety in modern times of individual freedom. That is to say, Ibsen deals with various forms of coercion to show how *unfitting* they have become. Apart from anything else we no longer have the myths to sustain coercion – a fact that the play also suggests.

Ellida's step-daughters, Bolette and Hilde, lead constricted lives, each in her own way. Bolette is something of a scholar, though unable either to study at home or to get away. For a long time she has run the house, catering for her father and younger sister. In the course of the play she seizes her chance by agreeing to marry Arnholm, a schoolmaster who used to be her tutor and once indeed, years earlier, proposed marriage to Ellida. Bolette is seventeen years Arnholm's junior and she does not love him, as he well knows. The point of this clear-eyed alliance is that each partner will give the other exactly what is needed: the girl will be able to study and the man to act as protective mentor.

Hilde, on the other hand, is too young for marriage and hasn't yet the faintest idea what she wants out of life, but now, in her late childhood, she needs Ellida's love. Lacking this, she is malicious, perverse, in revolt against even necessary constraints. At the close of the play she and Ellida reach out to each other, which is a satisfactory outcome. (But, since Ibsen was not concerned with make-believe psychology, the Hilde Wangel who four years later strides so devastatingly through *The Master Builder* has become not tame, but merely free from spite.)

We have noticed Arnholm's function in passing: he is the older man who offers Bolette freedom rather than constraint in marriage. Lyngstrand, now, is a naïvely egotistical sculptor who, despite his damaged lungs, will get on better at his art if those he 'loves' are kept at a distance. Here is freedom of another sort, the kind Ibsen introduced through Falk in *Love's Comedy* and Shaw later celebrated, not without irony, by means of Marchbanks in *Candida*. Ballested, too, fits the theme, for he – odd-job man, painter, carpenter, president of the brass band – 'actualises himself' cheerfully and too readily, thus constituting a pleasant parody of Ibsen's ideal.

As for the Stranger himself, Friman or Alfred Johnston from Finmark, he is one of Ibsen's visitors from the larger world that encloses the sphere of society, as is, for instance, the Rat Wife of *Little Eyolf*. The important feature of the Stranger is his indifference to the social rules: he is a guilt-free murderer and, of course, he believes that in consequence of their private rite of marriage he and Ellida should make off together. As we see him he is humourlessly and placidly anarchic, or to be more precise, he obeys unheard of laws of his own rather than the laws of society. He belongs to a region where people make vows and stick to them throughout a crazy, melancholy lifetime, the region of fairy tales and classical legends. To the extent that he possesses Ellida's soul, he does so not entirely as a result of the throwing of rings into the sea (which ceremony the young Ibsen actually performed with Rikke Holst[7]) but because of his calm and radical certainty.

Ellida matures at the moment of turning away the Stranger and electing to stay with Wangel. But our error would be to assume that she thereby climbs to our own estimable heights. We have always assumed ourselves to be free to choose spouses and life-styles, but that is not quite what Ibsen means. For we do as we do in disastrous ignorance of exactly those forces of which the Stranger is an emissary and Ellida has long been a slave. She chooses not one or more of the usual mechanisms of ego-defence but the path towards total self-acceptance. She ends approaching individuality rather than as a vain and fearful social unit.

In contrast, the heroine of Ibsen's next play, today the best known of Ibsen's creations apart from Nora Helmer, is vain to her dying breath and subject to social fear, yet for all that, her desire is precisely not to be a social unit. Hedda Gabler makes bold to stand apart from the pettiness and absurdity of her society, but in addition to her own weakness (her horror of ridicule, for instance), she is finally able to do this only by suicide.

Although Hedda is the most famous of Ibsen's leading characters, she is the least understood, and what has obscured the vision of many critics since 1890 when *Hedda Gabler* was published has been a moral net, as it were, which they – not Ibsen – have cast over her personality. It is common to dwell upon Hedda's obvious failings and her wicked deeds and to overlook the appropriateness of her scorn for society. Let us, for once, see the action from the heroine's point of view as a means of grasping Ibsen's own intentions. For Ibsen's attitude was far larger than Hedda's but contained Hedda's not as the antithesis of his more enlightened responses but as a fruitful part of his remarkably constant, if complex, scheme of values. Ibsen had more in common with his unprincipled heroine than with, say, Thea Elvsted or (and this is the important point) with the decent, balanced despisers of Hedda's neurotic cruelty whose voices have been loudest in discussions of the play these ninety years.

Hedda explains to Judge Brack in the second act that she married Jörgen Tesman because, as she puts it, 'I'd really danced myself tired . . . I had had my day.'[8] And the worthy Tesman was, she says, 'so pathetically eager to support me.' No doubt she felt that at twenty-nine she ought to be a wife. Whereupon this ill-matched couple, the handsome, proud, nervily fastidious woman and the eager, artless scholar, departed on a six-month trip, which for him was a combination of honeymoon and academic work. Before long Hedda was bored to distraction while Tesman remained cheerful, if concerned now and then that his wife seemed a trifle out of humour.

Hedda is the daughter of a general, which at that period in the history of Norway meant a fellow of martial inclinations but no experience in the field. Her surname in the title of the play is Gabler rather than Tesman to indicate, Ibsen wrote in a letter to his translator, that 'she is to be understood as her father's daughter rather than her husband's wife'.[9] Accordingly Hedda's ideals (for she undoubtedly has ideals) are in every respect the reverse of the standards by which she now seems obliged to live. It is misleading though not uncommon to say that she is 'mannish', equally wrong in view of Hedda's cowardice to talk of heroism, but such terms suggest the criteria Hedda has always had in mind. She longs not so much for glory in the conventional sense but for friends who share her sense that some domestic equivalent of glory is missing.

We are still trying to see Hedda in the most favourable light and so should remark that she is exasperated by the stupidity of her husband, his aunt and Thea Elvsted. From her point of view Tesman's unworldliness is simply crass. He has indeed the intelligence to be preparing a book on the domestic crafts of medieval Brabant, though the topic was plainly selected by Ibsen to suggest Tesman's limitations. So far as his social life is concerned Tesman rarely grasps things rightly, nuances and all. His armour is an almost imbecile amiability and he cannot see that his work has little more value than a hobby. Not once does he perceive that a faux pas of Hedda's is deliberate and sadistic. But the audience should appreciate that she is roused to cruelty by his obliviousness. According to Buddha unawareness of the Tesman variety is a sin: to Hedda, who scarcely believes in sin, it is nevertheless unendurable.

And this is the man to whom she has bound herself for life. He was brought up by two aunts, one of whom, 'a good-looking lady of benevolent aspect', is composed of the sort of niceness that is calculated to infuriate his new wife. For the Miss Tesmans of this world never understand how excruciatingly they demean everything in the eyes of such as Hedda. Jörgen has received a doctorate during his trip abroad and en famille this is going to be the cause not of dignified congratulations but of uncomprehending fuss. Of course his marriage is seen as a triumph. 'And to think', says Miss Tesman, 'that you'd be the one to walk off with Hedda Gabler! The lovely Hedda Gabler' (Act One). Hedda does not hear that snatch of conversation but it would seem to her typically complaisant.

Thea Elvsted now, a far more important character, manages unwittingly, or with the near-unconscious expediency of the woman who is essentially a helpmate, first to form a romantic extra-marital alliance with Ejlert Lövborg, then, after Lövborg's death, a partnership with Tesman as the pair of them begin to piece together the notes Lövborg made towards his new book. (Hedda has secretly and maliciously burned the fair copy.) In this way Thea, who has long stood in awe of Hedda, instals herself as a colleague of Tesman and no doubt a sharer of emotions with him, as Hedda herself could never be. But such happy, 'selfless' co-operation Hedda regards as a cheapening of life, a vulgarity. Tesman and Thea are collaborators in emotional dishonesty. Of Hedda's acquaintances only Judge Brack is free of such self-deception and he is a scoundrel.

Hedda wants, as Ibsen himself always wanted, tragedy not comedy – and, above all, not farce. In Act Four she desperately cried out, 'Oh, it'll kill me . . . it'll kill me, all this . . . farce.' At that moment the ridiculous Tesman is about to tell the maid that his wife truly loves him. She yearns for beauty and high drama while her husband wishes to babble to the maid. 'I say there is beauty in this deed,' Hedda declares, on learning that Lövborg has shot himself. It turns out that Lövborg's death was uncouth to say the least – as though Hamlet were to spend a few hours groaning on the stage – and this fact is another nail in Hedda's coffin. For Hedda is like her creator in being buoyed up by visions of terrible beauty, but also in respect of her cowardice. She is, at least until her last moments, an unheroic venerator of heroism. Of course, she has not a jot of Ibsen's talent, but some strands of Ibsen's own make-up went into the formation of Hedda, declining in ennui and neurasthenic loathing of the world's littleness.

We must not underestimate the fear that lies at Hedda's heart: it is moral fear of a kind that Ibsen himself surmounted. (He seems never to have overcome this physical cowardice.) Ibsen remarked in his rough, preliminary notes to the play, 'With Hedda there is deep poetry at bottom. But her surroundings frighten her. Think of it, to make oneself ridiculous.'[10] She is perhaps something of a 'schizoid character', one whose estimate of herself discounts the actual environment, with the result that the environment makes her nervous.[11] It is liable sooner or later to fill her with dread. She wants reality to match her imaginings but instead it mocks them. Thus Lövborg's death is not 'beautiful', as Hedda willed it to be, but a grotesque and painful business which begins in Mlle Diana's bedroom and ends in hospital. Earlier Hedda burned Lövborg's manuscript because, as she rightly realised, it was like a child born of the liaison between him and Thea Elvsted. What we must appreciate is that Hedda undoubtedly would wish to murder any child born to Lövborg and Thea. Destroying the manuscript, atrocious act though it is, is only a pale substitute for the atrocity she would like to commit. When they were at school together Hedda longed to torture and disfigure Thea by burning off her hair. Of course Hedda is jealous but her motive is more complex than that, for the ethos which Thea somehow manages to share with the brilliant and erratic Lövborg is an affront to Hedda's being.

Hedda is sterile culturally if not biologically. At the same time she realises, and rightly realises (for this is the hard point of the play) that the niceness of the nice people such as Tesman, Miss Tesman and Thea is of a piece with their illusions. And if they are not radically afraid it is because they have created a cultural and social sphere which more or less matches their feeble aspirations. Reality, Hedda knows, escapes them since it cannot be contained

by social decencies. Hedda hankers after some modern approximation to the ways of *The Vikings at Helgeland* and despite her
nineteenth-century irritability she is indeed related to the Hjordis
of that play as Thea is related to the pacific Dagny.

   Although she itches for a more stark milieu than the Norwegian
bourgoisie, she is fearful as Hjordis spectacularly never was.
Hedda's own drives are less sublimated than is common in a
woman of her age and class, while others in the play, including
even Brack, are unaware of their primitive motivations. It seems
that Hedda must die because she cannot fit into late nineteenth-
century society. Yet in another sense she pushes certain *fin-de-
siècle* tendencies to an extreme. Do we think of her suicide by
revolver bullet as a nineties sort of action solely because, in 1890,
Ibsen had her do it? Is it not also that Hedda finally responds to
her circumstances in a manner that a number of living persons
must romantically have dreamed of and a scattered few achieved
in circumstances compounded of romance and squalor? 'But,
good God Almighty . . . people don't do such things!' exclaims
Brack in the last line of the play. So he unwittingly reminds us that
some representative actions of a period are precisely actions taken
by alienated individuals. And who would finally deny Hedda a
sort of triumph, even a sort of justification?

   Certainly Ibsen shared Hedda's contempt for mediocrity, her
ignoble fears and her yearning for an unrealisable mode of life,
eternally lofty and vivid. Seen in this light, it was appropriate that
The Master Builder should follow (in 1892). For now, instead of
placing facets of his nature in unrecognisably different circumstances from his own, he wrote a play which critics have naturally
seen as 'autobiographical' in some sense. *The Master Builder*
assuredly is, in the first instance, about Ibsen himself; nor did he
shift his gaze very far from his own affairs to yield a general, faintly
parabolic meaning. For that reason alone the work will be better
grasped if we contemplate how Aline Solness relates to Suzannah
Ibsen, Hilde Wangel to Emilie Bardach (or some compound of
Ibsen's young women friends) and Halvard Solness to the
64-year-old author, dissatisfied alike with his career, his marriage
and his moral nature.

   Solness may well be the most lifelike character Ibsen created
and therefore one of the most lifelike in dramatic literature. Are
there many rivals for verisimilitude in the theatre who seem so
nearly to burst from image into chaotic life? Ibsen performed

supremely well the familiar author's trick of reducing a shapeless self to aesthetic proportions and did so partly by finding a tidy approximation to his own affairs.

Michael Meyer, along with other Ibsen scholars, notes that Emilie Bardach regarded Solness as a distinctly faithful copy of his creator. ' "I didn't see myself," Emilie said, on seeing the play for the first time in 1908, "but I saw him. There is something of me in Hilde; but in Solness, there is little that is not Ibsen." '[12] There is no corroboration of these remarks and in general, accounts of Ibsen's personality (even William Archer's) fail to give us a clear and detailed image of him. What can it have been essentially that Emilie spotted in Solness? She would have meant not a mere variety but a coherence of mannerisms. Now the core of Solness's personality is an overwhelming and *captivating* self-centredness. His rare sort of egotism is somehow combined with an habitually accurate view of the external world. Solness expresses his emotions with candour and finesse. He is frank and cunning at the same time. He exploits others largely, it seems, by means of a total, unabashed acceptance of himself. He is both a sharp observer of other people and, paradoxically, one whose every gesture invites the spotlight. He contrives to occupy the centre of the stage even when he must be shown up as flawed. In the dialogue between him and Hilde in Act Two Solness explains how his successful career as an architect was founded by the fire that burned down Aline's childhood home, a fire for which he had nervelessly hoped. Far worse, the shock of the fire gave Aline a fever and from her infected milk the twin baby boys died. In consequence of all this Solness prospered while Aline's vocation as a mother was destroyed. Solness asks Hilde if she doesn't believe that 'certain people have been singled out, specially chosen, gifted with the power and the ability to *want* something, to *desire* something, to *will* something . . . so insistently . . . and so ruthlessly . . . that they inevitably get it in the end'? (Act Two).[13] Thus Solness discourses on the inevitability of his triumphs and their shameful roots. He is a thief of happiness, his own as well as other people's. But the notable fact is that he is able so to expound his past life and his present feelings as to draw all around him into his orbit. He makes a strength even of his frailties – the capacity Ibsen acquired, or consolidated, at the time of *The Pretenders*. We know that Ibsen resembled Solness in being dour, possessive and self-contained. Sometimes he was brusque, which Solness never is, but he was expansive with Emilie Bardach as Solness is with Hilde. Emilie did not say that Ibsen was remorseful over Suzannah, but inwardly some such feelings must have troubled him.

What actual treatment of Suzannah is reflected in Solness's hope for a fire? Probably there was no specific and dramatic event, but instead Ibsen had gradually, in a thousand ways, exploited Suzannah's gifts; he had dried her up. He had also made her sad, or rather had aggravated her native sadness: in a humdrum fashion he had done to her what Brand more startlingly does to Agnes.

Until the 1890s the Ibsens had no proper family home to reflect both husband and wife. They owned few goods. When William Archer visited Ibsen in Rome in 1882 (that is, when Ibsen was fifty-four and had been married for twenty-four years) he found the place 'comfortable yet comfortless . . . well furnished, but with no air of home about it'.[14] For long Ibsen lacked, preferred to lack some ordinary family circumstances; he was a searcher and a wanderer, not a member of any community. Instead there were the sojourns in Italy and Germany, an endless quest and for Suzannah, since the quest was not hers, an unusual degree of sacrifice. For all his interest in his son Sigurd, Ibsen was overwhelmingly concerned with his plays, his ideas, his admirers and detractors. Suzannah gave up a great deal for her husband's career, 'lived in his shadow', and just before she died declared that 'Ibsen had no steel in his character – but I gave it to him.'[15] Yet all this brought him little contentment or joy. Was it not the entire situation, the woman sucked into the man's insatiable ambition, that Ibsen reflected in the marriage of Solness and Aline?

In the play itself we have the following piece of tormented, lifelike psychology: Solness explains to Dr Herdal (in Act One) that Aline suspects him of carrying on with Kaja Fosli and while this is untrue he does keep Kaja in his office 'because I somehow . . . enjoy the mortification of letting Aline do me an injustice'. When Herdal remarks that he cannot understand such behaviour, Solness explains that '. . . it's rather like paying off a tiny instalment on a huge immeasurable debt' – to Aline. He is so guilt-ridden about his wife that he savours her false suspicions; when she behaves wrongly it faintly relieves his guilt. There is another, equally dubious reason why he retains Kaja: if she stays so will Ragnar Brovik who loves her, and Brovik would otherwise set up in business as a rival architect. As it is, Kaja has vainly fallen in love with Solness. His constant though curiously palatable egotism infects everyone, until the trollish Hilde comes along.

In fact Solness is not ruthless but has what Hilde calls a 'fragile conscience' (Act Two) and his tragedy rests upon a combination of soaring ambition and sharp awareness. He would like to be bolder than he is without in the least blunting his responses. How well he understands Aline, for example. He appreciates how she was torn away from her childhood. The fire destroyed not only the twins and Aline's home but also her nine dolls which were like 'little unborn children' (Act Three). Her childhood vanished overnight: old silk dresses, family lace, jewels, the precious dolls, all the furnishings of her private world. Mrs Solness has not properly matured beyond that trauma and she is married to a man who once wanted to take the public world by storm.

And yet without Aline, Solness might never have become a successful builder, as Ibsen himself gained so much from his marriage to Suzannah. Now, at the time of *The Master Builder* the Ibsens were estranged from each other, not permanently separated but temporarily apart and each, in any event, emotionally isolated. Magdelene Thoresen, Ibsen's striking mother-in-law (whom he could perhaps have married and who was now if anything more vigorous than her daughter), remarked that 'They are two solitary people – each one alone – absolutely alone.'[16] In fact the Ibsens had returned to Norway, Suzannah having gone to Valdres and Henrik to the North Cape for a short spell. In August of that year, 1891, Ibsen went back to Christiania, where he renewed and intensified a friendship with the pianist Hildur Andersen. She came down from the mountains where she had been on a walking tour and the pair of them rapidly became such fond companions that they agreed to call 19 September their 'friendship date'. That of course is the date in the play when Hilde comes to claim her kingdom, reminding Solness that it was exactly ten years earlier that he climbed the church tower at Lysanger.

At the top of the tower Solness had told God that he would build no more churches, but only homes for human beings. This has naturally been taken to mean that Ibsen resolved to give up his ambitions as a poetic dramatist and concentrate on the sort of

prose works which, as it turned out, secured his reputation.
Presumably he made no instantaneous renunciation of poetry in
the theatre but after *The League of Youth* in 1869, pondered for years
until, in 1877, *Pillars of Society* started the unbroken series of prose
works. While Ibsen thought most highly of the prose *Emperor and
Galilean* (written with tortuous effort in that questioning period)
the peak of his poetic production was *Brand*, as early as 1866. In
other words, he once reached heights of a certain sort, grand and
unaccommodating, and thereafter returned to the foothills and
lowlands. *The Master Builder* makes it plain that he regarded
himself as a Brand who had given up the struggle. Instead of
leading the 'villagers' away from their trifling occupations he had
written plays precisely about those occupations. Nor can Ibsen
have given what he felt to be a sufficiently resolute example to his
own 'Agnes': no doubt he had exploited Suzannah, but had done
so for less than the highest purposes.

From our point of view it is fortunate as well as excusable that
he forsook poetic drama. *Brand* is tremendous but is doubtful that
he could, in the late nineteenth century, have made a great
reputation with more works in the same kind. (And if we are
thinking also of prose works of clear philosophic significance, we
should remember that *Emperor and Galilean* has never been much
appreciated.) Ibsen wrote in an optimistic, increasingly democratic age; the novel was the pioneering form of literature and
novelists aimed for verisimilitude in the treatment of commonplace subject matter. The antithetical, exalted sort of work
survived – or rather, was recreated – only in the operas of Wagner,
but in the main audiences and readers seemed to prefer prose to
poetry.

In effect Ibsen too, in the seventies, announced to God that he
would stop building churches. But twenty years later he started
building them again, though in a curious new fashion. In the
suicide of Hedda Gabler he gave a touch of grandeur to shoddy
circumstances. For Ibsen the highest deeds had always been
associated with defiance, renunciation and voluntary death.
Furia tempted Catiline away from the virtuous Aurelia, but
Catiline died knowing that the 'soul's true life' lies in unabating
self-division. Later, Lady Inger's death is likewise that of a 'great
soul', made up of contradictory, sometimes self-transcending
designs. The admired Margit of *The Feast of Solhoug* attempts

murder and ends in a convent; Hjordis in *The Vikings at Helgeland*
resolves to do battle with the fates and finally, so it seems, is
permitted to join the ranks of the Valkyries.

Now, for Solness, a simplification of Ibsen, to climb high towers
is to get dizzy and so risk death. It is ridiculous for a master
builder to fight shy of heights and for all Ibsen's achievements it
was unsatisfactory that he had ceased writing the one kind of play
he unreservedly admired. Devastating lack of recognition was
chief among several factors that impelled him to the writing of his
surpassing social dramas. What a blessing! But he remained
scared of his own still loftier aspirations.

Inexact though the comparison might seem, when Solness
starts to climb the spire, urged on by the radiant, unpitying Hilde,
he is like a warrior who after a prudent absence rejoins the battle.
For Ibsen saw death as heroic whenever it is the result of
maximum endeavour. The reason seems to have been that he
regarded the ordinary, accommodating sort of life (such as he
lived) as yielding only a patina of meaning rather than a rich
design. The young women Ibsen was friendly with in the nineties
(Emilie Bardach, Hildur Andersen and, for certain, Helene Raff
as well, for she replaced Emilie in his affections)[17] unintentionally
recalled him to the colours of his youth. They made him wish to
trample on his prudence and to live, or at least to write, as if only
glory mattered. For they whispered to him that he had failed to be
a hero in the cultural as well as the physical sense.

Naturally his response after all his years as the complete
dramatist was to make dramas which explored this very problem.
Eventually he reached new heights by lamenting his years of
failure to try for them. *When We Dead Awaken* is prose drama on the
frontier with poetry and it ends by celebrating an escape from
earthbound considerations. In short it is a new kind of 'church'.

Further, Ibsen regarded *When We Dead Awaken* as an 'epilogue',
though he did not know that it would be his last play. In 1900 he
wrote to Count Moritz Prozer, one of his French translators, 'You
are basically right when you say that the series which is concluded
with the epilogue actually began with *The Master Builder*.'[18] Now,
by ingenious means it might be possible to see all the last four
plays as forming a series, but only three of them obviously fit
together in such a way. *Little Eyolf* is the curious exception. *The
Master Builder*, *John Gabriel Borkman* and *When We Dead Awaken*

constitute indeed the progressive treatment of a theme: a
disappointed, guilty man of high ability becomes aware of his
need for salvation. But *Little Eyolf* (1894), following *The Master
Builder*, temporarily breaks the sequence and in some respects is
reminiscent of *The Wild Duck*.

It is a more austere and more probing play than *The Wild Duck*
but it betrays similar preoccupations. In essentials Alfred Allmers
is a combination of Hjalmar Ekdal and Gregers Werle, Rita
Allmers is akin to Gina Ekdal, and now it is a crippled boy, Eyolf
rather than the confused girl, Hedvig, who leaves behind the
grieving parents. The earlier work concerns the death of a child
brought about because her father is a self-centred dreamer
influenced by his meddling friend. In *Little Eyolf* a boy has been
lamed in infancy and is drowned in the course of the play, partly –
or, it might be argued, entirely – because his seemingly affection-
ate parents have never wholeheartedly loved him. In each case the
mother is more down to earth than the father, more sensual and
less given to theorising. There may well have been something
personal in this theme but little can be found in the biographies[19]
and the fictional point we should cling to is that Eyolf is pitied by
his father, resented by his mother and never valued for his own
sake by either parent. Moreover, he is a source of pain to them and
each by a different means seeks a pain-free life.

Alfred Allmer is a slightly built man of thirty-six or seven, a
'landowner, man of letters, occasional teacher'. In fact he is a
dilettante, though of a solemnly reflective sort. Since childhood,
despite his marriage, he has enjoyed a precious camaraderie with
Asta whom he has always supposed to be his half-sister, his
father's daughter by a second marriage. In Act Two Asta tells him
that she has discovered from a collection of her mother's letters
that the older Allmers was not her father, so that she and Alfred
are not blood relations. Nor have they ever regarded each other
purely in a manner appropriate to siblings but with subdued
sexual feelings.

First Alfred's father then Asta's mother died and the youthful
pair were left alone together. This was the happiest time of their
lives. She used to dress up in his old blouse and breeches and walk
about the house fancying herself as a boy. He liked to call her
Eyolf. Now Alfred remarks to Asta that 'our life together has
stamped each of us with the other's image' (Act Two),[20] meaning

that they are mentally twins. She still looks up to him and he, for his part, is unfailingly kind to her to compensate for the fact that his father never loved her.

At twenty-five Asta is still unmarried, largely because of this intense relation with her brother. On the other hand, Alfred many years before married Rita, a rich attractive woman who turn out to be possessive and sexually vigorous. Very shortly a boy was born to them whom they christened Eyolf. One day in their kitchen they urgently desired to make love, so Rita placed the baby on the table. While they were copulating Eyolf fell to the floor, permanently crippling his left leg. Now as a boy of nine he walks with the aid of a crutch, cannot play games or swim in the fjord and is 'undersized and fragile-looking'. 'But', Ibsen's description continues, 'he has beautiful and intelligent eyes' (Act One).

Rita has never felt especially guilty about Eyolf's deformity, for she is too taken up with her husband – his body, his exclusive companionship, his courteous, pensive personality. As she declares in the first act, 'Motherhood for me was in *having* the child.' She adds, 'But I'm not made to go on being mother to it.' 'It', not 'him'. Rita is unashamedly non-moral, having no use for family or civic duties. She wishes Asta would get married and leave the district instead of visiting them so often. Rita has loathed Alfred's writing which has regularly kept him from their bed late into the night and, as for the child (born to her with 'unspeakable pain'), he is merely half hers, whereas she requires only one human being who should be hers alone.

Until recently Alfred was engaged in writing what he now describes as a 'great thick book on "Human Responsibility" ' (Act One). He is the sort of man to whom ethical ideas are interesting while the practice of ethics is hopelessly dull. Eventually even the ideas lost their savour and Alfred went off into the mountains alone to meditate. He hoped to discover his true destiny and, it seems, he did gain an insight. For a day and a night he was lost and began to feel, as he reports to Rita in Act Three, that 'Death and I walked side by side like two good travelling companions'. His conclusion was that life is bleak and death unfrightening: it is preferable to fill one's days with some worthwhile task. So he returned home earlier than he had planned, now resolved to devote himself to Eyolf's education and upbringing. When Alfred

arrived, the night before the action of the play begins, Rita let
down her hair and got out some champagne, but he was tired.

The features I have mentioned form a large proportion of the
life-stories of the main characters to the time of the play. In no
other work does Ibsen more skilfully and abundantly weave the
past into present conversations and this is, as always, more than a
matter of stagecraft. His vision was to a peculiar degree one of
paying for the past. Nemesis was eternally real to him. Yet the
'arrogance' that solicits Nemesis he regarded simply as a feature
of human life; consequently, while it is possible to see Ibsen's
tragic characters as 'punished for their sins', it is wiser to see them
as suffering unavoidably, though each in a manner dictated by his
deeds. The nature of the deed determines merely the nature of the
suffering. It is not just that no one is 'without sin', but that no one
can be or indeed should be without it: the notion of immaculacy is
absurd.

What of Nemesis in *Little Eyolf* and in particular of the boy
himself? He is present for only part of Act One and in that time is
established as trusting, lively minded and unaggressive. But there
is no time, and possibly no need to give him much individuality.
The important event is, of course, his encounter with the Rat Wife
(a figure based, Ibsen said, 'on a memory from Skien').[21] Before
she knocks at Allmer's door Eyolf has been declaring that one day
he will go climbing in the mountains with his father, that he
wishes to be a soldier when he grows up and that he alone of the
gang of boys down at the jetty cannot swim. This is the kind of
thing that Alfred says 'gnaws' at his heart and indeed Eyolf's
deluded hopes are not less affecting because Ibsen omits to
emphasise them. Despite the title of the play the stress is upon
Alfred and Rita; upon self-deception rather than poignancy. Now,
echoing Alfred's remark (admittedly in too pat a fashion) the Rat
Wife enters and asks '. . . have you anything gnawing in this
house?' (Act One).

For the Rat Wife, as for many intuitive people, to predict is to
foster the advent of whatever is predicted. She does not prophesy
in so many words but manages to give the impression first, that
something undoubtedly is 'gnawing' in the Allmers household,
and secondly, that to follow her to their death is a proper fate for
innocent creatures who happen to be a pest to their hosts. She is
malignant but she entices into the water only those 'who are hated

and persecuted of men' (Act One). She carries out the unloved wishes of others and is therefore disliked and feared, but never turned away. She tempts Eyolf, but not openly. It is as if he gives meanings to words unconsciously, in the way of dreams: he 'knows' in an obscure corner of his mind not only that the local guttersnipes despise him but that he brings pain to those hedonists, his parents. Further, he should be wary of the water, while, as the Rat Wife says, the 'creepie-crawlies' enter the sea just because they are afraid of it. Thus, when the Rat Wife leaves the house Eyolf slips out after her. In Act Two it is recalled that as she rowed away, Eyolf, standing on the furthest point of the jetty, swayed after her as if he was giddy, and fell. It was an accident, yet not quite an accident. Most important, if Alfred and Rita had always simply loved little Eyolf the boy would have been less fascinated by the old woman.

When the curtain falls on the first act the cry has come up from the waterfront that 'The crutch is floating' and the child is missing. As Act Two begins Alfred Allmers begins the process, which he and Rita follow to the end of the play, of assimilating and interpreting the hideous fact of Eyolf's death. What ought to be made plain here is that the sort of analysis of themselves he and Rita conduct is an example of what most people are undeservingly spared. The Allmers do not belong to a special category and only the detailed manner of their blunderings is unique.

With little delay the husband concludes that the drowning is 'meaningless' and yet, he continues (Act Two), 'the world order seemed to require it'. He is right on both counts, though he does not unfailingly continue in such a stoic vein. He is right to see that Eyolf's death has no rational meaning and to realise that the incident, like all incidents, is a particle of the non-rational world order: without it that order would be changed entirely.

Also in the second act the Allmers learn that the boys down at the jetty saw Eyolf lying on his back, eyes wide open, at the bottom of the clear water. They never tried to save him. Those eyes, like the child's cry about the crutch, will haunt the parents for evermore. Alfred even wonders if the eyes were evil. Husband and wife accept that they are 'mourning a little stranger boy': Eyolf never really belonged to them because they did not want him as a distinct, irreplaceable person. There now appears no way out of a merciless awakening for the couple, unless they choose some form of insane make-believe. They acknowledge to each other that they

would rather live than join Eyolf 'on the other side'. They are
earthly creatures, wretched, loathe to leave even for heaven.

   All along there has been another aspect of their lives, barely
grasped by either of them. At the beginning of their marriage
Alfred was in terror of Rita: he feared, I suppose, the all-
consuming nature of her affections, for she is not a formidable
personality. But she was beautiful, she offered him 'gold and
green forests' (money and land) and anyway it was desirable for
Alfred to free Asta from her attachment to him. But this
emancipation is so far incomplete, and Asta has to be pushed (in
the third act) into going away with Borghejm, the road engineer
who wants to marry her. Alfred, remember, used to call her Eyolf
long before the baby Eyolf was born, a fact he disclosed to Rita in
that 'devastatingly lovely moment' (Act Two) just before the boy
was lamed.

   For all Alfred's rationality (and he is superficially a sensible
man) he has sometimes confused Asta and Eyolf – again
somewhat as characters or items may be 'condensed' in a dream
image. He has confused the sister who is no sister with the child,
the first incestuously loved and the second scarcely loved at all.
Only in Act Three, when Asta realises that Alfred and Rita want
her to complete their lives for them by permanently substituting
herself for the lost child, does she resolve to marry Borghejm.

   When Asta goes Alfred and Rita are left, finally and fittingly,
without defences. Only then does Rita conclude that she will live
for the community, specifically for the poor boys who play down
at the jetty. Such an ending, with its echoes of Comte and George
Eliot, and indeed its anticipation of a common ethic of today, is
suspect, the one serious flaw in the play. Ibsen in fact asked a
friend, Mrs Caroline Sontum, after the first performance, 'Do you
think Rita will really take care of those naughty boys. Don't you
think that it's just a Sunday mood?'[22] If he had included that
doubt in *Little Eyolf*, then the play might occupy a secure, instead
of a precarious place among the greatest tragedies. But audiences
would have found it unbearable.

   The pervasive aspect of Ibsen's attitude towards life which
some critics still do not find bearable is his individualism – to use
that work in its full nineteenth-century sense. For good or ill he
admired people who have no respect for society, since he had
none. We have commented on this in passing: it is now time to
discuss the matter more fully, in regard to the last two works. In

an Ibsen play the difference between a character for whom we are expected to feel admiration and a merely decent character, is that the latter fits comfortably into a social group. By and large the women are more interesting and will serve here to illustrate the point. At first the opposition is between Aurelia, loving wife of Catiline, and the temptress Furia; it is of course Furia whose baleful spirit enriches the play. Now, if this was a juvenile attitude on Ibsen's part, it nevertheless persisted, though in a far more sophisticated form, through his mature works and into his old age. After *Catiline* the sequence in the early plays of Signe versus Margit, Ingeborg versus Alfhild, and Dagny versus Hjordis gives way eventually to the more intricate polarities of Beata Rosmer and Rebecca West and of Thea Elvsted and Hedda Gabler. I have omitted to mention Inger Gyldenløve because she is not contrasted with a righteous or amiable woman, and the potential rivalry of Kaja Fosli and Hilde Wangel, which comes to nothing. The only instance in Ibsen of the contrary tendency, a clear preference for the good woman, is the shining superiority of Solveig over the Woman in Green in *Peer Gynt*.

Now, in the last two plays the opposition is subtler still, though it rests upon the same tacit assumption. In *John Gabriel Borkman* the hero's wife, Gunhild, is unpleasant not because she is vengeful but because she places society above her criminal husband. On the other hand, her sister Ella Rentheim is appealing because her generous love for Borkman makes her indifferent to society. And in *When We Dead Awaken*, as we shall see, Maja Rubeck, though earthy, sensual and so, one might assume, healthily 'bad', is also a compromising realist, a member of the same category as Regine Engstrand in *Ghosts*. The heroine, Irene, is a proper partner for Rubek in his abandonment of the world. There lies the true distinction: the good are worldly and therefore unsatisfactory to Ibsen, while the bad are unworldly (a spirit, for instance, such as Furia, a suicide such as Hedda Gabler) and consequently, whatever their faults, respected by their creator.

John Gabriel Borkman has lived in isolation for thirteen years, five years in gaol for fraud and eight years keeping to his room. For that period Gunhild, Borkman's wife, has occupied the same house, never exchanging a word with him, and expecting that one day their son Erhart will somehow restore the family honour. To the age of fifteen Erhart was brought up by Gunhild's twin sister Ella Rentheim, and now, although he is back home with his

mother, he wishes to follow his own path in healthy disregard of
her wishes.

A certain Vilhelm Foldal, a clerk, was ruined in consequence of
Borkman's crime and is now pretty well Borkman's only visitor.
Foldal's daughter, Frida, has gained a commercial qualification
as a result of coaching by Erhart, who also arranged for her to
study music. For some time Frida has lodged with Mrs Wilton, a
beautiful divorcee whom, we discover in Act Three, Erhart plans
to marry. He has no interest in furthering Gunhild's designs.

But Borkman's guilt is not confined to fraud. Like Bernick in
Pillars of Society he forsook the sister he loved to aid his career. He
took Gunhild rather than Ella because renouncing Ella was a
secret condition of his appointment to a bank directorship. So he
condemned Ella to a sterile life. Now, in Act Two, she tells him
that 'The great sin for which there is no forgiveness is to murder
love in a human soul.' 'You are guilty of double murder,' she says.
'The murder of your own soul and of mine.'[23]

These are the characters and circumstances surrounding
Borkman, but what matters, as always, is the hero's disposition.
This is not a given but product of will wrestling inevitably, as its
raison d'être, with environment. Michael Meyer remarks that 'In a
sense the play is about what Ibsen's marriage might have been
like had he failed as a writer.'[24] For what we now recognise as
Ibsen's talent was never a guarantee of success. Nor would the
talent, lacking the twists and turns of his fortune, have developed
in the manner that it did. That is so with every artist, for talent is
not an ingrained quality that meets the external world, but, like
disposition as a whole, is made up of a myriad such encounters.

It must be understood that Borkman is a man of strong ability
reduced through his criminal impatience to an obscure and
powerless life. His comparison of himself with Napoleon, his
posture of right hand thrust into jacket breast, is not supposed to
be the antic of a dreamer. When Ibsen has him tell Foldal, in Act
Two, that 'The masses, the common herd ... they don't
understand us, Vilhelm' he is not satirising Borkman from a
democratic standpoint, but rather recognising the sort of sentiment he himself might justifiably have uttered if his ambitions
had come to nothing. It is nevertheless true that here is an
illustration of a subtler mind enclosing a blunter one, since Ibsen
had the wit to exploit his self-conceit in order to win success.

So Borkman is 'like a Napoleon who has been maimed in his

first battle' (Act Two), or like an Ibsen ruined by the reception given to his early plays. But Borkman has also broken the law and his offence was betrayed to the authorities by a certain Hinkel, a lawyer who had repeatedly been rejected by Ella Rentheim and believed Borkman to be behind the rejections. In fact Borkman killed both love and pity in Ella who has since lived 'as though under an eclipse' (Act Two). Borkman is ludicrously candid with Ella when he tells her that, though she was the most precious thing in the world to him, 'in the last resort one woman can always be replaced by another' (Act Two). Ella is amused, bearing in mind his ghastly life with Gunhild.

What raises Borkman above the careerist level? He has a visionary capacity, or more precisely, combines the visionary and egotistical. When he speaks in his lyrical way of the 'iron-hard, dreamless world of reality'; when in Whitmanesque terms he contemplates a network of communications spreading out from Norway; when, above all, he rapturises about turning minerals into treasure for the millions, we are meant to accept him as a man of insight, not a self-justifying crank.

For he sees how we might use material elements to produce spiritual refinements. Indeed, so far as he is concerned veins of metal in the earth are wholly alive, crying out to be borne to the surface, turned into bridges, ships, locomotives. But he alone is the magician who has the power to release them.

He is also a king, for when, with Ella, he climbs the hill behind the house he indicates distant mountains and proclaims them to be his kingdom. He fancies he hears his factories working full blast down in the river valley. This is not hallucination of the usual sort but Borkman's 'poetic' awareness of his thwarted destiny, for he thinks at times in such metaphorical terms, like a primitive. But Ella tells him, not unlovingly: 'You will never enter triumphant into your cold dark kingdom' (Act Four). It becomes clear that Ibsen has all along been talking about his own gift for making poetry out of prosaic materials, for transmuting dull facts into bright and lasting drama. And he has yet again dramatised his own guilt over using others and disowning a part of himself.

After *John Gabriel Borkman* the central, determining feature of Ibsen's personality still remained to be expressed and *artistically* mastered. For whatever Borkman's specific crime, whatever the particular faults of Borkman, Solness and for that matter earlier heroes and heroines, there lay unexamined a basic flaw in Ibsen's own life from which cracks and fissures spread outwards, so fruitfully, through the plays. I have suggested earlier in this book that Ibsen as a boy 'resolved' (perhaps unconsciously) to justify his family's claims to superiority by transmuting their ordinary bourgeois ambitions into the highest goals.[25] He wished to be a hero who rises above common social and psychological limitations. Early in 1850 Ibsen, spending a last, short holiday in Venstøp, went for a walk with his sister Hedvig, and told her that he intended to scale the heights 'in greatness', as he put it, 'and in love'. Since Hedvig was a normally unaspiring girl, more or less indifferent to greatness, she asked, 'And when you have done that?' He replied, 'Then I want to die.'[26] To Hedvig, in other words, such deeds as her brother had in mind could scarcely replace or even co-exist with ordinary social procedures. Henrik, on the other hand, already regarded these procedures as mere background or raw material. He would 'go through the motions of living', so to speak, in pursuit of love and historic significance.

So the young Ibsen set out to make use of himself and everyone else who might prove serviceable. The guilt he increasingly expressed in the last plays (though not, of course, in them alone) was, whatever its particular occasions, the general guilt of a grand exploiter. Just as an aspirant saint might in earlier periods have seen the world as a gymnasium for his spiritual exercises (though he would have needed to outgrow that vision in order to attain his goal), so Ibsen saw around him only the stuff of his art. Paradoxically he, like Flaubert, was regarded as a realist because he despised the real.

To compound this 'error' (and we should keep reminding ourselves that the so-called error was the source of our profit) he betrayed his high calling by writing such plays as *Pillars of Society*, *A Doll's House*, *An Enemy of the People*, plays of the lowlands rather than the heights. Yet his nature was that of an artist to whom the actual remarks of Norwegians in the second half of the nineteenth century were important only for the poetry that might be made out of them. In the period of the Icelandic Sagas details of daily life were insignificant or gained some small significance solely in relation to the deeds of Sigurd, Gudrun, Brunhild and the rest. But Ibsen in his age of realism had gone so far against the grain as to give the impression that humdrum items – tricks of speech, clothing, furniture, debts, sanitation systems – were important in themselves. Thus he had won success as a photographer rather than a true poet.

That, of course, is a reduction of Ibsen to the level at which many apprehended him and where, it seems, he was dejectedly liable to place himself. In fact his heroic strain had all along, tacitly or quite explicitly, qualified the prosaic material. He helped to resolve the distinction between poetry and prose, but he nevertheless felt that he had betrayed his youthful promise. *When We Dead Awaken* is about the tarnishing process and how to leave it behind. The play also sets art and life squarely against each other, asserting that an artist may not simply live, and if he drifts into doing so had better die. This is an exalted view of art the function of which is seen as quasi-religious. The writer (sculptor, painter, composer) has the hieratic role of reminding people of the world's paltriness.

The antecedent events of *When We Dead Awaken* are uncharacteristically simple. Arnold Rubek, a sculptor of international renown, made his name with a piece he called 'the Day of Resurrection'. It depicted his 'vision of how the pure woman would wake on Resurrection Day . . . filled with a holy joy at finding herself unchanged – a mortal woman – in those higher, freer, happier realms, after the long and dreamless sleep of death' (Act One).[27] Note: the woman had not become a spirit, but was somehow still mortal and fleshly. He used a model, Irene, who gave him not only her 'naked beauty' but also, as she says (Act One), her 'young living soul'. To him she was indeed a picture of loveliness, but just the same a mere model to be used and discarded.

At first the figure of the woman stood alone on its plinth. Then after he and Irene had parted, Rubek progressively added fresh figures, 'their faces animal beneath the skin' (Act Two). Further, he moved the young woman away from her commanding position, making her a 'middleground figure' (Act Two). And now Rubek himself is prominent in the group, a man dipping his soiled figures into water, racked by guilt.

He and his wife are presently staying at a spa hotel in a seaside town, each restless in a different way. Rubek can think of nothing he positively desires, while she, on the contrary, wants a regular supply of vivid sensations. Once he promised to take her up a mountain and show her 'all the glory of the world'. (Act One), but now he is uninterested and anyway, so he says, she is no mountaineer.

Into these doldrums come Ulfheim, a purely sensuous, gluttonous, predatory man, a hunter both of animals and women, and Irene herself, a pale, thin figure in 'creamy white cashmere', accompanied by a black clad nun. Ulfheim's crude assertiveness fascinates as well as repels Maja, and when the pair of them wander away from the hotel lawn, Irene joins Rubek to accuse him, tonelessly, of having 'killed' her. Since those sittings years before she has posed naked in peep shows and variety halls and been involved with two men, a South American whom she married and drove mad and a Russian whom she knifed to death. But can we believe her? Irene declares that she has been in a padded cell and even now she is on the borderline of insanity.

Ulfheim and Irene are diametric opposites, he as material, she as immaterial as human personalities can be. They are the extremes, while Rubek occupies a point on her line, so to speak, and Maja a point on Ulfheim's. From a realistic point of view the personalities and the action of this play are too schematic. Yet the very schematisation, combined as it is with colloquial speech pregnant and insistent enough to border on poetry and with various attractive minor artifices of scenery and clothing contributes to the work's singular quality. It is mistaken to worry about improbabilities, since *When We Dead Awaken* is something between allegory and naturalism, done obviously not in a whimsical spirit but as a deadly earnest portrait of the author's own life-problem. It is also that rare sort of play, a tragedy happy in its outcome and barely unhappy in its unfolding.

That unfolding is quite straightforward, in brief an exposition of the central feature of Rubek's (or Irene's) nature. For the Maja–Ulfheim pole of the action serves only to illustrate by contrast Rubek's way of art. All his life Rubek has placed 'The work of art first . . . the human being second' (Act One). No matter that he prefers his works of art even to himself: his object has been precisely to exclude human grossness and muddle. Rubek does not reject Irene's charges that she gave him her 'young living soul' and that he then discarded both her and their 'child', 'The Day of Resurrection'. He knows she is right, for he has few illusions now. Nor does he mind when Maja, in Act Two at a mountain sanatorium, wishes to go down into the forest with the bear-hunting Ulfheim.

Part of the second act is taken up with Irene's probing of Rubek as they talk in the sanatorium grounds. He was unmoved, she says, by her nakedness, for he was 'an artist . . . and not a man' (Act Two). As he talks of his various accretions to 'The Day of Judgement', she draws her knife to murder him and holds back only to hear what he's going to say next. He is 'soft and spineless' (Act Two), but for all that she invites him to spend a summer night with her on the mountain. The night will be perfect, beautiful and sexless. The pair of them will be in the world but as near as possible out of it.

In Act Three Maja and Ulfheim, in the midst of a zestful row, continued down the mountainside, while Rubek and Irene climb upwards. Irene knows she is already 'dead', though he still deceives himself that both of them might survive. Finally she convinces him that life is over for both of them. They decide to go through the mist 'to the very top of the tower [the mountain], lit by the rising sun' (Act Three). As they vanish into the cloud Maja can be heard below singing 'I am free' and then, on high, an avalanche overwhelms her husband and his deathly new bride.

Irene is the last embodiment of Ibsen's lifelong vision. He and his beautiful partner have always, in different guises, held aloof from the world. Sometimes they have defied society and been detested by orthodox people. She is bad or decorously mad, perhaps both: at any rate her outcast nature signifies that she will not play the world's games. The woman is not safe, of course, not a comforter in the usual sense, for in fantasy at least, her creator desires spiritual dangers. He keeps a line of communication open from his highest ideals down to his lowest instincts. Unlike most of us he does not obliterate his sense of the instinctual origins of his ideals. Irene, like her predecessors, is sexually lovely but promises no actual sex. She is forever intimate and, so far as the hero is concerned, forever chaste.

Ibsen observed so discriminatingly (was, in other words, such an incomparable 'realist') not because he welcomed life but because he found it disquieting and pointless. His heroism lay, if anywhere, in refusing the consolations of religion, social change and scientific development. Perhaps, therefore, his way of escape was simply aesthetic, building beauty out of what would otherwise seem ugly or merely dull. If so, it is hard to see how a less reprehensible form of escape can ever be found.

Part II
Shaw

5 Lilith's Champion

The published biographical material about Shaw falls far short of what will soon be available and at the time of writing we are still awaiting the first comprehensive biography. Even so, I do not think it is premature to interpret some well known facts about Shaw's childhood and youth, the pre-GBS phase, so as to show the personal origins of his 'legislation'. We can infer from the 'best evidence' available (to use a lawyer's phrase) why he embraced certain doctrines. For the value, and for that matter the precise nature of a doctrine is not separable from its sources.

Like Ibsen, Shaw was brought up in a household where social expectations outstripped attainable standards. His father's flour and cereals business sharply declined and at the most dramatic moment, Shaw tells us in the Preface to *Immaturity*,

> My father, albeit ruined, found the magnitude of the catastrophe so irresistibly amusing that he had to retreat hastily from the office to the empty corner of a warehouse, and laugh until he was exhausted.[1]

George Carr Shaw, this fellow of the remarkable sense of humour, was 'the least formidable of men'.[2] He was also a wretched, self-despising drunkard until 'a mild fit, which felled him on our doorstep one Sunday afternoon, convinced him that he must stop drinking or perish'.[3] The drunkard's moroseness and the uncontrollable laughter at a time of failure are not, of course, irreconcilable. On the contrary, both proclaim a posture of helplessness before society. Shaw senior managed to regret even one of his rare achievements, though Shaw himself mentions the matter only to illustrate the origins of a rhetorical technique. Thus the father took his little boy for a first dip in the sea.

He prefaced it by a very serious exhortation on the importance of learning to swim, culminating in these words: 'When I was a boy of only fourteen, my knowledge of swimming enabled me to save your Uncle Robert's life.' Then, seeing I was deeply impressed, he stooped, and added confidentially in my ear, 'and, to tell you the truth, I never was so sorry for anything in my life afterwards'.[4]

Certainly this anti-climactic manner is perfectly Shavian, but there is more than an anecdotal trick; there is also the distaste for Uncle Robert delivered inoffensively and probably an outrageous desire for Uncle Robert's death so phrased that no outrage can be felt. Shaw likewise managed to say what he wished, however scurrilous or subversive, so that no one resented his views.

The common impression of George Carr Shaw formed by the biographers is that of an ineffectual man whose wife and children were more or less indifferent to him. Yet according to a boyhood friend of Shaw, Matthew Edward McNulty, Shaw hated his father. Whatever the truth we should not forget that the father was a considerable nuisance whose drinking cut the Shaws off socially and whose poverty and mildness caused him to acquiesce for a while in the sending of his son to a Dublin Catholic school, the Central Model School in Marlbrough Street. Certainly, in a Shaw play (that is, a play riddled with the devices of competition and self-assertion) someone like his father would obviously be playing for sympathy, dramatising his melancholia, seeking to avoid retribution, secretly longing for the downfall of his more robust relatives. It seems likely that George Carr Shaw did influence his son in a paradoxical way, but disappointed him also. I think that Shaw as a boy must normally have felt deprived of even a small degree of paternal support or resistance. By rendering himself so easily disregarded the father helped the son to grow up with a sense that reality as a whole is at the mercy of our manipulations.[5]

The older Shaw plainly felt beaten not by reality in the large sense but by certain social customs. He was a younger son and came of a line of younger sons with the result, as Shaw demonstrates in the Preface to *Immaturity*, that he judged himself by the criteria of a moderately 'good' family, though he was almost always hard up. Another important social fact is that Protestants in Ireland were the ascendant minority. They were not necessarily better off than Catholics but regarded themselves as essentially superior people. One of the most exasperating positions was that of the poor Protestant, since the milieu had somehow failed to provide an appropriate niche: one needed either to find such a niche or to slip away silent and defeated. This general situation explains, by the way, why the young Shaw felt wounded and cast out by his few months of attendance at the Central Model School, not in other respects a devastating fate. However, in terms of the subjective experience it is no great exaggeration to speak of Shaw's 'blacking-factory episode', because he was so shamed by being thrown among the children of Catholic tradesmen.[6]

Nor were the members of Shaw's mother's family, the Gurlys, quite so well established as he seems to have believed. The biographer John O'Donovan has pointed out that in fact two eighteenth-century lawyer-forebears bought cheaply some no doubt poorish properties in and around the town of Carlow.[7] In addition, at one stage in the family history the Gurlys owned sixteen acres of land. It is true that Shaw's mother, Lucinda Elizabeth (Bessie) Gurly, inherited £1500 from her mother (ultimately part of a sum bequeathed by Bessie's maternal grandmother), but even this not contemptible legacy could be used only to augment some other source of family income. Bessie's mother died young, her father seems to have been a waster and she was brought up mainly by a domineering, hunchbacked Aunt Ellen. Then at the age of twenty-one she was courted by the gentlemanly bachelor of thirty-seven, George Carr Shaw. He was not unqualifiedly eligible since, apart from the difference in age, he was cross-eyed and rumoured to be a drunk. When Mr Shaw assured Bessie that he was a teetotaller she discounted the tales of alcoholism as malicious and of the very sort to be used to influence her by her vile family. As it happens Bessie was anxious to marry in order to evade both her father's home (now complete with a second wife) and the house of Aunt Ellen. Consequently the wedding proceeded and according to Shaw his mother discovered on the honeymoon that her husband was in fact a thorough drunkard, after which she rapidly descended into a 'hell' of 'shabby-genteel poverty'.[8]

More should be said at this stage about Bessie's nature. She was a dreamer, for that is what Shaw presumably means when he says that 'She had plenty of imagination, and really lived in it and on it.'[9] Mrs Shaw's would not have been the disciplined imagination of an artist but an intense capacity for transmuting her desires or

fears into self-centred images and dramas. Further, she overrid-
ingly wished to rise in the world, or – to see matters from her point
of view – to be restored to her rightful place among the Dublin
rentiers. For the time being she was living in poverty in an
unprepossessing house with an incompetent husband and, by the
year 1856, three children. Even though she disliked her father, her
Aunt Ellen and other members of her original family it was
important not to be despised too much by them for making a bad
marriage against their sound, if selfish, advice.

Bessie's attitude towards her husband and children was
amiably unloving: they had no priority in either her limited
affections or her scheme of things. Obviously they all had to be
cared for to some extent, but we exaggerate rather than falsify if
we picture the father as defensive and self-reviling and the
children blundering unguided through their early years. It is
clear, anyway, that so eccentric a figure as Shaw must have been
largely self-taught in youth. All his life he had the autodidact's
independence, the tendency to come upon things wide-eyed and
unconditioned by school, professional colleagues or social group.
For we must remember that George Carr Shaw's drunkenness
limited the circle of acquaintances his family formed. They were
not asked out, so Shaw taught himself in matters social as well as
academic. As a boy he at least knew how to handle the cutlery but,
on the other hand, he did not realise that elders and betters
expected some conversational deference from him. As a young
man he studied books of etiquette in the reading room of the
British Museum. In his teens, however, he was at once shy and
self-assertive, a hobbledehoy with little enough grace. Even when
he acquired his celebrated Irish fluency the whole manner was
plainly willed, like an actor's; he assembled the lineaments of his
mature personality.

Mrs Shaw dreaming of social elevation had no worldly-wise
friends who could offer advice, effect introductions or in any way
direct her to an orthodox channel. At the beginning of her
marriage Bessie, who was distinctly impractical, had no idea how
to climb to her coveted social plateau. From the range of her
excessively good education one acquirement seemed serviceable:
music. This, an art-form rather than a branch of commerce,
presented itself in the course of time as her best means of making
both money and reputation. It was probably in 1858 (when
George Bernard, the youngest child, was two) that Bessie became

a pupil of George Vandeleur Lee, teacher of singing who lived in Harrington Street, very near the Shaw's Synge Street house. After some two or three years' training with Lee, Bessie rose from being a member of the chorus of his Amateur Musical Society to the position of prima donna. Throughout Shaw's infancy, in other words, his mother was preoccupied with what she regarded as the truly important business of her new-found career. She must regularly have been out of the house practising with her musical colleagues, or, if at home, engrossed with the full power of her imagination in rehearsals, scores, public engagements, newspaper reviews, artistic rivalries and the like.

In the late fifties and the sixties Lee's star was climbing the Dublin sky. In particular a concert his society gave in 1864 to mark the Shakespeare Tercentenary Celebrations made his name locally and helped the group as a whole to move from an amateur to a semi-professional status. At the same time Lee's increasing celebrity made him intolerable to some more orthodox Dublin musicians and in 1873 he was so humiliated by Sir Robert Prescott Stewart, Professor of Music at Trinity College, that he fled to London.

Stewart in fact gleefully showed up Lee's inadequacies as a conductor, and it is true that Lee was not in the ordinary sense a competent musician at all. Perhaps he was always something of a charlatan or, at best, with no formal qualifications, a 'mesmeric' personality and an idiosyncratic method of voice development (about which he wrote a book) he succeeded in maximising his pupil's capacities. The chances are that he was a good teacher who loved the exhibitionism and the power of teaching but had little interest in some laboriously solitary feature of his craft and no regard for music as an academic profession. He was a showman, histrionic through and through, and at all times, elated or downcast, the centre of attention. Was it not he who gave Shaw the notion that success, indeed power itself, is largely a matter of personal style?

For, of course, Lee paraded before the young Shaw exactly the qualities lacked by Shaw's dejected father. Lee did this all day long since in or about 1865 the Shaw family moved with Lee to 1 Hatch Street and the six people lived there until Lee went to London, closely followed by Mrs Shaw, her two daughters and, within a year, George Bernard himself. In the end George Carr Shaw was left alone in Dublin, his entire family having made off to

London to be near the music teacher. It may be a mistake to see
this desertion in anything but the obvious manner as a humiliation for George Carr Shaw. Perhaps it brought him some relief as
well. The biographers, following Shaw himself, seem to have
regarded the father as too sweetly passive to feel resentment or
despair. We cannot know the truth, but this simple version seems
unlikely. What is certain is that George Shaw's personality was
plentifully threaded with gestures of futility, and his career was
crowned by his being tossed aside for a Roman Catholic of
overwhelming panache who made a sort of triumph out of an
ignoble flight to England.

But of what nature were young Shaw's relations with Lee? Was
the latter in any sense a second or substitute father? Of what kind,
for that matter, was Lee's partnership with Mrs Shaw? It is
generally assumed that Lee was a ladies' man and the tale is that
he conducted some kind of flirtation with Lucy, Shaw's eldest
sister, presumably when she was in her middle or late teens. Just
the same, Lee's gallantries (if any) either with Bessie or with her
daughter might have been purely verbal. And for Bessie, possibly
for Lucy Shaw as well, Lee was professionally a useful man.
Carnality is so plainly missing from Shaw's plays (missing, that is,
to a degree unmatched in any other writer one can think of who
deals comically, seriously or even peripherally with romantic
entanglements) that it would be strange indeed if he had grown up
in a house where he could subliminally sense, if not comprehend,
strong sexual harmonies or conflicts. And Shaw, in the preface to
London Music in 1888–89, fairly explicitly denies any sexual relation
between his mother and Lee.[10]

Shaw was deeply impressed by Lee ('a man of mesmeric vitality
and force.')[11] but he did not positively like him.

> We never felt any affection for Lee; he was too excessively
> unlike us, too completely a phenomenon, to rouse any primitive
> human feeling in us. When my mother introduced him to me,
> he played with me for the first and last time; but as his notion of
> play was to decorate my face with moustaches and whiskers in
> burnt cork in spite of the most furious resistance I could put up,
> our encounter was not a success; and the defensive attitude in
> which it left me lasted, though without the least bitterness, until
> the decay of his energies and the growth of mine put us on more
> than equal terms.[12]

That is plain enough and there is no reason to doubt it. Yet it was surely Lee who provided the foundation of the theme of success upon which Shaw in his plays (despite his socialism) came to compose many variations. Lee is not merely Higgins, for example; he lies behind all those Shavian men of superficially different sorts who have in common the constant capacity to gain attention, to brush aside opposition, to win arguments and sometimes, when necessary, to 'charm the birds off the trees'. Further it seems certain that Lee unwittingly provided the model for the personality which Shaw created for himself in his late twenties. I do not suggest that the mature Shaw simply copied Lee – far from it – but that he adapted to his own purposes and capacities what he discerned as the essence of Lee's winning ways.

It is true that by the time Shaw undertook this course of self-determination he had come a long way from the gauche teenager who in his Hatch Street home found himself so readily thrust aside by Lee and sat drinking in the nuances of his mother's (and later of sister Lucy's) ambitious manoeuvres. At least two of the women in his house (Elinor Shaw, who died at twenty-one, is an altogether vaguer figure) were inordinately resolute, always driving towards some objective. They loved neither George Bernard nor anyone else and saw life as an upward journey rather than a series of occasions for emotional indulgence or altruistic behaviour. Lee was the man they both used, but he used them in turn. These were businesslike forms of intercourse, later modified by Shaw, presumably, into the association of Higgins and Eliza.

What we must bear in mind is that Shaw never thought of himself as anything other than a man of destiny. His boyhood was a preparation for some splendid adult fate; his adolescent job with a firm of Dublin land agents was from the beginning *obviously* a mere phase in his career, and later his humble years in London were years of watching and waiting. I mean, of course, that that is how Shaw saw his early life, long before there was any justification for doing so. He did not know precisely or even roughly what great future lay in store for him, but of the greatness he had no doubt. Logically such an attitude as young Shaw's is absurd (as I imply), and yet to the extent that it passes beyond daydreams it ensures the sort of triumphs it serenely expects. Nor is the reason hard to find, for such a person evades or treats flippantly every avenue that would lead to mediocrity, and follows (if sometimes in a clumsy fashion) the signs that point to conquest. Thus there is no *secret* of success.

One such hopeful sign was the personal style of George Vandeleur Lee. Shaw observed that Lee gained his ends because his every gesture proclaimed that he would do so. Even Lee's material failure in Ireland magically became a sort of success. When he was hounded out of Dublin he not only drew most of the Shaw family after him across the Irish Sea but rapidly established himself as a maestro in Park Lane. It is true that Lee eventually deteriorated into a perfect quack, so that Mrs Shaw had nothing more to do with him,[13] but the years of his genuine accomplishments were impressive. Shaw must have pondered how this sort of thing was done, or rather, since the method was transparent, how he could acquire the skill to follow it. He was up against the paradox of confidence: the virtual coincidence of expectation and achievement.

Of his early years in London Shaw once remarked, in revealing terms:

> I had not then tuned the Shavian note to any sort of harmony; and I have no doubt the Lawsons [a family he was in the habit of visiting] found me discordant, crudely self-assertive, and insufferable.[14]

Perhaps we can take the musical metaphor here seriously enough to assume that many expressions of Shaw's individuality (gesture, tones of voice, speech-patterns, opinions and so on) were to begin with discordant with one another and with the occasion; then after his transformation, these elements flowed together into a Shavian harmony. His will to dominance was the same before and after, but by the second stage it had grown almost *aesthetically* impressive. The change was brought about as Shaw, through fearful repetition, learned to ignore the pairs of eyes fixed upon him and to concentrate upon his own performance. Confidence grew in him as he began to think of life as a whole, as a complex of techniques to be mastered. Such was the elementary and powerful lesson Shaw absorbed from the example of Lee, and from Lee's practices as a music teacher.

Shaw's method, as is well known, consisted of inveterate public speaking. After some three years of walking the streets of London (reaching in time a condition of 'indescribable seediness'), of haunting the National Gallery, Hampton Court and of course the British Museum, he happened to join the Zetetical Society to whose members in 1879 he urged himself through his first speech. He resolved to speak thereafter at every opportunity; his skill and pleasure increased while his nervousness dwindled to vanishing point. Still, he had no theme, no message; he was an entertainer. Then in 1882 he heard Henry George at the Memorial Hall, Farringdon Street, and was shown the economic basis of society. He read *Das Kapital* in French, or so he claimed. Now he had his socialist theme, which was greatly strengthened when he joined the Fabian Society and met Sidney Webb in 1884. The following year Shaw gave his first genuinely public speech: we have a record of it and the manner is perfectly his own.

Shaw was twenty-nine in 1885, by which time he had grown into GBS. That same year he belatedly lost his virginity with a widow named Jenny Patterson. The evidence clearly suggests that from then on, with the two principal exceptions of Charlotte Payne-Townsend (Mrs G. B. Shaw) and Mrs Patrick Campbell, Shaw did his best to reduce his relations with women to a series of more or less enjoyable flirtations. I do not mean that he must have avoided sexual intercourse but that he certainly subordinated it to his more manageable social pastimes. So far as Shaw was concerned sex was less the goal of an enterprise than a peculiarly uncontrolled intervention. 'It is not the end he cares for,' wrote Beatrice Webb. 'It is the *process*. His sensuality has all drifted into sexual vanity – delight in being the candle to the moths.'[15] However, he seems never to have flirted with Charlotte but simply married her in the most 'sensible', chaste and unromantic manner, while he did uncharacteristically lose his head (at the age of fifty-six) over Mrs Patrick Campbell. But Shaw's sexual reluctance can be regarded only as an aspect of a ruling ambition: he wanted to bring everything in the world into the stockade of his imagination.

Shaw's mature personality was a coherent set of devices for controlling all social experiences. He wished to sweep others before him, like Sir Andrew Undershaft disposing not only of his family but of the armaments (and therefore, to a degree the political affairs) of European nations, or like Lady Cicely Waynflete running rings around Brassbound and his gang. I offer these two examples because each entails the dominance through rhetoric of such situations as in life ultimately reduce rhetoric to screams or silence. Undershaft has to deal with masters of *Realpolitick*, Lady Cicely with cut-throats. Now Shaw was fully aware of the discrepancies between his plays and actuality, but he was, if you will, a sort of Hegelian who believed that external facts must gradually be taken up into ideas; that an ideational or spiritual reality in this sense takes precedence over phenomenal events.

In the same vein, he was never a realist in the Western empirical sense. Reality to Shaw was the principle exhibited by an action rather than the action itself. Consequently his task as a playwright was, for instance, to disclose the relation between the manufacture of armaments and the Salvation Army. That the latter actually depends on the former could best be revealed, he supposed, in a comic and not meticulously credible play. By such means Shaw hoped 'Hegelianly' to change the world; for example, to acquaint not only the officers of the Salvation Army but all high-minded individuals with their dependent places in the social scheme.

Shaw's habitual interest in underlying principles was the legacy of a youth that had been empty of love and free from restrictions. His mother taught him very little because she was, as he puts it in *Sixteen Self Sketches*, a 'Bohemian anarchist with ladylike habits'.[16] She was determined that her children should be free because she as a child (brought up by Aunt Ellen) had been so rigidly controlled. Shaw's father, likewise, scarcely taught him at all, through a sense of personal inadequacy. 'Who am I', he said in effect, 'a business failure and an alcoholic, to instruct a child?' Later, Lee must have shown off a good deal to young Shaw (and incidentally recommended the disastrous attendance at the Central Model School), but evidently did not pass on rules of behaviour or facts of social life in any regular manner. The result of this general neglect was that Shaw needed to discover the workings of society. Because he did not absorb any of the usual bogus explanations (moral, political and customary) he was compelled to find certain 'true' explanations. He took it for granted that hitherto orthodoxies had been shared hypocrisies and that rivalries, often involving deceit, constituted the pattern of human relations. He looked with reasonable though not exemplary care at superficial indications: at clothes, modes of address, business customs and so on, taking these to be guides to the unuttered rules that govern our lives. His great desire came to

›e to disclose these rules and where necessary strive to change
hem for the better. Shaw grew into a reductionist, one to whom
Das Kapital would have seemed, in the 1880s, a marvellous
:learing-away of the obfuscations of the centuries.

But that is only one side of the picture. There is also what might
·easonably be called the theological side: Shaw was an iconoclast
>ecause the gods were false, not because there can be no divinity.
While he needed 'genuine' explanations and principles to control
he flux, he needed also the sense of a far-distant, infinitely vast
and immaculate objective. Obviously he himself was human,
all-too-human, infinitesimally a part of the movement towards an
all-embracing, spiritual totality – a totality not unlike, so it seems
:o me, the Absolute of Hegel's *Phenomenology of Mind*.

It is possible to account for this vital factor in Shaw's make-up.
We might begin by recalling that in *Sixteen Self Sketches* Shaw
writes that after realising one day in boyhood that his father was
drunk he never afterwards 'believed in anything or anybody'.[17] In
other words, he didn't 'believe in' his mother or his wife or Mrs
Patrick Campbell. He certainly lacked faith in contemporary
political and cultural leaders (though he overrated the dictators).
Historical personages in the plays are sometimes venerated less
for what they are in themselves than for what they portend. Thus
Caesar rises above the generality of men but is not unreservedly
admirable. Even Joan as a wry saint in the epilogue to her play is
only a forerunner of some unimaginable future condition.

The necessary faith for Shaw was that there should be a golden
future *beyond imagination* to look forward to. At the end of *Back to
Methuselah* Lilith foresees the 'goal of redemption from the flesh',
matter superseded by 'pure intelligence'. 'It is enough,' says
Lilith, 'that there is a beyond.'[18] It was enough for Shaw also, for
he was the supreme apostle of life as never-ending progress. Life is
the antithesis of matter, for it is spiritual and therefore on the
opposing side of the Manichaean divide. At some primordial
stage Life invaded and took up its abode within the 'whirlpool of
force', a vortex of pure materiality. Lilith is not merely, as she is in
Semitic fable, the first wife of Adam, but the originator of life. She
will eventually pass from existence into legend, while Life will
sweep onwards for evermore.

The value of Shaw's doctrines is not our present concern and
the subject is pursued in Chapters 6 and 8. The important point to
dwell on here is his need for a sense of limitlessness. From an

emotional standpoint he solved the problem of his own finitude by
recognising his part in infinity. What mattered was the universal
chain of events from which one absolutely could not fall away.

Shaw required certainty to compensate for the insecurities of
his youth. To have unreliable parents is common, but it is rare to
find no consolation in any conceivable society or scheme of values.
Shaw's kingdom, as he said, was 'not of this world'.[19] The world
indeed was what he wished to fend off. But he could not do this by
pretending to himself that a satisfactory society was just around
the corner or that the members of some reformist group were in
principle, if not always in practice, admirable. The process of
reform is venerable, not its more or less grubby participants.
Shaw came to terms with the misgivings forced upon him by his
father and mother. Between them they robbed him of emotional
anchorage. His mother did not love him but did not exploit him
either; she left him free. His father did not love him and exposed
the world as Vanity Fair. So came about Shaw's total scepticism;
he had no social certainty to fall back on. He found solace in the
one *progressive* fact of life: that creatures have succeeded one
another in a hierarchy of consciousness. This fact was purely
natural and therefore surpassed all the villainies and stupidities
that men could practise. Men might indeed wipe one another out,
but nature would then produce another highly conscious species.
Nature is inexhaustible and man a trivial offshoot. Once Shaw
became aware of that and further realised that he might aid what
he anthropomorphically thought of as nature's 'intentions' he
gained a confidence that nothing could weaken. All Mrs Bessie
Shaw had ever wanted was to be a local winner. She wished to
'show them', to acquire prestige in the eyes of her family and their
peers. Her son translated this petty ambition into a doctrine of
cosmological progress and felt invincible through identification
with the invincible forces of life.

6 Shaw's Quintessence

A Freudian study of Shaw cautiously and convincingly suggests that the subject, among other psychic manoeuvres, externalised his aggression; incorporated his mother, thus aligning himself with the mother against the male; transformed his all-consuming narcissism; made his own aspiration and despair into boundaries of the cosmos, and sought (as is clear indeed in *Back to Methuselah*) to 'remake sexuality and eliminate death'.[1] We shall return to some of these observations later in the chapter and for the moment it is enough to remark that such a man as this Shaw would tend to appropriate whatever he encountered. A vaguely similar impression of him used to be common enough, though it has receded in our better informed and blander times: at any rate, my present aim is to explore rather than contradict that earlier view. To begin at the beginning, readers have assumed since 1891 that by means of *The Quintessence of Ibsenism* Shaw in some degree assimilated Ibsen to the Shavian sphere: the only quarrels have been about the legitimacy of the process and how far it misrepresents the Norwegian. At one extreme Huntley Carter, for example, writing in 1912, declared that Ibsen had been 'butchered to make a Fabian holiday',[2] while in the opinion of J. L. Wisenthal (1979) Shaw's exposition of a 'basic attitude' in Ibsen is 'not only highly interesting in itself and an excellent guide to Shaw's own plays, but . . . an invaluable source of insight into an essential aspect of Ibsen's work'.[3]

Before we go any further I should mention that several Shaw critics have already dealt with his treatment of Ibsen, so that my purpose here is just to stress a few points as a prelude to discussing Shaw's own literary ways. First, then, it is necessary to bear in mind that he never claimed to have given a balanced account of Ibsen, but on the contrary acknowledged his partiality. In the Preface to the first edition of *The Quintessence of Ibsenism* he states that what follows 'is not a critical essay on the poetic beauties of Ibsen, but simply an exposition of Ibsenism'.[4] The remark is

117

meant to be disarming, though it contains two unexamined
assumptions: first, that the 'poetic beauties' in Ibsen are extrinsic
to the 'arguments' and secondly, that those arguments amount to
a doctrine of 'Ibsenism'. Thus the Ibsenism of the title is not a set
of organically connected characteristics but a thesis – of which,
however, its originator might not have been fully aware. For, as
Shaw remarks,

> I have also shewn that the existence of a discoverable and
> perfectly definite thesis in a poet's work by no means depends
> on the completeness of his own intellectual consciousness of it.[5]

Ibsen's thesis, we learn from the Preface to the second edition of
The Quintessence of Ibsenism (1912–13), amounted to an 'attack on
ideals and idealism'.[6] According to the Preface to the third edition
(1922) the Great War, a war of ideals, would never have taken
place 'had the gospel of Ibsen been understood and heeded'.[7]
Shaw means that the First World War could not even have been
conceived by people who reacted only to observable particulars
and not at all to general beliefs. But that is generally true of wars
and Shaw is unwittingly saying that human life would be entirely
different (in other words, non-human or alternatively, 'fully
human') if we were all 'realists'. In practice realism and idealism
are mixed together and Shaw's notion is that every pioneer raises
up an ideal that is marginally less untrue to facts than the ideal it
replaces. So there is a progressive reduction in the number and
strength of the ideals by which man is governed, and the objective
of this process (to be realised far in the future) is a wholly
empirical way of life.

The vanguard of mankind is composed of two classes of
pioneers, one of which undermines obsolescent codes while the
other creates fresh moral refinements. Some pioneers belong to
both classes, for instance Shelley who sought to remove the taboo
against the marriage of brothers and sisters and to make everyone
a vegetarian. (That Shaw offered Shelley as his example of a
double pioneer suggests that he would not have minded readers
detecting his small but distinct debt in this preliminary argument
to *A Defence of Poetry*.)

It is important to recognise that we are dealing not with a
rationalist who objected to various activities because they lacked
reason but with one who merely employed reasoning as a weapon.

'In process of time,' Shaw cheerfully says, 'the age of reason had to go its way after the age of faith.'[8] The end for which we should be striving is not arid rationality but abundant life. This paradise not of serenity but of vigour will be reached only when the last public duty has been repudiated and each man is left with only the duty to himself. When 'man's God is his own humanity ... he, self-satisfied at last, ceases to be selfish'.[9]

The interesting fact is that Shaw set out to enlist Ibsen in these Shelleyan endeavours, for what is lacking throughout *The Quintessence of Ibsenism* is any recognition that Ibsen might have believed the very opposite, namely that vigour is actually fostered by enmity and obstruction. In Shaw's vision at the outset of his career as author man is everywhere in chains which impede the movements of his soul as well as his body. He is therefore dull, fatigued, immoral and more than a little mad. When he has cast off his chains and stands free of his dungeon; when, in other words, there are no impediments to his desires, he will be healthy in body and spirit and no longer liable to sin. For his selfishness and his disgust with himself are caused solely by restrictions.

Such restrictions are often cast in the form of ideals, a term we employ for fantastic beliefs designed to mask terrifying facts. Death is the most appalling fact, so from earliest times men have covered its face with the ideal of personal immortality. Every soul survives, according to its quality, in a suitable region. An ideal has likewise been formed to disguise each reality which people find unnerving. Those who most dread some piece of the real world believe implicitly in the ideal which hides it. For instance, the ideal of the womanly woman, to which Shaw turns his attention in the third preliminary section of *The Quintessence of Ibsenism*, is enthusiastically upheld by people of both sexes who are scared of diverse and merely human woman. Ibsen himself confronted that particular idea by creating so 'unwomanly' a creature as Rebecca West. Yet not even Ibsen was admitting the fact of diversity so much as offering a less ridiculous ideal. According to Shaw that is all anyone can do.

At this point, before proceeding to the main body of the *Quintessence*, we should distinguish one of Shaw's beliefs from both Ibsen's attitude and a common modern attitude. Despite the vilenesses of our period many people are convinced that humanity has improved over the centuries in terms of ethics, health, government and law. There is a common assumption that we are

Part II: Shaw

or ought to be, on balance, happier than our forefathers. (And much of whatever joy they experienced depended, people say, upon illusions, so transparent to us.) Likewise, every right-thinking person today tries to aid the further progress of mankind: there is really nothing else to do but go forward gathering increments of happiness, health and justice.

So far as Ibsen was concerned, on the contrary, nineteenth-century Norway was not comprehensively better than the ninth, the age of the Vikings. It was possible indeed that our race took a disastrously wrong turn in forsaking the sea for the land. Man seemed not to be improving, since there was no reduction in the quality or number of chicaneries with which the good by definition were obliged to contend. All that mattered fundamentally to Ibsen was the noble spirit which flickered here and there in every generation. A small number behaved in accordance with nature and were by that stoic test commendable.

Shaw's point of view was different again. On the one hand there absolutely must be improvement but on the other hand, as he explains through Tanner in the seventh section of 'The Revolutionist's Handbook', *Man and Superman*, 'We must frankly give up the notion that man as he exists is capable of net progress.' That was written in 1903, but as late as 1944, in *Everybody's Political What's What*, he answers his own question, 'Is Human Nature Incurably Depraved', by saying in effect that we must assume that some cure will eventually work. His procedure eminently but almost desperately reasonable, was to examine contemporary facts afresh, from a bird's-eye view.

So there was from the beginning a glaring difference between Shaw and Ibsen, but in the *Quintessence*, for all its high quality as literary interpretation, this difference is muted and disguised. Towards the end of the essay, in the section called 'The Lesson of the Plays', Shaw rightly says that 'What Ibsen insists on is that there is no golden rule, that conduct must justify itself by its effect on life and not by conformity to any rule or ideal.' He adds that we should observe of Ibsenism that 'its quintessence is that there is no formula'.[10] True indeed and probably the most important single thing to say about Ibsen's writings, but throughout the preceding essay Shaw has given the impression that Ibsen set out positively to 'legislate', as it were, against all codifiable legislation. He has Shavianised Ibsen's meaning partly by bringing out a 'discoverable and perfectly definite thesis'.

If it is argued that Shaw would have found it hard to interpret Ibsen in any other fashion at a time when people were not merely discovering theses in the plays but discovering the wrong ones, we might still say that he should have emphasised from first to last that Ibsen's beliefs were anti-doctrinal.[11] Shaw failed to do so because of his own didacticism and unyielding habit of generalisation. For him to observe was to generalise, and so to draw moral conclusions. Everything in Shaw is a typification; nothing is solely what it is but exists for the sake of an idea.

Today many believe that the mind by its nature makes structures, but a complex structure must always be reduced to fit the form of an idea. So there is a world of difference between an Ibsen who refused to narrow structures into ideas and a Shaw who could scarcely refrain from doing so. Ibsen discouraged exactly what Shaw demanded: the drawing of general conclusions from particular fictional instances.

Partly because of its origins in a paper Shaw read to the Fabian Society in 1890 *The Quintessence of Ibsenism* is a mixture of accurate exposition and progressionist misrepresentation. When Shaw falsifies he does so, more often than not, because he wishes to minimise those elements in Ibsen that suggest how impotent, beyond narrow limits, man's thought actually is. *Brand*, for example, with which Shaw begins, is not in his reading an essentially ambivalent story of a man heroically too high for ordinary living yet not high enough for sainthood. Instead it is a study of one who 'dies a saint having caused more suffering by his saintliness than the most talented sinner could possibly have done with twice his opportunities'.[12] It is clear though that Ibsen cared less about the suffering Brand causes than about his hero's constancy. What Shaw did not realise (he discussed the play without seeing or reading it) is that Brand, far from vainly trying to live up to an ideal, really does live in the most down-to-earth manner according to the gospels. It is fidelity to practical, not idealistic gospel tenets that causes the suffering and gives the play its paradoxical quality. Nor, of course, is Brand a villain, as Shaw maintains, but Ibsen in his 'best moments'.[13]

Conversely, when Shaw turns his attention to *Peer Gynt* he is right to see it as an anti-idealist play which advocates paying attention to the concrete here-and-now. Only at the end of his long, farcical life, and perhaps not even then, does Peer give up his ideal which, as Shaw remarks, consists of 'the realisation

of himself through the utter satisfaction of his own will'.[14] Peer
Gynt's will, in familiar fashion, distorts or ignores the realities
which surround him.

Following the section on *Peer Gynt* Shaw conducts a skilful
analysis of *Emperor and Galilean*, then towards the end of his
remarks tries to ram that play into his scheme by saying that
'Julian, in this respect [the divergence of his ideals from reality] is
a reincarnation of Peer Gynt'. But Julian is no respect resembles
Peer Gynt, since his doomed opposition to the 'world-will', in
other words to burgeoning Christianity, is based not on Gyntian
wilfulness but on a perception of the anti-philosophic nature of
Christianity. Indeed he thinks of it as deathly and of Jesus as the
'pale Galilean'. If Christianity is the thesis, Julian represents the
antithesis, and from both the synthesis of the 'third empire' will
eventually come.

The next division of *The Quintessence* is called 'The Objective
Anti-Idealist Plays' and chiefly deals with the works from *Pillars of
Society* to *Hedda Gabler* (though the earlier *The League of Youth* is also
included here, since it is of the same kind). Shaw's method is to
summarise the plot of each play, emphasising the specific
contra-idealist element. Thus *Pillars of Society* satirises the ideal of
duty to society; *A Doll's House* exhibits an ideal and therefore
misguided husband and wife; *Ghosts* is an 'outspoken attack on
marriage as a useless sacrifice of human beings to an ideal';[15] *An
Enemy of the People* assails 'commercial–political ideals';[16] *The Wild
Duck* shows up the idealist Gregers Werle who masquerades as a
realist; *Rosmersholm* is concerned with 'the danger of forming ideals
for other people';[17] *The Lady from the Sea* reveals the origin of
ideals in unhappiness, and finally, Hedda Gabler is susceptible to
romantic ideals.

It is not just that Shaw's view of these plays is too schematic but
that the scheme is misleading. Ibsen himself must have realised
that cold, deliberate liars, however common in life, are the stuff of
more melodramatic effects than he was aiming for. Since their
conduct cannot be explained in the usual manner, which is to say
palliated, they tend to make fiction as meaningless as reality. On
the other hand, if people are going to deceive themselves they tend
to reach out for some handy social formula. That the formula itself
is at fault is obvious, but is Shaw's rather than Ibsen's emphasis.
Shaw wished to get rid of conventional formulas and wrote his
plays for that very reason. But for Ibsen, while each formula was

more than a theatrical device, it was yet only a local expedient for a timeless human weakness. For example, Hedda's 'romantic deals' are themselves at the service of her spite and exasperation. Everything depends on whether one believes human nature to be the cause or the product of cultural conditions. Ibsen was rather of the first persuasion, Shaw emphatically of the second.

Shaw's discussion of the later works is called simply 'The Last Four Plays', but subtitled 'Down Among the Dead Men'. In the opinion of J. L. Wisenthal, 'Shaw was never much interested in pathology, but he is a good deal closer to the complexities of Ibsen's plays in 1912–13 than he was in 1891.'[18] That may be roughly true but it is an exaggeration, since the preceptor's tones are as pervasive as ever and figures in Ibsen are still held up as blundering sinners from whose errors we are overwhelmingly intended to profit. Shaw's is an evangelical manner while Ibsen's view includes anger and poetic zest, a relishing of irony and a most unShavian *amor fati*. Shaw gives the impression that Ibsen wrote *The Master Builder* so that fewer people would behave as Solness or Hilde. Solness has sacrificed his wife and is 'himself sacrificed to a girl's enthusiasm';[19] consequently the play has the function of a homily against exploitation. But, as Shaw could not have known, Solness is a simplification of Ibsen and the play expresses not only the bite of Ibsen's conscience but also the recrudescence of his youthful dream.

In Shaw's eyes *Little Eyolf* shows us the reality of the ideal home of romance (*égoisme à deux*) and how the right sort of individualism is no longer self-centred but reaches out to the species. Our consideration of Ibsen's career suggests that it is more likely that he doubted not only Rita Allmers's final decision but the purity of all altruism.[20]

John Gabriel Borkman is naturally represented as an unqualified denunciation of the money-voluptuaries, those moral imbeciles whose lust for money is a disguised lust for precious metals. Borkman, being of this class, makes a criminal error, sacrifices the Rentheim sisters and becomes the centre-piece in 'the grimmest lying in state ever exposed to view by mortal dramatist.'[21] The conclusion of the play exhibits no uplift whatever and Borkman's progress is from melancholy near-madness to joyful complete madness. In fact, as we have seen, Ibsen represents Borkman's dreams as the half-crazy neighbours of genuine greatness, his vision as a mere distortion, not a reversal, of Ibsen's own.

The play that above all others should not be read moralistically is *When We Dead Awaken*, yet Shaw grasped it as a treatment of the 'woman question', in which the male partner in each of the two couples exploits his female. Ulfheim and Maja are 'Stone Age' man and woman, so Maja welcomes her enslavement, while Rubek, who belongs in the most cultivated modern category, does not think of Irene as having a personality of her own. He callously uses Irene and she, years later, takes him up a mountain in order to find 'an honest and natural relation in which they shall no longer sacrifice and slay one another'.[22] As they go up they meet the Stone Age pair coming down. There is a storm and Ulfheim is brave enough to carry his 'willing prey' to lower slopes. Rubek and Irene, being 'beyond the fear of death', climb higher. Only Irene is free from blame and to show the inadequacy of the other three is Shaw's whole concern. Ulfheim and Maja are relics of man's savage past, beneath consideration, while Rubek is a nineties aesthete to whom others may conceivably be of artistic use. Ibsen himself is quite outside the play, a preacher offering his 'ensamples'.

At this stage a reminder is overdue: Shaw's analysis of Ibsen's plays was far ahead of his contemporaries, including the shrewdly appreciative William Archer. *The Quintessence of Ibsenism* is rightly regarded as a classic both of Ibsen studies and of Shavianism. No one that we know of – not even the undergraduate James Joyce writing in the 'Fortnightly Review' in 1900 – seems to have had a better understanding of *When We Dead Awaken*. Even so, Shaw could not perceive that so great a dramatist, so momentous a European event as Ibsen might not be conducting a humanist crusade. Since Shaw wished to improve people he assumed that the satirically observant Ibsen had the same paramount desire. It is true that Ibsen sometimes entertained hopes of improvement (in his private utterances rather than his plays), but such hopes never amounted to a faith, while to Shaw, on the other hand, they unified as well as expressed his personality. Nothing made sense to him except as a potential, a plant struggling towards the light or a deformity waiting to be mended. Here is the appropriate place to begin a sketch of Shaw's *literary* nature in terms of his reformist goals.

We have noticed in the last chapter that Shaw's fluent, witty, unfalteringly self-assured manner was formed before he had any firm opinions to offer. While he was finishing his second novel, *The*

Irrational Knot, he joined the Zetetical Society and promptly, though agonisingly, set about becoming a 'performer'. Through speaking regularly at meetings of the society he began to satisfy a hitherto frustrated requirement of his nature: he held the stage by a series of increasingly polished speeches. Annihilated were the discordant London scenes outside the hall and the clumsy gestures of the pre-Shavian personality. Now only Shaw's style mattered since, as a matter of fact, his theme could be anything under the sun, or at least anything consistent with bravura tones.

Shaw must then have loved the magical quality of the orator–actor, because such a man was complete and elegant beyond anything one might encounter in the streets. In time the new manner was well nigh perfect; nor should anyone simply say that Shaw was busy substituting artifice for reality, since the adopted personality embodied his intimate needs. However, the most noteworthy fact is that Shaw's first need was for aesthetic wholeness: this scorner of aestheticism was obliged first to practise art for art's sake.

To be exact, his own sake and the sake of art were nearly the same, so that the oratory was also a method of self-invention. The speeches has to be almost flawless since in creating himself he was aiming for a *finished* state. He was striving for harmony, seeking to design himself as one designs a piece of music.

The hunt for a mould to contain the entire, assertive Shaw had long been in progress when he joined the Zetetical Society and continued for some time afterwards, for, as Colin Wilson astutely remarks, four of Shaw's five novels were 'mirrors', recording his 'search for a hero'. Wilson continues: 'The shy, awkward young man from Dublin wanted to know what he ought to do with his life; that is, what sort of a person he wanted to become.'[23] Read in this light the novels, except for *Cashel Byron's Profession* (in which the search for a hero is suspended), make a kind of sense they otherwise lack. Each one reveals Shaw trying out a model for himself. The model embodying Shaw's desires most completely is Sidney Trefusis of *An Unsocial Socialist* (written in 1887, five years before the first play, *Widowers' House*). Trefusis is a rich, eloquent revolutionist, cleverer by far than the other characters, much after the style of some heroes of the plays.

What the later Shaw hero exhibits is control – of his social situation and, through his ideas, of the larger world. To imagine him worsted or seriously suffering is absurd, since he absolutely belongs in his original context, yet because he speaks of life in general, because he is so much a messenger and an apostle there is always the temptation to say, 'Yes, but how would you fare in such and such an awkward situation?' However, before Shaw could conceive a dramatic hero of this sort he needed to support the commanding manner with a body of doctrine. Before we go any further let us try to work out why this should have been so.

According to Colin Wilson, who has paid more attention to this matter than other critics and biographers, it is important to grasp that Henry George gave the future dramatist 'an answer to the purely practical problem of what [in 1882] to do next'.[24] I am sure this is true but why should the answer have been provided by socialism? Specifically it was provided by Henry George's recommendation that privately owned land be taxed so heavily that it would become for practical purposes the property of the community. Since this was proposed as the solution of an array of economic and political problems, I suggest that Henry George convinced Shaw that all problems have simple solutions. The Georgian clues were first, that elementary answers may be given – indeed, must be given – to even the most complicated questions, and secondly, that personal quests for identity and purpose were illusory. Such a quest, it now seemed, had been imposed on the young Shaw by the economic system. He began to lose his feelings of guilt and inadequacy, having been persuaded that they were a legacy of pre-socialist generations.

Shaw immediately came to believe that many human sorrows and most of human culture were founded upon folly, that is, upon the tendency to overlook plain explanations in favour of Laputan monstrosities of learning, to which university professors, for example, devoted their lives. Thus in the past a few men had grabbed land, later giving it to their sons, and upon this elementary foundation had been erected vast systems of culture and government.

If there is something wrong with this simplifying mode of thought, then some of the most respected minds have been guilty of it. But Shaw's eureka-moment influenced him entirely and put an end to serious problem-solving. He would never torment himself like a Marx or a Freud, since he no sooner saw a problem than he found its solution. The labour of his writings would shortly start but the labour of fundamental thinking was over for him before it began.

But why should a playwright, an artist, think fundamentally about his subject matter? Of course, there is no compelling reason why he should and it was Shaw who chose to be a diagnostician of society. Social ills did not impose that role upon him, but rather, in the eighties, he voluntarily moulded himself to it. He embraced a task and thereby finally assembled his personality. So ardent did he become that he found contemptible any past writer of suitable talents who had not urged reform. He despised Shakespeare for having no creed and no programme. Contrariwise Shaw himself never wrote a play which lacked a clear social message and even then felt it necessary to support some of the plays with prefaces. (As a result Shaw is less liable than other authors to be interpreted in any way but his own.)

He would never have written a line purely to amuse people, make money, create a pattern, solve an intellectual problem, achieve fame or 'express himself' – that is, if there had been a non-didactic self to express. He was a moralist before he was a man of letters. Like the art of Bunyan, which he by and large admired, his art was intended to be instructional. More precisely, Bunyan is much more poetical than Shaw, so that bits of his allegory need to be construed, while Shaw is crystal clear. Bunyan 'set pen to paper with delight',[25] greatly enjoyed writing the first part of *The Pilgrim's Progress* and was then ashamed of his frivolity until he remembered that even God's laws were originally propounded 'By types, shadows, and metaphors'.[26] And people have always read Bunyan for pleasure, finding the narrative the main source of interest. Just the same, a number of readers in every generation have fitfully tried to emulate Christian. Similarly, from the beginning people have both enjoyed Shaw's plays and been influenced by them. The first play *Widowers' Houses*, spread abroad the belief that everyone's money is tainted in a free-enterprise society.[27] Shaw helped to create our present climate in which businessmen claim to work for the benefit of others.

The moral passion in Shaw, then, was primary. It was not fundamental in the psycho-analytic sense but so far as we are concerned, working chiefly with the surface material of the writings, it remains the constant governing factor. He wrote to put things right, which he seems to have imagined as a process not of change alone but of metamorphosis. Moralists of the past had tried to make others better, either to please God or as an end in

itself, but they never imagined that the pattern of human life
would be essentially altered if some people, or even a great many
people, mended their ways. The urgings and admonitions of the
Bible are uttered on the assumption that man must always fight
temptation and that, whatever happens, the world will be as God
wills. However, for Shaw, to reform men's ways was to straighten
for ever the entire crooked disposition of humankind as part of
nature. It was to remove man from the natural sphere. In the
distant future people would order their affairs justly, without sin
or sorrow. Alternatively, of course, our race would be swept aside
to make way for a higher species.

Bad behaviour affronted Shaw because he saw it as misguided
and absurd. Wickedness, however cunningly practised, was
stupidity. To him the word 'sin' must have been an archaic term
for a kind of incomprehension, so that virtue could be taught (as
Socrates believed). And wisdom was a human attribute with the
result that man needed first to know sin, then in the course of time
to transcend it. Therefore the Serpent was a necessary figure in
man's moral evolution, since as Shaw's Serpent says in *Back to
Methuselah*, 'I chose wisdom and the knowledge of good and evil;
and now there is no evil, and wisdom and good are one.'[28]

What is at stake here? The vision is not merely couched in
predominantly comic terms but is by its nature non-tragic or
anti-tragic. It is the perfect antithesis of the Aeschylean ethos.
The tragic assumption is that nothing can be radically changed,
while Shaw's comic attitude amounts to saying that everything
must be changed – according to man's wishes. (*Heartbreak House*
and *Saint Joan*, despite their less than optimistic tones, are
qualifications rather than refutations of this usual view.)

But the Shavian doctrine of infinite amelioration could only be
sustained by a use of words to replace rather than reflect daily
experience. Indeed Shaw's object was to force experience into
submission, to be the captain of his soul not by self-acceptance but
by self-transformation. To do this he needed, as we shall see, to
mask and divert a multitude of defiant impulses.

Margery M. Morgan writes of Shaw:

For his temperament matched the mood of nineteenth-century
commercial imperialism at its zenith: vigorous, self-confident,
optimistic, productive.[29]

That is true so far as it goes, but no nineteenth-century commercial imperialist dreamed of extending an empire through infinite time. 'They have accepted the burden of eternal life,' says Lilith of Adam and Eve at the end of *Back to Methuselah*. The fantasy is meant seriously: we shall 'end' by defeating death and living eternally, not in heaven but on earth. So Shaw seems never to have accepted that progressionism means the death of every variety of the supernatural.

He postulated – quite artlessly – a relation between man's conscious will and the circumambient universe. The universe 'intended' the advancement of species from simpler to more complex forms, so that enlightened man with his growing knowledge of evolution must obviously intend the same. Thus Shaw conferred purpose upon the purposeless forces of the universe: the physical earth itself was man-like in working towards objectives. So far as we know, however, purposeful activity in the full sense is attributable to man alone, since even lower animals have nothing more than the most immediate or instinctual objectives.

But Shaw believed that there were universal, non-human aims to which human beings ought paramountly to contribute. In the preface, 'Three Plays by Brieux', he speaks of 'the identification of the artist's purpose with the purpose of the universe, which alone makes an artist great'. This means that our species, which emerged on the planet by haphazard if explicable means, should follow its artist–pioneers in accommodating its wishes to supposed universal wishes. In fact, some people, in modern times notably Shaw himself, have projected their own hopes on to the universe as a whole and then claimed absolute validity for those human hopes. The scarcely conceivable universe-as-a-whole cannot be presumed to have aims, though a myriad miniscule fragments of it blindly undergo mutations. Shaw confused struggle with purpose, perhaps because humankind provides purposes for its own struggles. The truth is that every living thing contends incessantly with its environment as the very condition of life, but there is no reason to suppose that those countless tiny engagements are governed by a grand strategy. Shaw rejected Darwin in favour of a development of Lamarckianism by means of which he forged for himself a set of extra-human possibilities: he imposed his own aims upon the natural sphere, so that anyone with different goals was cosmologically out of order. Is this not a sort of theism?

Along with many of his contemporaries Shaw held that evolution was creative, more or less as people may be creative. In other words evolutionary changes were, so to speak, 'designed'. The artist especially, if not exclusively, had the supreme role of conceiving forms towards which the life-force should obediently proceed. This assumption can be caused to sound modest (since one places oneself at the disposal of the sovereign evolutionary power), but it is overweening. To begin with, scarcely anyone now supposes there to be a 'life-force' in the Vitalist meaning of a principle governing all the energies in creation. And if there were such a principle, why should it take account of artists' trifling images?

The point is that this teleological foundation was candidly meant to serve ethical purposes. Since Shaw saw immorality as blind discord, he wished to foster a society – a world society – which should proceed harmoniously (for all its individual 'melodies') towards his goal of spiritualised, or insubstantial man. Such a creature would lack not only passions in the spectacular sense but almost all of what we know as human nature.

For it was human nature itself, pretty well in its entirety, that Shaw eventually wished to leave behind. The process had its visible beginnings (discounting whatever fertilisation took place in boyhood) in the 'dawning', as he famously called it, of his 'moral passion'. Jack Tanner so describes his development in Act One of *Man and Superman*, but Shaw remarks in the preface to *Immaturity* that Tanner speaks for him. Shaw says that he lost Christian faith at the time when he began to grow moral.

> It is worth adding that this sacrifice of the grace of God, as I had been taught it, to intellectual integrity synchronised with that dawning of moral passion in me which I have described in the first act of Man and Superman.[30]

Tanner's account, incidentally, does not mention synchronisation with the loss of Christianity. In conversation with Ann Whitefield he explains that the moral sense is not a cold dictator controlling passions but itself the strongest of passions, 'that turns a child into man'. (Not, by the way, into a woman, for despite his

feminism, Shaw seemed to see a difference between the sexes
here.)

> All the other passions were in me before; but they were idle
> and aimless – mere childish greedinesses and cruelties,
> curiosities and fancies, habits and superstitions, grotesque and
> ridiculous to the mature intelligence. When they suddenly
> began to shine like newly lit flames it was by no light of their
> own, but by the radiance of the dawning moral passion. That
> passion dignified them, gave them conscience and meaning,
> found them a mob of appetites and turned them into an army of
> purposes and principles. My soul was born of that passion.[31]

Tanner's words are quite well known but it is not immediately
clear what they mean. In some way the mob of appetites turned
into an army of purposes and principles. How can greed, for
instance, be caused to shine by the radiance of moral passion? The
alteration in the youthful Shaw must have amounted to a fresh
gratification of instincts by 'higher' means than those hitherto
employed – the usual process, in other words, though unusually
well executed.

Daniel Dervin, discussing a rather different feature of Shaw's
development, provides a clue when he mentions his 'ability to
transform reality by looking at it in a different way'.[32] Suppose
every passion was stood on its head so that cruelty, a mode of
dominance, ceased to be the hurting of others and became an
attempt to change them, while curiosity changed from schoolboy
inquisitiveness to adult moral scrutiny. As for greed, if Shaw
(through Tanner) meant acquisitiveness, then the plays abound
in Shavian appropriation, as opposed to self-surrender.

Shaw found that he could alter the character of an actual event,
or, I suppose, realised that its character is given by us. Thus,
when he was touring the Western Front in 1917 he saw everything
through a veil of characteristic and to my mind inapt language.
'As they entered the Ypres salient,' writes Stanley Weintraub,
'Shaw observed a headless body lying by the roadside.'[33] Such a
sight was possibly no longer ghastly to the soldiers, but civilian
Shaw expressed no feelings about it either. Perhaps he concluded
that it was just the sort of misshapen thing that men's misshapen
purposes produce in war, to which he had already given the

correct or Shavian solution. In short the Western Front, like all his mature experiences, did not shake the rigid pattern of his personality. That day his ears were partially protected against the shelling by plugs but, as he said, he heard the Germans ' "sending them over" as persistently as the gentleman next door to Mr Nickleby sent cucumbers and marrows over the garden wall'.[34] The words, the absurd simile from Dickens, the entire attitude suggest that Shaw was Shavianising the scene. He transformed the grisly landscape by 'looking at it in a different way'.

Gazing towards Vimy Ridge he 'pitied the boredom of the artillerymen', and later at Arras he thought the cathedral looked better as a ruin than it had done intact.[35] Perhaps the gunners were bored and perhaps the cathedral did look better, but these comments still seem off-key, routinely facetious. For all Shaw's fulminations against the war he seems to have understood it theoretically and in one sense unimaginatively, for he blanketed the sights, sounds and smells by posturing and chatter.

It is barely a digression to ask at this point how far an imaginative writer may be relied upon as a guide to his own original vision. He says he wishes to express himself, but how much does he do so? Naturally his language, coming as a rule from common stock, is to some extent a falsification of his experience. The words themselves function as 'liars', since they cannot match the original experience. Let us say they represent bits of his experience he wishes to emphasise in some oblique fashion; indeed that selection, that emphasis, or if you will, that semi-deliberate falsification, constitutes his personality, so far as we know it. He imposes meanings and values upon situations which would otherwise be conventional or chaotic. To be precise, there is only chaos upon which convention confers fairly meaningless meanings and artists confer their individual meanings – though these quickly enough harden into new conventions, or are forgotten.

I am not concerned with 'universal truth' but with personal truth, and the point is that the author's own awareness is altered by him from its pristine muddle into whatever reaches the manuscript. The raw personal experience is in part preconscious and scarcely knowable – though it may sound a warning bell against falsehood. Now, is it not reasonable to suggest that the more a writer retains a sense of that preconscious hinterland the more trustworthy he is?

Retaining a sense of those shadows and half-lights does not necessarily mean mentioning them or even hinting at their existence in one's writing. Among prose writers consider Bunyan and Samuel Johnson. The first, one of Shaw's paragons, does suggest that his words are mere inadequate signs, not the truth itself, and anyway rise from his total mind like peaks above uncharted territory. Yet even when we are reading Johnson, so different from Bunyan, so magisterial and seemingly comprehensive, we still know that the words are of the surface and black chasms yawn beneath them.

Shaw on the contrary implies that there is nothing of consequence left to say: he has plumbed his topic. The truth is verbal or at least may be tamed by someone of sufficient verbal skill. It is likely that he externalised not only his aggression but his mental life generally and viewed his preconscious as either simply functional or, in large part, a rubbish bin of contingent and disposable observations. I think he thought in words not images and wrote almost as rapidly as he thought.

Allied to this is the fact that Shaw barely allowed himself to contemplate stark physical matters. The last thing he wanted to do was subject his mind to concrete detail, or his spirit to the material world. If an author proposes to describe a battle, a murder, a rape, he may use words to give the happenings a certain character, but if he is willing to separate mental attitudes from physical events he makes himself humble. His skill then goes into mimesis and he copes with the violence by acknowledging it. Conversely, when he describes an invisible mental process there is little or no check on his accuracy and with very little ingenuity he may be able to pass off preposterous psychology as realistic.

Shaw's psychological accuracy was high indeed, but instead of building a world upon that solid foundation he refused to accept as final the brutish facts revealed by his own observations. Nor did he fancy that a better ordered society must reduce the so called defects in human make-up. On the contrary he realised (and made plain in 'The Revolutionist's Handbook' and first chapter of *Everybody's Political What's What*) that unevolved man will spoil any moves towards a model society. His answer therefore was that we can evolve only by first knowing the facts of our present and historical condition. But what is questionable is the sort of creature Shaw wished man to become. Why is the creature admirable? Is it desirable or necessary that our race should grow less physical as we become an even cleverer breed of animal?

For it is clear that Shaw regarded physical matters as beneath him and beneath any civilised modern person. The physical was the inferior which must be outgrown. He was himself distinctly 'non-physical', an erratic bike-rider, a sparing vegetarian, a husband who abstained from sex, a cerebral rather than a sensuous artist.

He also managed to suggest that internal conflict is old-fashioned, misguided or purposely self-generated. It is egotistical drama to lighten dull hours or impose on other people. Daniel Dervin has pointed out that the mature Shaw seems not to have been aggressive towards himself: the enemy was without and he was inwardly at peace.[36] Nor would he have hurt a fly since his pugnacity flowed upwards into words and ideas. To see this clearly compare anything in Shaw with the events in Ibsen's plays: beside the latter's mishaps, murders and suicides there is, as a forceful episode, only the burning of Joan of Arc, softened by Joan's apparition in the Epilogue.

The kind of criticism I have been conducting might be thought irrelevant and unfair on the grounds that Shaw, after all, wrote comedies. Just the same, even Shaw's feeblest plays (those of the thirties, in the main) are comedies with a social purpose. Such a purpose was his *raison d'être* and possibly, in view of his loveless childhood, helped to hold desperation at bay. Shaw's stance, however, implies the view, which is never quite expounded (though he comes near to expounding it in *Back to Methuselah*), that human life as a whole might be transformed into joyous, energetic play. We should aim to abolish pain and thereafter frolic as if in the Elysian Fields. Meanwhile we can at least think in a sprightly fashion, anticipating our proper destiny. An interesting illustration of the influence of such an attitude upon critics is provided by Margery M. Morgan in her *The Shavian Playground*: she concludes by stating, correctly and approvingly, that to Shaw 'thinking itself is creative play at the service of life'.[37]

Shaw believed what Margery M. Morgan says he believed and she is right to stress the credo. It is or comes near to being, his 'quintessence', as a writer. It is also a modern attitude to be distinguished sharply from the Dionysian sort of licence, or play, which according to Nietzsche gave birth to tragedy itself among the Greeks. The ancient revelry occurred in the teeth of suffering while Shaw's hopes can only be realised as suffering declines, or paradise is regained.

For thinking to be pure play it must either be of no account, as in a rule-bound game, or Shavianly omnipotent. If it might ever be the former, wouldn't our lives – and not *our* lives alone – then be insignificant? Perhaps they are insignificant, but can we live without the notion of significance? Heaven itself was never a sphere where anything mattered in human terms, for it was purely goal and apotheosis. As for omnipotence, a dream which is never quite discarded, that can be imagined, in so far as it is imaginable, only as boredom and futility.

But is there a third possibility, a 'way' in the philosophic sense, which Shaw should have confined himself to demonstrating without the supernatural pretensions? This way is already present in his writings and contributes to their charm, though it is of a surprisingly cavalier sort for a man often thought to be a puritan. It consists of exerting one's mind to the utmost, yet lightly, without solemnity, under all conditions short of physical hardship. The manner is witty but not facetious, and imperturbable so far as humanly possible. All strong emotion is seen as a snare and basically a pose; anguish is treated as a mode of self-dramatisation. One is energetically relaxed, courteously clever, honourable without priggishness, at ease with many sorts of man, hating none. The aim is to surpass tragedy rather than deny it. Indeed, Shaw's plays, to which we now turn our attention, should be judged according to how successfully they overcome the primitive and always rather magical spirit of seriousness, thus helping to substitute a fitting human standard for Procrustean ideals. Even so, Shaw would never concede that his yearning for change amounted to a faith and that it is not ideals alone that restrict us but the natural sphere itself, within which we ingenious beings may fight or romp or repine, but to no purpose which surpasses our necessarily *hostile* conditions of life.

7 Shaw's Plays of the Nineties

Few writers of Shaw's stature can ever have found their exact medium so randomly and with so little enthusiasm as he. His entry into the theatre (at thirty-six) was neither the start of a long embittering struggle, as had been Ibsen's fate, nor, for that matter, a triumphant Marlovian eruption. Instead events and aptitudes collided in a haphazard and mildly promising manner.

In 1884 William Archer met Shaw for the first time in the Reading Room of the British Museum where Shaw was alternately studying *Das Kapital* and the score of *Tristan and Isolde* Shortly afterwards Archer suggested that the pair of them collaborate in writing a play, he to provide the scenario and Shaw the dialogue. Accordingly Archer devised the play of a work to be called 'Rheingold', whereupon Shaw composed two acts using up the whole of Archer's plot. Archer did not like Shaw's material and the project was shelved.

The second phase took place in 1892 when J. T. Grein, the Dutchman who had staged *Ghosts* at the Independent Theatre started looking for a new piece in English. Shaw suggested that Grein herald a new play by G. B. Shaw, then rapidly added a third act to the dust-gathering Rheingold script and, with reference to the biblical phrase, 'widows' houses', called the result *Widowers Houses*. The play was first produced at the Independent Theatre on 9 December 1892. Half the audience cheered, the other half booed and Shaw rounded off the evening with a speech which one critic found more remarkable than the play.

Even as late as the nineties Shaw was only toying with the notion of writing for the theatre, because, according to his account in the Preface to *Plays Unpleasant*, he was running out of steam as a journalist. He did not plan to become a dramatist, nor can we say that he put pen to paper because he had found a creed. Despite the example of Ibsen, he thought poorly of the profession of playwright. He wrote *Widowers' Houses* for something to do and in the hope of making a little necessary money. To begin with, his art was primarily for his own sake and in a secondary way to show up social shortcomings.

We can readily trace some of the main influences upon *Widowers' Houses*. First, it was calculated to be an 'Ibsenist' play, since so-called Ibsenism was in vogue, because Shaw himself had contributed to that vogue, as that was the sort of thing Grein wanted for his theatre and since Shaw's mind was by now naturally moving along what he regarded as Ibsenist channels. In other words the work was designed to anatomise society and to be anti-idealist in *The Quintessence of Ibsenism* sense. Above all, it had to stand conspicuously apart from the 'Parisian' kind of divertissement then monopolising the London theatre (for in 1892 Pinero had got no further than his early farces and Wilde had only just written *Lady Windermere's Fan*).

In terms of its principal idea *Widowers' houses* is Marxian, Henry Georgian and in particular Dickensian. The argument is reminiscent of Dickens's novels after 1860, especially *Bleak House*, *Great Expectations* and *Our Mutual Friend*. If we compare those novels with the work of any earlier English author, however moralistic, it is plain that Dickens – and perhaps he alone – spread abroad the notion of society as an organism whose degeneracy in any of its parts even its best protected members cannot withstand. This view had become Shaw's and *Widowers' Houses* illustrates it by means of slum landlordism. A proper focus on the play shows that it is not precisely about Sartorius's ownership of slum property but about common guilt. It was cheerfully intended to be offensive to share-owning middle-class audiences and at least seductive to any who might be taken by the doctrine of interlocking social obligations. (How different, by the way, from Shaw's admired Bunyan, whose hero, in the manner of seventeenth-century puritanism, removes himself from the City of Destruction.)

Shaw's knowledge of housing matters was accurate enough, since it had been gathered not just from socialist books and pamphlets but also from a degree of personal and practical interest that led to his becoming, in 1897, a vestryman for the borough of St Pancras. And he was far more concerned than Ibsen had ever been to present the relevant unaesthetic facts to his audiences. After reading the play, Oscar Wilde wrote to him, 'I like your superb confidence in the dramatic value of the mere facts

of life.'[1] Such documentary evidence interested Shaw quite a
much as the psychology of his characters and more than the
quality of his prose, which he justifiably took for granted.

For he wished to disclose how rented housing was managed in
London and other cities: such bluebook sort of information was
intended to be the core of the play around which the characters
the settings and the petty romance of Blanche Sartorius and
Harry Trench should grow. I am not indicating the relative merit
of these elements, since the character of Blanche is the best thing
in the play, but their original order of importance in Shaw's eyes
His starting point, fruitfully qualified even in this play but never
afterwards quite abandoned, was the view that much of our
behaviour and all our culture depend upon economic circum
stances. He wanted to explain some of these circumstances to
West End audiences, not vaguely in the usual dramatic fashion
but in concrete terms.

In at least one respect Sartorius is a typical landlord, for he is a
fairly scrupulous man rather than the gloating villain of melo
drama. Nevertheless, he is a credible wrongdoer, for he grasps the
facts of his occupation while refusing to see them in a moral or
imaginative light. Sartorius is not even callous but fails to exercise
his imagination, presumably sensing that his entire social being
would crumble as soon as he did so. It is the preference for social
sentiment over accurate observation that Shaw is fundamentally
attacking, though he would never draw Ibsen's conclusion that
society tends to distort individuals' perceptions, which alone have
some chance of accuracy.

Sartorius is meant to be correct in his view that the people
renting his St Giles's, Marylebone and Bethnal Green houses
would wreck any decent place they occupied within a week. At
present they use banisters for firewood. 'When people are very
poor, you cannot help them', says Sartorius in Act II, and Shaw
would have agreed, with the rider that poverty must therefore be
eliminated. Sartorius is also right to demonstrate a chain of
responsibility: first the slum-dwellers themselves, next the own
ers' henchmen, then owners in the class either of Sartorius or of
Lady Roxdale, the ground landlord, and finally people like Harry
Trench, the mediocre young lover in this play (a virtual parody of
a romantic lead), whose income is derived from a mortgage on
Sartorius's property. This pervasiveness of corruption and
accountability is a subdued, prosaic version of the condition

Dickens presents in *Bleak House*, in which novel disease and depravity reach out into the land from the germ-laden London alley, Tom-all-Alone's.

That in daily life a landlord would have Sartorius's clear grasp of his place in the economic chain is perhaps unlikely, as is Sartorius's one flash of nevertheless involuntary wit: 'I am an Englishman; and I will suffer no priest to interfere in my business' (Act II). Shaw was not meticulous whenever he saw a good or goodish joke looming up. For example, Lickcheese, Sartorius's whining rent-collector who turns cocky capitalist by Act III (and is thus the forerunner of Doolittle), is proud of his contemptible skills. 'Look at that bag of money on the table,' he boasts to Trench and Cokane in the second act. 'Hardly a penny of that but there was a hungry child crying for the bread it could have bought.' And here we see the beginnings of one strand of Shaw's originality: no one else has caused villains (and dolts as well) to define their own qualities so clearly, yet brag of them so as to draw audiences to the opposite conclusions. It is Lickcheese too who first realises the opportunities for profit presented by a Royal Commission on housing and as usual he expects praise for his shrewdness. He fails to appreciate that gentlemen camouflage such 'common sense' even from themselves.

But despite the moderately effective social satire, what now brings the play alive, ninety years on, is the psychological satire (neither funny nor remotely exaggerated) in the portrait of Blanche Sartorius, She who, it seems likely was drawn not from Florence Farr, the actress who first played her, but from Jenny Patterson, the widow by whom Shaw was first seduced, constitutes the realistic element in Shaw's originality.[2] For here he imitates life with a capacity approaching Ibsen's own. Throughout his career he brought off similar feats from time to time, but he never seriously cultivated his mimetic gifts because he was too intent on stressing either the comic or the moral principle of each important character.

'Blanche is pure Shaw,' writes one critic, meaning that her counterpart cannot be found in other dramatists.[3] But her literary uniqueness suggests that Shaw observed her, not that he invented her. Anyhow she is less pure Shaw than, say, Ann Whitefield, because at this stage he had not quite yielded to his zest for explanation. Blanche is not to be explained and indeed her quality lies in her evasion of a reformist playwright's categories. Shaw had noticed what people were generally blind to, that such a woman – a dissimulating husband-hunter, non-moral, squeamish over plebeian dirt, intelligent chiefly in the realm of practical behaviour, occasionally vicious and prepared to be physically savage as well as physically enticing, moreover to be savage as a means of enticement, in short a healthy, unscrupulous brute – abounds in society. Blanche's memorable scenes (in Act II when she half throttles the maid and at the close of Act III when her ferocity with Trench is, as Shaw says, 'erotic') are the memorable scenes of the play.[4] When a trait of Blanche, the squeamishness, can fairly be attributed to her Surbiton upbringing, Shaw emphasises the fact, but in general her traits are not obviously *caused* by anything, let alone by anything so comparatively superficial as her social position. To a degree she is culturally unassimilated, a specimen of the beings Shaw already knew he must reckon with in order to push mankind up the evolutionary slope.

In addition, a trait of Blanche Sartorius is scarcely developed in comparison with the treatment a similar characteristic receives in Shaw's second play, *The Philanderer* (1893). No one doubts that two distinct characters, Blanche herself and Julia Craven of *The Philanderer* were both derived from Mrs Jane (Jenny) Patterson, with whom Shaw's relations had continued since 1885. The characteristic Shaw copied from this lady was self-dramatisation: indeed Julia Craven is through and through a performer, and consequently a creator, of her passions. She has behaved passionately all her life and her physical features express her deliberately turbulent soul.[5] For Shaw is contradicting the common notion that one's emotions take one over; he is saying through Julia that emotions are self-assertive devices.

Once again a Shaw play is all but stolen by a woman, though it is called *The Philanderer*. The title means that it is about Shaw himself, in the person of the hero Leonard Charteris, but it is Charteris's antithesis, Julia, who shines brightest of all and does so by escaping the categories of comic art.

At first Shaw seems to have had no particular intention of following up the modest success of *Widowers' Houses*. In this brief dormant period he endured an actual scene rather like the scene around which he later built the first act of *The Philanderer*. On the evening of 4 February 1893 he was dallying with Florence Farr, presumably at her house in Ravenscourt Park, when Jenny Patterson gained admittance and lengthily harangued the pair of them. Far from acting the imperturbable philosopher, Shaw was openly distressed by this (and finally got Jenny back to her own house at four in the morning), but a short time afterwards he fashioned the episode into the basis of another so-called 'Ibsenist' play.

This time the work is avowedly if impishly 'Ibsenist' in the sense that the breed of new woman (which as a breed Ibsen had never remotely advocated) is important to the plot. Charteris, having wearied of Julia's importunity, has taken up with Grace Tranfield, a genuine new woman, so to speak, being sensible, resolute and independent minded. Julia's arrival at the Tranfield flat puts an end to the love-making of Grace and Charteris; Grace retires to her room and the other two are left to argue about their blighted friendship. The quarrel is ended when the fathers of the two women arrive, so that the rest of the first act it taken up with more explanation and further exhibition of Charteris's faithless nature – which the audience is expected to find engaging.

The following day at the Ibsen Club, of which improbable institution most of the cast are members, a certain Dr Paramore learns that a disease he has won prestige for identifying, 'Paramore's Disease', does not exist. At first he is inconsolable, but when he returns to his Savile Row rooms he is visited by Julia and soon finds himself proposing to her on the grounds that she is as sincere as she is beautiful. Despairingly Julia agrees to be his wife. Later in Act III Charteris, now happily bereft of Julia, learns that Grace Tranfield will not have him. The last lines of the play are interesting: Julia declared herself to be 'worthless', because she hasn't the courage to kill Charteris; Grace says 'Never make a hero of a philanderer', and the rest of the cast now gathered at Paramore's, look at Julia and feel themselves to be 'for the first time in the presence of a keen sorrow'.

The play has been, or has seemed to be, about artifice of one sort or another: Julia's cultivation of her chagrin, Paramore's wretchedness when deprived of his disease, even perhaps Charteris's self-conceit as a philanderer. Finally everyone becomes aware, for the very first time of a 'keen sorrow', and this befalling a woman who has appeared to be the complete poseuse. Likewise, the hero's sub-Wildean conversation and the mere inclusion of the unlikely Ibsen Club have made the play seem a thorough comedy of manners. Yet the conclusion emphasises sorrow and this is evidently a deliberate or semi-deliberate volte-face.

What is Shaw's verdict on Charteris's, which is to say his own, philandering? It has served to fend off obligations, restrictions, exasperations, boredom, and it is to the point that Charteris excels at seeing through social stratagems. What he cannot see, and what Shaw himself therefore could not see, is that such stratagems are not necessarily restraints on vigour but may be parts of vigour. He still suffered from the belief that we shall all grow livelier when we stop posing, or to be precise when there is no need of posing. And the paradox remains: the liveliest person in the play is a play-actress entirely. Julia finally becomes the tragic figure she has long impersonated. Even so, the Julia-character, who will accompany Shaw for much of his career, is already in the process of being turned by him into a concept. At present she still bids fair to burst from her comic frame and her creator wishes to enclose her more securely. He cannot contain Julia in his moral categories and this failure whispers to him that the categories might be vulnerable. He must find a way of linking the ethical with the natural – of which, for all her 'unnatural' histrionics, her affectations, Julia is an insistent reminder. It is this quest that puts him on the long road to Lilith and the absorption of matter into spirit.

Real drama, says Shaw in the Preface to *Mrs Warren's Profession*, is the 'presentation in parable of the conflict between man's will and his environment'. By real he does not mean realistic but undistorted and by environment he means natural as well as social circumstances. But all drama, even the paltriest, reflects that conflict in some fashion and what matters is the vitality in a play. The 'unreal' in relation to drama is merely the devitalised.

A little later in the same preface Shaw remarks that there is a tendency for us to blame 'human nature' (his inverted commas) for the evils we suffer. Accordingly he suggests that we had better change our nature. This means, for example, that a woman of roughly the Julia Craven variety should be brought to wish herself a woman of the Grace Tranfield variety, especially since the latter seems to have a greater chance of happiness. Indeed Grace is the model he now pursues as part of his aim to show audiences, and to show himself for that matter, the alternative – and therefore, who knows, the solution? – to the problem of Julia. The result is Vivie Warren of *Mrs Warren's Profession* (1894).

Vivie is not quite a paragon, for in the argument with her mother in Act III (the doctrinal kernel of the play), she insists that 'Everybody has some choice' and that there are no unavoidable, determining circumstances. She is then chastened by Mrs Warren's account of her hard and solid youth in the 1860s and 70s. Curiously Shaw fails to point out that the mother is perfect proof of what the daughter is maintaining, since Mrs (Kitty) Warren and her sister Liz, both made their way against all manner of obstacles, by means of white slavery. While their two half-sisters wore themselves out by the regular East End processes of overwork and self-neglect, these two adventurous girls took to brothel-keeping and made money hand over fist. It seems, then, that Vivie's confident outlook is an underestimate of life's problems not a downright error. She is right to scoff at social determinism and remains, in Shaw's eyes, no more than marginally flawed.

Shaw went out of his way to contrast what he regarded as the seamiest sort of career with what he saw as exemplary female aspirations. On the one hand is Mrs Warren, part-owner of whorehouses in Brussels, Ostend, Vienna and Budapest, an accommodating survivor who must normally consort with such an insensate blackguard as Sir George Crofts; and on the other hand is Vivie, clever mathematician, ambitious businesswoman and, as she turns out, creature of serene conscience. In the past the clear reverse of a Mrs Warren would have been some model of spiritual endeavour; for Shaw the right balance is struck by a professional woman who prefers work to romance and idleness. Vivie welcomes legal problems, drinks whisky, reads detective novels for pleasure and hates holidays. She is, of course, attractive as well as being 'prompt, strong, confident, self-possessed' (Act I), yet she states in the fourth act (and the judgement is not finally modified by doubt or irony) that 'there is no beauty and no romance in life for me'. These negations are somehow marks of honour. And, of course, romance and beauty, in the forms of art, music, and the picturesque, have never disturbed or enlightened Mrs Warren either. These seeming opposites, mother and daughter, are temperamentally somewhat akin, for they both wish to manage affairs and live without sentiment. (To be sure,

Mrs Warren affects sentiment as a gambit or a source of pleasure, but she doesn't believe in it.)

There is here, for the first and far from the last time in Shaw, a suspect biological contrariness. I mean that through Vivie he is rejecting not only sentiment but the plain sexuality which sentiment is designed to mask. Vivie Warren is Shaw's early ideal (of which a later and more spectacular version is Joan of Arc) and is so because she is at once nubile and in a manner 'sexless'. She has the capacity to allure men but prefers not to do so. Both are important: the ripeness and the refusal. When Vivie learns in Act III that the charming scapegrace Frank Gardner, is her half-brother, not merely courtship and flirtation fall away but mating and reproduction themselves. She abjures these primary activities, for ever it seems, without the smallest regret. Shaw's argument (and in Shaw such dramatic unfoldings always amount to arguments) has an air of common sense but it is dubious. Vivie's may be a reasonable decision, but neither she nor her author seems fully to realise that it must also be either a personal sacrifice or the way of a specialised individual. In other words, Vivie's virtue, or cheerful indifference, is no more a general answer to what Shaw sees as the burden of sexuality than it is to the world of Mrs Warren.

It is true that none of the men in the play is up to Vivie's standards. Praed is safely unconventional, theoretically anarchistic, soft and easily shocked. Vivie has her romance with Frank Gardner and the pair of them seem to be baby-talking their way to a union until it emerges that both are offspring of the Reverend Samuel Gardner. Crofts, who makes a crass bid for Vivie, is beyond the pale. She comes to feel that nothing is left for her except work, on the grounds (though these are not admitted) that everything else is tainted, unmanageable, irreducible to sense. In the closing scene Mrs Warren ('a conventional woman at heart') stresses the worldly argument: society is a network of corruptions to which one must submit as the alternative to self-immolation. Despite some similarity there is this important difference between Mrs Warren and Vivie: the brothel-keeping mother is an orthodox social creature, while the daughter defines herself by her distaste for the confusion and deceit of ordinary social life. Though Vivie's character and situation are quite different from those of anyone in Ibsen, she is distantly derived from Nora Helmer. She is Shaw's characteristic explanation of why a personable young woman would wish to forsake the normal woman's destiny.

Vivie's rejection of the marriage market is also connected with her resistance to what Shaw regarded as the delusive sphere of beauty, illustrated in the play by poetry, Wagner, Venice and Verona. Beauty and romance are snares; the real is the prosaic; value lies in preference for the real. That beauty is a perspective of the real and romance need not be confined to fantasy never crosses anyone's mind, for this is, more than the later works so named, a play for puritans.

Since *The Quintessence of Ibsenism* Shaw has been pursuing the one theme of the folly and wickedness of ideals. An ideal may be anything from an agreeable picture of society which camouflages the management of the slums to exclusive romantic love; from veneration of a painted medieval city such as Verona to the fancy that pretty, decorative brothels subsist without crude commercial foundations. There is an ideal woman composed of bogus female psychology and likewise the ideal man, a dashing soldier perhaps. There is an ideal of warfare, reinforced for example by Tennyson for whom a sparse Crimean valley is a place of deathly beauty. Contrariwise, according to Shaw, the reality of war is as fatiguing and farcical as it is hideous.

What he could not properly contemplate was the truly mixed nature of things, for he was a perfect dualist. Eventually, by the stage of *Back to Methusaleh*, he would absorb matter into spirit, but there is no need for such a desperate remedy unless you discern two contrasting principles at the outset. If spirit is understood to be a sublimation of matter the problem vanishes. That Shaw could not think in such terms seems to establish that he remained a sort of Platonist or Gnostic.

For that very reason he excelled at giving the devil his due, while dismissing the world and the flesh. Worldliness, or despiritualised social activity, did not interest him in the least, and he found the flesh actually boring as well as contemptible. But in man's spirit the bad angel lurks sullen or sprightly alongside the good. Shaw respected attitudes contrary to his own when they transcended self-interest, and the expounder or personification of such an attitude is Shaw's bad angel. He is not malign but merely says what Shaw would say if he were speaking for the opposition. Just the same, the devil is 'wrong', for the play has been written largely to refute him. Thus he takes the form of the Inquisitor in

Saint Joan, whose reasoning is more skilful than Joan's. Indeed the devil may be a worthy fellow, as he is in *Arms and the Man* (1894).

The straightforward response to this play is to take it as a denunciation of war as romantic heroism. The sophisticated response is to note the balanced arguments and neat Scribean construction. The truth is that Shaw does cast doubt on military glory, but builds qualifications upon that elementary position so as to seem more accommodating than he really is. The debate is zestful but the thrust of the play remains what the simple observer has always assumed it to be.

Nevertheless, *Arms and the Man* is the nearest thing to a flawless play. It is without a moment of boredom and not a phrase seems redundant. Each remark either makes or develops a point, yet there is no stagey pithiness and, as a matter of fact, no Shavian swaggering. 'Technically,' Maurice Valency says, '*Arms and the Man* is a textbook example of the well-made play.'

> The exposition is at the same time thrilling and informative . . . [It follows] the best Scribean practice, through the convergence of the main plot and the sub-plot, the superposition of the Bluntschli–Raina–Sergius triangle – the triangle of the principals – upon the triangle involving Sergius, Louka and Nicola, the triangle of the servants . . . Nothing neater – or more artificial – can be imagined.[6]

Valency's full account of Shaw's new dramaturgic skill is complete and unexaggerated. As an artefact *Arms and the Man* is a great advance on its predecessors: *Mrs Warren's Profession*, for instance, takes four acts to say, if anything, less. What should be added is that in this play Shaw freed himself from the realistic, or Ibsenist, conversation he had hitherto attempted. Now there is fully fledged Shavian dialogue, too pointed for realism though scarcely epigrammatic. For that reason alone, I think it true to say, we take the characters more seriously than we take most of Oscar Wilde's. Here at least Shaw's people speak well and do so unostentatiously. He has found the right verbal level for one whose fervent teachings will always be couched in comic terms. Although nearly every remark in *Arms and the Man* is a progress of some sort, never does a character seem to be legislating unequivocally on behalf of the author. To the extent that Bluntchli is such a mouthpiece, the opposing (or 'devilish') view of Sergius is fairly presented. It is at worst an exaggeration to think of the play as an elaborate Socratic dialogue in which Socrates himself is a little absurd.

In the first act, however, there is no effective counter to Bluntschli's politic view of war, since Raina, whose bedroom he has entered to dodge the bullets of Bulgarian soldiers is so youthfully and (charmingly) silly. 'Some soldiers, I know,' she contemptuously says to him, 'are afraid of death.' 'All of them, dear lady, all of them, believe me,' replies Bluntschli. Yet it soon emerges that in the recent Bulgarian cavalry charge the leading horseman, instead of pulling on the reins in what Bluntschli maintains is the usual horrified manner, hurtled onwards towards the guns, an operatic hussar in a real battle. Naturally this madman turns out to be Raina's fiancé Sergius. In other words, Raina's hero-worship is so far justified, despite her naïveté and Bluntschli's sensible observations.

Sergius in fact is an interesting, even admirable fellow, or at any rate he is no less admirable for being a picture-book soldier. Not only is he no coward but he is no fool either. Apart from anything else, his valour in war doesn't prevent him from declaring war to be 'A fraud . . . a hollow sham like love' (Act Three). In the second act he says he finds the 'higher love', meaning Raina's, 'very fatiguing' and he begins to prefer the beautiful servant Louka. Coincidentally Raina starts to tire of her own ecstasies.

What exactly is at issue here? It is not simply the romantic versus the practical attitude, and to the extent that it is a variant of the usual quarrel between 'idealism' and 'realism', then at least the ideals (of Sergius) are scarcely censured. To begin with, Bluntschli regards himself as a professional soldier: in Act I he declares that his is the 'professional point of view'. Professionalism as against amateurism is certainly a small part of the question Shaw is dealing with. Bluntschli is concerned to survive, preferably to win, but his defining quality is his rejection of heroics and glamour, except when these might be useful. War is the human activity in which he has become professionally involved and which, through sheer practical intelligence, he manages tolerably well. But if war is not an evil to him it has no merit either. Now Raina comes to accept this expedient attitude to life and the couple will no doubt make a good match, intent on running their own lives in a businesslike manner. They will cultivate their garden.

What the bourgeois Bluntschli (son of a Swiss hotel owner) is up against is the aristocratic ethos, which bedazzles the Petkoff women. Raina is the daughter of an aspiring bourgeois mother, Catherine Petkoff, who, according to Shaw's stage directions (in Act I) 'is determined to be a Viennese lady', and Major Petkoff, who is 'naturally unambitious except as to his income and his importance in local society' (Act Two). Raina has artlessly venerated what she believed to be noble ways and finally she comes home to herself as the future wife of a Swiss capitalist.

As for the servants Louka and Nicola, they are both plebeian of course, but only Nicola has the plebeian virtues. He will manage one of Bluntschli's hotels efficiently and profitably, since his sole concern is money, or work purely for the sake of money. He is useful, philistine, efficient, happily materialistic. Neither bourgeois aspiration nor aristocratic honour has ever entered his head except as qualities to be despised, so that even 'getting on in the world' will simply be a by-product of his industry. Louka, on the other hand, is a healthy, libidinous creature who opposes her courage to Nicola's 'cold-blooded wisdom' (Act III) and needs only the scent of economic freedom before she embraces Sergius's creed of preferring her 'own will and conscience' (Act III) to everything else in the world. In other words she is a natural aristocrat who respects nothing so much as her own soul.

The Byronic Sergius himself differs most markedly from Bluntschli in this: while the latter believes that virtue must by definition benefit others, the former assumes it to be the same as one's personal sense of honour. To Sergius a virtuous act on someone else's behalf may be a good thing, but it is no great thing, nothing to be proud of, for it then has an 'ulterior motive'.

In the portrait of Sergius, indeed in the play as a whole, Shaw was not inventing paradoxes so much as bringing out the paradoxical nature of social reality. In war there are the Bluntschli and Sergius attitudes (among others), as in the sphere of courtship one woman might be something of a Louka, another of a Raina. Shaw himself fairly plainly preferred the combination of Bluntschli and Raina but he was not dismissive about Sergius and Louka. The attitude of the second couple when reduced to theory is not readily defensible – though of course one might say, so much the worse for theory. Further the second couple are less likely than their opposites to lessen, or frankly even to notice human suffering. Bluntschli is more morally aware than Sergius, not so liable to produce suffering and possibly more respectful of the individuality of others. That Bluntschli is also less honourable in the classical sense is no doubt part and parcel of his extra moral awareness. And if there is a single strand running through all Shaw's writings, it is this very championship of the 'moral', meaning his belief that individual merit and universal freedom are bound together. He assumed that to suppress the individuality of another is to suppress one's own. If some are unfree all are unfree.

What Shaw consistently yearned for was a kind of personal liberty which never impinges on the liberty of others. When 'man's God is his own humanity . . . he, self-satisfied at last, ceases to be selfish'.[7] By 'humanity' he meant not the generalised quality of humanness but one's own impulses, preferences, observations, feelings; in short, one's individuality or specificity. This presumably unique bundle of traits he saw as pent up not by other individuals but by social codes. Such codes usually crystallised into ideals and at the heart of each ideal was a plain untruth.

For example, one such untruth still persisting well after the end of the nineteenth century was that a 'proper' or unperverted woman was more tender-hearted and illogical than a proper man. Another contemporary untruth concerned the superiority of the man of action over the dreamer, who might be a scholar, a poet, an artist, a philosopher, or just a wool-gatherer. This superiority was regarded as a fact, not a fashionable estimate. Part of Shaw's purpose in writing *Candida* (1895) was to qualify that judgement, but he would not have sought to do so if he himself had not been a dreamer who required his dreams to come true, or in other words to be realised by men of action. Mere artists were scarcely admirable and he was not of their number. Thus part of Shaw respected the Reverend James Mavor Morell while another, more fundamental part was a finely strung Marchbanks.

It is often assumed that Morell was based on Stewart Headlam, the Christian Socialist vicar, though Shaw apparently said in a letter to the 'Evening Standard' of 30 November 1944 that, as Margery M. Morgan puts it, 'the nearest model to Morell was Stopford Brooke, with touches of Canon Shuttleworth and Fleming Williams'.[8] All that matters is that each of these men contributed to Shaw's essential portrait, which is of a competent, decent, manly man who links Christianity with socialism.

Morell's bookshelves include 'literary landmarks in socialism' such as *Das Kapital*, *Progress and Poverty* and *Fabian Essays*. Morell is vigorous, efficient and politically 'enlightened', a leader and a crusader. Moreover, the fact that he is energetically good, distinguished as much from dully respectable people as from scoundrels, means that he is the perfect foil for Eugene Marchbanks who is to orthodox eyes nothing more than a selfish, effeminate parasite.

Morell and Marchbanks are plainly antithetical from one point of view, but from another they are different degrees or types of goodness: limited unimaginative good as against creative anarchical better. Morell knows for certain what is good and scrupulously does it, while Marchbanks finally goes out to make an unknown new world. An aspect of Shaw himself is in Morell, whose speaking engagements and other forms of responsible citizenship reflect the author's own life. Morell is the Shaw who attended so many Fabian meetings, became a vestryman for St Pancras, concerned himself with the dry-as-dust machinery of public causes. To make Morell, Shaw, apart from observing Steward Headlam and the rest, subtracted his own Marchbanks propensities. Thus Morell is a pedestrian version of the pontificating Shaw whose morality is settled and elementary. Morell declares La Rochefoucauld a 'rotten cynic' for saying there are convenient marriages but no delightful ones (Act One). We rather look down on this parson for being so simple minded, and he has indeed the simplicity of less than half a complete human being. Morell believes that 'God has given us a world that nothing but our own folly keeps from being a paradise' (Act II). That is a piece of self-caricature by Shaw, not in the sense that he personally would have been no more than tempted to such an utterance but because the words convey only the ground brass of his belief. All the Shavian melodies and variations are missing. When Morell declares that 'Wicked people means people who have no love' (Act III) he is thinking of *agape* rather than *eros* and offering a perfect Shavian sentiment.

According to Maurice Valency the action of *Candida* might express Shaw's regret 'in having lost the poet in choosing the preacher'.[9] But what if poet and preacher were at one in Shaw, so that the polemical dramas are precisely his form of poetry? It is certain that Shaw attempted to wed morality and anarchism. His preaching is always against authority; doing good consists in upsetting the apple cart for other than selfish motives. When he flirted with the dictators he did so, I fancy, on the foolish assumption that their radicalism would release their people's energies.

Even Morell wishes to upset the apple cart; even he aims to change the social system, for he is a Christian Socialist. The trouble is that he has no idea of the immensity of his task or even of its necessary dreariness. Certainly he does not appreciate that it must entail what he presently sees as wickedness. For he is shielded at every turn by a woman who makes him master in his parsonage, just as his parents and sisters coddled and lauded him in his childhood home. Morell's practical decency is part and parcel of his impracticality. His competence over parish organisation is an actor's competence gained at the expense of the stage-hands. 'Ask the tradesmen', says Candida, 'who want to worry James and spoil his beautiful sermons who is it that puts them off' (Act III).

Candida herself is not complex but simple; she is a simplification of the familiar sort of woman who essentially helps men. It is important to grasp that Candida is of no personal interest whatever – as Marchbanks comes to realise. She is 'interesting' only to the men whose interests she reflects. She has no aspirations of her own, no dreams, and keeps her feet stolidly as well as sensibly on the ground. She sees through ideas because the first thing she asks herself is: What sort of need in the man gave rise to this idea? Ideas are neither true nor false in her view but the necessary codifications of needs. Alternatively they are the outward and visible signs of souls, and it is the inward soul that matters. Marchbanks says in Act III, 'A woman like that has divine insight: she loves our souls, and not our follies and vanities and illusions, or our collars and coats, or any other of the rags and tatters we are rolled up in.' She is, as Shaw not very flatteringly suggested in a letter to schoolboys at Rugby, a 'dear nice woman'.[10]

From a down to earth point of view that is all Candida is. She might additionally be a Shavian version of Ibsen's Svanhild in *Love's Comedy*, who chooses the solid businessman Gulstad, rather than the poet Falk. What should we make of the much-discussed fact that an autotype of Titian's 'Virgin of the Assumption' hangs prominently in the Morell's drawing room? This picture at least suggests that Candida is more than a 'dear nice woman', that she

approaches the sublimation of feminine guardianship expressed
in Titian's Virgin, a pure, bountiful figure of infinite mercy.
Candida is perhaps the mother Shaw never had. He must have
regretted that deprivation, but was he not also pleased about it,
even proud of it? For the missing mother was a source of his talent
as well as his pain. No wonder the attitude to Candida is
ambivalent. Having lacked a loving mother, Shaw at once
venerated such a woman and saw her triviality. He was free like
Marchbanks, but not therefore unqualifiedly joyful.

Candida is a generalised creature to the extent that she
articulates what many actual women only feel. Perhaps any
woman who could divine her own motives so shrewdly and
precisely as she would not be confined to those motives. There are
many men whose wives or mothers have something of the
Candida nature and are therefore outraged at a bald illustration
of it. And there are women who despise Candida because they
themselves have never wished to help a man silently and without
recompense. But Candida herself seems to remain a shining
illustration of a commonplace type. To a man who could never
forget that she does no more than guard his soul she would prove
unendurable.

At the close Marchbanks recognises these implications. Candida would mean the sacrifice of his ambitions and of his very
nature. She could not defend his soul without ruining it, since he is
a real pioneer. She must hold him back, submerge him in her love.
He says he does not want happiness and he does not want love
either. Or rather he wants them as moments and phases in his life,
not as permanent states. How would Candida help him to be
miserable and unloved, which conditions, as a poet, he also needs.
I mean, of course, that he must face life whereas Candida's whole
function is that of shield.

Candida, a 'mystery', was followed in the same year, 1895, by
The Man of Destiny, a 'trifle' or alternatively, as Shaw put it, a
'commercial traveller's sample'. But a proper sample gives the
flavour of the whole and in that sense this one-act play is not a
trifle. Its chief and considerable interest is that it tells us more
about Shaw's self-image. At thirty-nine he cast himself as the
27-year-old Napoleon, just after Lodi, already a general but a fair
way from his future glories. Shaw believed he was a man of destiny
like Napoleon and the play unwittingly tells us why he had that
opinion.

It is clearer in this work than in some other plays of Shaw that he regarded mankind as overwhelmingly competitive, though he saw most people as credulous or silly into the bargain. Napoleon, on the other hand (or Shaw), is 'imaginative without illusions and creative without religion, loyalty, patriotism or any of the common ideals'. He has been poor, has known failure as an author, has suffered humiliation as a time-server, has even pursued his *métier* crassly, and indeed various ordeals 'have ground the conceit out of him'. What this means, though it is uncertain that Shaw appreciated as much, is that he, Napoleon or Shaw, has lost both honour and shame. Everything's a fraud and one must shamelessly live by one's wits.

Napoleon's secret is simply that he thinks and acts in the most expedient way, taking it for granted that the world-pictures accepted by his contemporaries, namely the revolutionary and the reactionary, are mere fables to be used. Shaw himself regarded history as a pattern of errors which he could readily detect. So far at least, he was an adventurer like Napoleon and could respect Napoleon's clear-sightedness. However, it was his self-defining and unNapoleonic task to point out contemporary mistakes and above all to reveal the general character of mistaken beliefs. People err, he thought, because they cannot accept the sheer nothingness of life without evolutionary purposes. In Shaw consciousness of that purpose was only then forming and would crystallise in *Man and Superman*. But for the present his sense of social futility was exuberant rather than depressing, because he believed that some transcendent realisation was at hand. As for Napoleon, he was then more than now commonly thought of as a great man, a being of miraculously superior gifts. Actually the 'greatness', Shaw says in effect, consisted in prodigiously sharp wits and devouring ambition. If the ambition was finally pointless, well then, so is everything else – unless it is included in an evolutionary design.

What we see in *The Man of Destiny* is Napoleon as adventurer contending with two other adventurers, the Lady and the Landlord, and one aristocratic blockhead, the Lieutenant. Giuseppe the Landlord is normally master of those he serves. He thinks that Napoleon, if he becomes emperor, will be 'everybody's servant under cover of being everybody's master'. The Lady who has arrived to lodge at the inn and rapidly finds herself Napoleon's antagonist has earlier, while masquerading as a youth, robbed the blockhead Lieutenant of mail from Paris. Now the Lieutenant supposes the Lady to be the youth in disguise. As Napoleon tries to recover the letters and despatches which he rightly assumes to be hidden in the Lady's bosom, she hints that she wants only one letter, a compromising message of love from a woman to the Director, Barrass. Napoleon gets his all-important despatches and finally he and the Lady, as accomplices, burn the love-letter.

The story is trifling and what matters is Shaw's portrait, amusing yet serious, of a wholly competitive world. Napoleon is busy making himself supreme through his assumption that human values are devices. Fear alone is what makes soldiers fight; 'goodness is want of character'; the English hide their shopkeeper mentality behind a camouflage of principles; the highest and lowest classes in a nation have no scruples while the middle class (of which England is entirely composed) have expertise hindered by scrupulosity. And so on. The play is an occasion for Napoleon to make such pronouncements, for the Lady to prove herself his equal, for the Landlord to display his Bluntschli classlessness and the Lieutenant his Hotspur senselessness. This is the vain world of which Napoleon would be master. He is master of nihilism, yet he is certainly Shaw himself.

Shaw's gusto, then, is for the present a gusto of negation. And his mood is more than playful; it is positively joyful. At this stage of Shaw's career as between a superior character and the rest there is not a difference of high and low, of examplar and benighted others. Thus Shaw insisted that Candida was not very remarkable; no one of quality would try to emulate her, especially as she is merely travelling with Morell as his guardian. Napoleon's direction, on the other hand, is his own, and he is the leader of bemused peoples, but he and they are alike in just moving forward for the sake of it.

Does the same reactive energy lacking positive aims still govern *You Never Can Tell* (1896)? Possibly the skill, zest and variety of this play mean that Shaw has achieved a technical breakthrough, rather than a wider vision. At all events, the vision involves the simulacrum of tragic insight rather than the reality. The exceptionally high spirits (even by Shaw's usual standards); the ending which seems to reconcile ways of life as well as people; the sheer diversity of the characters and the quasi-tragic personalities of Gloria Clandon and Fergus Crampton suggest that Shaw has found a technique to accommodate both his buoyancy and his puritanism. To put the matter another way, he has worked out how to appear to fit passionate reality into a comic and artificial scheme and that is why people speak of the play as a 'tragic-comedy'. But it is really a radiant comedy which includes some appurtenances of tragedy.

Here for once is a play with a faintly Ibsenist pressure of the past upon the present. Mrs Lanfrey Clandon, having separated from her husband Mr Crampton, has made a reputation with a series of best-selling books on twentieth-century life (for example, 'Twentieth Century Parents') and has brought up her three remarkable children in Madeira. Now this family, Mrs Clandon, Gloria the eldest daughter, and the twins Dolly and Philip, have returned to England and are staying at a South Coast hotel. The action combines two principal stories: the reunion of Mr Crampton with his family from whom he has been estranged for eighteen years, and the winning of Gloria Clandon by Mr Valentine, an impecunious dentist. These two serious or semi-serious sequences are woven into a predominantly light-hearted pattern. From another, perhaps better perspective these tales form the main structure around which curlicues and pretty foliage abound.

It seems that Shaw's intent was to accommodate two of his old and solemn, not to say nagging concerns within the Shavian vision – which specifically excluded solemnity. Such concerns pressed to be included in Shaw's cock-a-hoop personality and the *weltanschauung* of the plays. Gloria Clandon declares in Act II of *You Never Can Tell* that 'Everything comes right if we only resolutely think it out.' No doubt the sentiment is Shaw's and he was at this stage thinking out the problem of his father and the equally unShavian but infinitely wider 'problem' of human passion. In a strictly limited sense Mrs Clandon is Mrs Bessie Shaw, Crampton is George Carr Shaw, Valentine is the young, unestablished George Bernard and Gloria is any sterling young woman whose nobility the author hoped to match – not indeed by noble qualities of his own but by his combination of cleverness and ethical assurance. (If there is the slightest hint of a supergo in Shaw it reveals itself here where he needed to prove himself the equal of a passionate woman of integrity.) Of course, these dramatic characters scarcely resemble the originals and all that matters is that the principle of each owes something to a principle discerned by Shaw in an actual individual.

The biographical connections in *You Never Can Tell* are more diverse than I have so far suggested. The teenage Philip, for example, has the forwardness of George Bernard at his age, before the future playwright had learned about the deference expected of youngsters. Both Philip and Dolly are stylised Shaw children, lively, clever, unabashed and with little understanding of the ways of society. They treat their father Mr Crampton, when he arrives at the hotel, gaily and without a trace of concern. All the coldness of the Shaw family is here. But they are also enticing, bouncing dolls or indeed Harlequin and Columbine whose costumes they don at the hotel fancy dress dance, thus turning themselves into an 'exquisite and charming apparition' (Act IV). In other words, these twins are engaging versions of Shaw children, transformed from Dublin hobbledehoys into delicate, amusing creatures from Madeira, but retaining the essential unconventionality.

Crampton, who must by some means be harmonised with these figures of mischief and their clever, fanciful mother, his wife, is a bitter, dull and above all suffering mortal. In fact George Carr Shaw was by all accounts a self-reviling man rather than a cross-grained complainer like Crampton, but the aspect of his father that Shaw is dealing with here is the social inferiority, the tendency to be outclassed by his wife and children. That is Crampton's painful feature and it is notable how expertly Shaw has worked so mortifying a matter into a debonair play. Crampton is neither a figure of fun, which he could so easily have been, nor an object of pity. Yet his humanity makes him the inferior person of the play, if not in a contemptible sense. Shaw saw suffering humanity as the mode of being to be surpassed by his own glittering creations. In this way Shaw's father enters the Shavian sphere and a reconciliation is effected between the clumsiness of a real man and the style of an artificial family. Crampton is mellowed, the burden falls from his shoulders and all become simply friends. Was it an unworthy dream on Shaw's part?

Perhaps not, but it was a piece of wishful thinking, a determination to judge the world from a comic standpoint. Crampton is sympathetic, not a butt, though his claims (George Carr Shaw's claims) are not truly met. It seems that Lanfrey Clandon married Crampton without the least affection for him and that was the hurt from which, after eighteen years of anger, he recovers only in the fourth act of the play. It is suggested that the lovelessness drove him to drink, while Shaw's father, we understand, was already an alcoholic before his marriage. Nevertheless, something of the relations of the Shaw parents is reflected in the play, and Crampton's being drawn back into the Clandon fold, as he is charmed first by Gloria (who realises in Act IV that she is by temperament her father's daughter) then by the twins is at best Shaw's regretful dream, at worst a piece of flippancy.

Gloria Clandon is yet another variant of the woman of feeling, natural antagonist of Shavian man. Her feelings are not appreciably stagey, as are those of Julia Craven in *The Philanderer*, but in her battle of wits with Valentine, the 'duellist of sex', Shaw suggests that Gloria's seriousness, her sense of honour and dignity are of lower value than Valentine's quick intelligence. Her pride, says Valentine in Act III, has been 'nothing but cowardice', and he is not refuted. Her type of heroic gravity can be regarded from a certain point of view as inferior to the 'lightness of heart' which is Valentine's talent. Gloria is teased out of her high-minded attitude, or if you will, is robbed of her nobility. 'I respect nothing that is not noble,' she declares in Act II, yet Valentine's persistence and amiability win her over. Beforehand there was little to suggest that her nobility was an affectation and therefore liable to comic change. In this way, however, Shaw breaks down the spirit of seriousness. He might well have defended such a procedure (though I cannot recall that he ever did) on the grounds that earnest ways belong to man's burdensome and superstitious past.

The union of Valentine and Gloria will serve to illustrate a general point about Shaw's methods of presenting his characters. As a rule he explains and describes them when they make their appearances. They are immediately provided with attitudes and often with motives too. No doubt he retained something of the traditional novelist's technique and was anxious into the bargain that readers, producers and actors should apprehend exactly his creations rather than characters part-invented by themselves. Sometimes, however, the meaning of a play, or at least one of its signal features, consists of a change of nature and a self-discovery. Valentine is an agent of change in Gloria. She is described in Act I as 'all passion'. 'A very dangerous girl, one would say,' Shaw proceeds, 'if the moral passions were not also marked and very nobly marked, in a fine brow.' But when Gloria accepts Valentine at the conclusion of the play her reasons for doing so are obscure. It is an amusing volte-face but it would also be a puzzle, even perhaps a disappointment, if we wished to trouble our heads about it.

Here I suppose Shaw simply contrived a dramatic effect and at the same time sought to establish that he himself could obtain such a first-rate girl if he chose. But generally in Shaw's plays positively good behaviour, on the rare occasions it occurs, is not deemed to require explanation: it is simply admirable. Bad behaviour, on the other hand, is assumed to need at least summary diagnosis. It is as if human psychology were to Shaw specifically the study of bad, or in other words commonplace actions, while deeds of genuine altruism or self-sacrifice are just joyously acceptable. They are not a problem from any point of view.

One of the clearest instances of this feature of Shaw is to be found in *The Devil's Disciple* (1897). The play is melodramatic, predominantly serious and exemplary. Nobody is quite villainous but one man emerges as a true pilgrim. It is something of an adventure story with a Shavian or anticonventinal meaning. We might distinguish Shaw's homiletic intentions from the adventure-story pattern of the work. The outcome, like the outline of the plot as a whole, belongs in part to conventional romance; no one we respect finally suffers, and individuals get their deserts. But Shaw's principal purpose was to recommend self-discovery and pure altruism, which ways lead through vicissitudes to at least temporary triumph.

Each of the three acts of *The Devil's Disciple* is dramatically effective almost in its own right, and the third is the most exhilarating. The first act is striking enough because of the distinctiveness of the characters, the threat of a hanging as the British troops draw nearer and the reading of Timothy Dudgeon's will. Mrs Dudgeon, 'without knowing it, the most licentious woman in the parish'; Christy, her simpleton son; Anthony Anderson, the presbyterian minister too much of a man of action to be a wholehearted parson; Judith Anderson, his pretty, sentimental and youthful wife; little Essie, the bastard teenage daughter of Uncle Peter Dudgeon; Lawyer Hawkins and finally Richard Dudgeon, the rapscallian son: all these individuals, each so clear-cut that merely to put them together would make a 'drama', are gathered in Mrs Dudgeon's house for the reading of her late husband's will, while rumblings of rebellion disturb the New Hampshire countryside. Since nearly everything is bequeathed to Dick Dudgeon instead of the malevolently respectable widow, there is interest enough of a familiar sort, but already the chief sources of fascination are that Judith Anderson seems attracted to Dick Dudgeon, that Dick declares himself a votary of the Devil and that the British intend to hang one prominent citizen of Websterbridge.

For all that, Act II does more than retain the interest of the audience as a result both of Dick Dudgeon's allowing himself to be taken by the British in mistake for Anderson and of Judith's growing love for Dudgeon. The situation is no less in keeping with a standard tale of romance because the two men are equal to the last degree in terms of manliness, courage and personal charm. It is Judith who is a little unsatisfactory, for this is a play more or less 'without a heroine'. Most important is the fact that underlying the conventions of the romantic tale is the challenge not to simple, recognisable tyranny but to the far subtler tyranny of non-creative living. Anderson's rebellion, when all's said and done, is still a rebellion of one set of orthodox values against another. But Dudgeon is satanically in revolt against 'goodness' itself, in so far as goodness is construed as self-denial.

The third act is splendid, if barely probable. (Indeed the entire play is improbable and faintly allegorical.) For Shaw has saved one of his best characters, Burgoyne, until now. In fact Burgoyne is one of the best characters in the Shaw canon. The question is: How should we regard him? Is he near to Shaw's self-ideal, a superior Caesarean figure, or is he, on the contrary, merely a politic man, hiding a certain shabbiness behind his wit and intelligence? It seems to me that Burgoyne is best seen as an honourable aristocrat in precise opposition not to scoundrels but to a rare moral being, such as Dick Dudgeon. He is 'classical' where Dudgeon is Christian. The distinction is reminiscent of the Ibsen of *Catiline* and *Emperor and Galilean*. Burgoyne hangs rebels exactly as a Roman general would have done: it is the imperial way. But he has no pettiness, no ill-feeling, no revengeful cruelty, no master-race ideology and no fear either of rebels or of his governors back in London. In the political context of 1777 he is not an innovator but a status quo-ite. On the other hand,

Burgoyne's very alertness to every nuance and his independence
of convention suggest that he too is capable of originality, and
perhaps the only valuable sort of originality.

But Anderson rides up in time, Dudgeon is spared and Judith is
restored to Anderson who 'finds his true profession' (Act III) as a
Captain of the Militia. Dick meanwhile finds his as a parson.
Shaw's Blakeian or Shelleyan view is that those who revolt against
current morality are the elect. Dick's master is the Devil in his
Luciferian aspect. The Devil is worthy, not for tempting people to
sin but for challenging God. God or God's obsolete morality is the
tyrant.

Neither in the Preface to the play nor in the play itself did Shaw
account properly for Dick Dudgeon's behaviour. Dick is not
world-weary or in love like Sidney Carton and Carton's
nineteenth-century counterparts. He is not an ideologue or a
victim of angst in twentieth-century fashion. Louis Crompton
rightly remarks that 'Man, in his best moments, is for Shaw in the
grip of a transcendent social will which has the force of moral
necessity.'[11] But whence comes this will? It is as much outside
human psychology as 'divine revelation' itself. To give oneself up
to be hanged is glaringly different from risking one's life for
another in an emergency – Shaw's own misleading parallel.[12]
People do such things, but every time there is a peculiar personal
reason, so that 'good deeds' require analysis every bit as much as
'bad'. Shaw really did have a sense of union with mankind at large
and with a universal moral principle, which could only have been,
for him, a force greater than man as a species and towering to the
skies over any individual. Like most believers he evidently felt it
superfluous to expound this principle, and it seemed likewise
unnecessary to understand Dick Dudgeon. But since Dick's
behaviour is not explained, it is for us *invalid*, a piece of stirring
unphilosophic nonsense. The paradox is that *The Devil's Disciple*, a
'play for puritans', succeeds triumphantly, not as a lesson but as
antipuritanical entertainment, and to an appreciable extent
because of Burgoyne. If there is a lesson, it is somehow involved
with the portrait of a superior worldly man, the reverse of a
puritan.

Shaw later wrote that when the novelty of the 'Diabolonian
position' had worn off, *The Devil's Disciple* would be exposed as the
threadbare popular melodrama it really is'.[13] It is indeed popular
melodrama, though not threadbare at all, and it has that

character partly *because* of the Diabolonian position, no longer a novelty but still a fraud; an ideal, as a matter of fact, of exactly the kind Shaw thought he wished to destroy.

In referring to Burgoyne just now as both superior and worldly my intention was not to be paradoxical on my own account but to reflect Shaw. Burgoyne is superior because he is aloof from common prejudices and he is worldly in the sense that he is free of ideals. (The worldliness of many people is part and parcel of their shared ideals.) But how was it possible for Shaw himself to be both overwhelmingly a moralist and at the same time worldly? How could he so respect such a man as his Burgoyne? If Shaw's kingdom was 'not of this world' on what grounds did he approve of Napoleon and Julius Caesar, two of the world's commanders? *Caesar and Cleopatra* (1898) begins to answer such questions.

There is a Prologue and an 'Alternative to the Prologue'. The former expounds the relevant chapter of Roman history in terms of Caesar versus Pompey, and this, according to Shaw, means the creative man versus the rule-bound soldier. Caesar is figured not as the complex patrician but as a classless adventurer who makes up his own rules as he goes along. These two types are of course reconcilable, but Shaw simplifies greatly. Julius Caesar's actual *bon vivant* tendencies, his prodigality, his positive sensual love for Cleopatra and his general sensuality, his 'covetous desire to be king', as Plutarch puts it, even his zest for soldiering: all these features and more are eliminated or played down. Nevertheless, the real Caesar's unassuming mateyness remains in the play and his all-important replacement of convention by commonsense.

Further, in the Prologue Shaw declares that since the forties BC there has been no improvement (and possibly a deterioration) in the human race. His belief is that men are pretty well as they have been throughout recorded history, but here and there an Alexander or a Caesar (or a Shaw) rises above his fellows. (The 'Alternative to the Prologue' merely though plausibly shows the superstitious terrors and warlike ethos of the Egyptians of Cleopatra's day. Presumably these are not features we have positively outgrown so much as ancient parallels to our own savage ways.)

The five acts of the play itself are meagre in terms of narrative (so different from *The Devil's Disciple*) but thoroughly provided with historical detail and ample as regards their chief purpose, the portrait of Caesar. It is a history play in Ibsen's or Herman

Hettner's sense of a work based on history but primarily of psychological and ethical relevance to the author and his contemporaries.[14] Shaw, indeed, seems to have believed that his Caesar was more or less the Caesar of history, but the character is really Shaw's valuation of himself at his best. That is to say, Caesar behaves as Shaw would have wished to behave in the same circumstances. Naturally in projecting his ego-ideal Shaw is also setting up a hierarchy of values. Caesar – therefore Shaw – occupies the pinnacle. and this is not so much a sign of vanity as a recognition that the great unCaesarian or unShavian majority are enslaved by their habits of mind and body and caught in cultural snares. For that very reason we shall have to consider whether Caesar is substantially more than a critic of society, for his solutions to problems are simply unprejudiced and objectively 'correct'.

Caesar addresses the Sphinx: 'You and I are strangers to the race of men'. The Sphinx is the symbol of Caesar's genius and Caesar thus describes his own nature: 'part brute, part woman, and part god – nothing of man is in me at all' (Act I). He is naturally a 'brute', being composed of animal or fleshly elements. He is 'part woman' because women in Shaw's view, unless they are deceived by a masculine culture, are non-moral agents of the Life Force, and Shaw himself is such an agent as well. Caesar resembles a woman in exploiting or ignoring rules rather than believing in them. 'Part god' implies a yet greater independence of rules, for Caesar is like a god in creating his own rules, or to be precise in making a godlike response to every fresh situation. The point about gods is not their powers but that they are laws unto themselves. The nature of each is formed without obedient or even defiant reference to society, and something of that divine transcendency is supposed to be a property of Shaw's Caesar. Just the same, each god has his own distinctive nature (for instance, he is warlike or sagacious), while Caesar adapts himself thoroughly to every turn of fortune.

In comparison with Caesar, Cleopatra is intentionally of little interest. When we first meet her hiding on the Sphinx she is a 16-year-old bundle of wilfulness, credulity and craft. She never seriously advances beyond that stage but instead learns from Caesar various tricks of dominance. Little of Plutarch's Cleopatra remains and it seems Shaw really saw the historical woman as a capricious Victorian girl. It was so necessary for him to rob

Cleopatra of the variety and power usually attributed to her: that celebrated compound of animal cunning, persistent ruttishness, genuine affection, regal authority, theatrical talent, delightful conversation and savage cruelty – the whole enveloped, at suitable times, in cloth of gold luxury. But Shaw dismissed as total fable what must have been only the distortions and simplifications of legend. His Cleopatra is designed to demonstrate his Caesar's easy superiority. Indeed, Shaw absolutely could not make a Cleopatra worthy to stand beside his Caesar and the play might as well be called 'Caesar and Others (including Cleopatra)'.

Several of the other people are brief, serviceable character-sketches. Ptolemy Dionysius is no more than a misfit, a normal boy forced into the role of king; Theodotus is a minor satire on the figure of learned man at court, quick, pretentious, schoolmaster-ishly spiteful; Pothinus is simply a sharp, headstrong fellow, for his eunuchism is of no account.

Rufio is more substantial, Shaw's counterpart to Shakespeare's Enobarbus before the latter's doubts set in at Actium. And as Enobarbus verifies the fascination of Cleopatra and the self-betrayal of Antony, so Rufio's bluntness enhances Caesar as the supremely self-confident captain with whom it is never necessary to be tactful.

Lucius Septimus represents the martial code which Caesar finds offensive. What is interesting about him is his flat, unruffled acceptance of traditional ways: he kills Pompey because 'woe to the vanquished' (Act II) is the natural law. Losers are automatically killed or enslaved.

Ftatateeta, Cleopatra's nurse, is a striking historical realisation because of her ancient, uncomplicated delight in master–slave distinctions and blood-lust cruelty. A victim is purely a regale-ment, and of course one might be a victim oneself. In the 1890s Ftatateeta must have required a nice enough exercise of the historical imagination and I doubt that the twentieth century has brought the type back to life, for the murderousness Shaw depicts here as a feature of the ancient world still seems too unevolved and animal-pure for modern times. Ftatateeta would rather die or suffer unspeakable pains herself than think ahead, take precau-tions, check her instinctual drives.

Shaw, who could create such a convincing creature, neverthe-less could not resist such anachronisms as Apollodorus and, more blatant still, Britannus. The latter's incongruousness was denied by Shaw[15] yet it is nonsense to argue that a stuffy, face-saving, post-1850 gentleman could have been found in the forests of Gaul. Apollodorus, the young patrician peacock, practitioner of art for art's sake, who happens moreover to be daring, chivalrous and skilled with the sword, is Shaw's amiable picture of an Alexandrian nobleman. As an artist he is a 'famous patrician amateur' (Act III) and therefore acceptable to Britannus. But in truth Apollodorus is simply Elizabethan.

Caesar himself is qualitatively on a different plane from other characters, and this is entirely a matter of his being free of the usual vices. He is unpetty, unvengeful, unsensual: the prefix is necessary because Caesar does not positively possess antithetical qualities. Admittedly, he abhors legal executions and still feels ashamed of himself for having had Vercingetorix put to death. (No one mentions the Cilician pirates whom the young Caesar had crucified for holding him hostage.) 'Natural slaying' (Act V) or spontaneous murder is different, as indeed it is. Books are merely tools, Caesar argues, of little intrinsic value. Therefore he has no qualms about the burning of the great library of Alexandria (and this must still give a jolt to scholars). As for 'great books', these are simply works that 'flatter mankind' (Act II). Any truthful book would promptly be destroyed. (More accurately, I suggest, it would promptly be misinterpreted.) Caesar has no 'hatred in him', as Cleopatra recognises in the fourth Act. She must learn, he says, not to 'protest or contradict', for these are ignoble ways (Act IV). In short, as Shaw puts it, Caesar, 'having virtue has no need of goodness'.[16]

What Shaw meant by this distinction needs working out, even after his own brief explanation.[17] Certainly Caesar makes no show of specific virtues such as prudence, temperance and the rest, for these constitute what Shaw understood as 'goodness'. (If, by the way, Caesar had been healthily libidinous in the play he would have been more impressive as well as more authentic, but also quite unShavian.) On the other hand, 'virtue' as a general quality seems here to mean the absence of any wish to harm others, so that Caesar's martial exploits are to be seen purely as a pastime. Shaw's Caesar has no aggression; he conspicuously lacks the common kind that wears a moral disguise. His originality is of a piece with his open-eyed observation of the people around him, whom he judges without rancour or rivalry. He accepts what is present to his eyes and has no personal desires to speak of. To be more exact, each of his desires is a precise response to a unique situation. In that sense he has no 'character'. Such seems to be what Shaw meant by 'virtue'. If only he had said as much, instead of wasting time on the usual sort of polemics.

Shaw's hero, then, manifests a lack, a negation of vice rather than any positive moral quality. Vices are negated effortlessly, not trampled down. There are no temptations. Caesar is neither charitable in the Pauline sense nor loving in any sense. If he had to sacrifice himself he would do so without fuss, heroics, or even regret. There is something wrong with the conception. The turmoil of a human being has been smoothed away and replaced by a few petty inconsistencies. The result is that Caesar is a paradigm masquerading as an individual, and indeed, real individuality, the source of creative power (or, as one should say, the *being* of creative power) is missing entirely. Caesar is Shaw's first attempt at a *solution* to humanity and therefore displays the opposite of many human traits. But this opposite is a vacuum. Shaw would not acknowledge that creative capacity is first of all utterly specific to the creator and secondly bound up with his human 'viciousness' – if that's what we want to call it. It does not spring from purity and while it may help to determine values, is not itself virtuous. Nor does it necessarily lessen human suffering.

Chief among Caesar's paradigmatic attitudes is, as we have noticed, the loathing of behaviour calculated to harm others. The category includes judicial as well as private deeds. People are necessarily killed in battle and in moments of domestic fury, but planned killing is another matter. Caesar rages against military executions. It is clear enough in this play and far clearer in *Captain Brassbound's Conversion* (1899) that Shaw was horrified by the deliberate preparation of murder for any reason whatever. Brassbound is transformed from a brooding avenger to a straight-forward leader of men, and by this means Shaw disputed the romantic Monte Cristo pattern of paying back an oppressor.

The situation which gives rise to this, Shaw's last play of the nineties, is of a familiar nineteenth-century sort, namely that one man has resolved to destroy the destroyer of a loved one. The processes of justice have been used to perpetrate an injustice and so, it seems, the person responsible must be punished by extra-legal means. Brassbound is the son of an English father, Miles Hallam, and a Brazilian mother. Hallam owned an estate in the West Indies which he left in the hands of an agent. The agent

seized the estate and since he had retained both the Attorney
General and the Solicitor General, the only lawyers on the island,
nobody could bring an action against him. Miles died and his
Brazilian wife, an uneducated woman, turned to Miles's brother,
who happened to be a London solicitor, but he justifiably said that
he could do nothing for her. In consequence the wife threatened
the brother with violence, was briefly imprisoned and then forced
to leave England as the only alternative to being certified as a
lunatic. Indeed she has been driven mad by her misfortunes, and
died abroad, rambling and penniless.

Years later the lawyer brother Sir Howard Hallam, visited the
island, in the absence of the rogue land agent as it happened, and
simply took his opportunity to recover the estate. Because Sir
Howard had himself risen to Attorney General by now, no one
was competent to act against him.

But Brassbound has long yearned for revenge on this man
whom he regards as the cause of his mother's doom, and seizes his
chance when Sir Howard arrives in Mogador for a touring
holiday, accompanied by his sister-in-law, Lady Cicely Waynflete. Brassbound is a trader–smuggler, late of General Gordon's
army, who with his unsavoury gang occasionally accompanies
tourists on trips to the interior, and when Hallam engages him as
escort the fly engages the spider. As it stands the situation is
scarcely plausible but what matters is Shaw's determination to
show how a man with motive and will for revenge might be
brought, not to a display of foregiveness but to sublime indifference. The world must go on; what do I or my enemy matter?

Brassbound's thirst for vengeance, or alternatively retributive
justice, is by many people's standards impeccable, in the sense of
humanly natural. Who could let Sir Howard go scot free without
feeling something between mild shame and poisonous resentment? In that sense Shaw's example is well chosen. But Brassbound, idealistic fellow that he is, is up against not Sir Howard
alone but also Lady Cicely who is Shaw's representative in a
remarkably complete sense. Lady Cicely's undoubted feminine-
ness is oddly unimportant, for what matters is her Shavian
technique (the technique of Shaw as a private person, not merely
as a playwright) of countering every 'lower' manifestation (anger,
spite, fear, and so forth) with a sort of beaming, no-nonsense
reasonableness. In fact Lady Cicely's arguments are not up to
much, but they halt opposition in its tracks. Whatever anyone

says or does, she plucks from the air some sweetly conclusive remark, so that she could be defeated only by a bearish show of logic. She herself is something of a dialectician, but her dialectic is at the disposal of her benevolence.

Lady Cicely, good-looking, thirtyish, dressed with cunning simplicity, is mistress of every situation. (This was Shaw's own style, never to be out of countenance, and to win every argumentative point.) An ambush by the tribe of Beni Siras which results in the wounding of Marzo the Italian; a menacing dispute among the British group, Sheikh Sidi el Assif, and the Cadi of Kintafi; Brassbound's assassination plot and finally the judicial enquiry presided over by Captain Kearney of the United States cruiser 'Santiago': these desperate matters are all in a day's work. Lady Cicely is faced at one time or another by freebooters, by the surly fanatic Brassbound, by proud desert chieftains and by the gruff manliness of American soldiers. All and especially Captain Brassbround are charmed as if by Orpheus, and the metamorphoses take place where, in life, an English lady would be raped, thrown aside, in all probability murdered.

Let us take account of some of Lady Cicely's sentiments, for they reflect Shaw's own. When told that the natives of the Atlas Mountains are dangerous she asks, 'Why? Has any explorer been shooting at them?' (Act I) 'All men,' she tells Brassbound, 'are children in the nursery' (Act I). In Act II she remarks that 'Men are always thinking that they are going to do something grandly wicked to their enemies; but when it comes to the point, really bad men are just as rare as really good ones.' A little later in the same act Brassbound tells her, '. . . you have belittled my whole life to me', to which she disarmingly replies that no one could belittle the many 'kind and brave things' he must have done. Lady Cicely tells Captain Kearney at the hearing, 'Then the escort ran away – all escorts do' (Act III). Finally in this brief list of illustrations, she assures Captain Brassbound that 'I have never been in love with any real person; and I never shall' (Act III).

Lady Cicely's attitudes are incorrigibly Rousseauesque. People do harm because they have been constrained, and it is wicked to retaliate against one's so-called enemies. Is it not clear that Lady Cicely's assumptions, though they are at one with her manipulative cleverness, belong to her *innocent* world in which her own aggression has been transformed into benevolent tyranny? She is innocent because she does not know that tyranny is itself the cardinal fault. 'Benevolence', after all, is not inevitably a good thing and may crush someone as readily as other forms of behaviour. Lady Cicely belittles Brassbound's whole life, as he says, without once realising that he has defined himself by adventurous exploits and vengeful broodings. He absolutely is an avenger and something of a Conradian freebooter, so that when he comes to act as a mere responsible leader he will have no purpose and no self to speak of. He will have been rendered decently null.

And this on a large scale can now be seen to be what Shaw was after. It was a position he moved towards as the nineties progressed, and when he grew able to conceive his own exemplars he produced first Caesar then Lady Cicely, characters curiously distinguished by their lack of character. The morality Shaw aimed for was a depersonalising morality. The matter is effectively masked, since Caesar and Lady Cicely have strong stage 'presences', and she especially is a delight to behold. Each has an audacious attitude and much charm, nourished of course by the idiosyncracies of the actor and actress.

But real personality is by definition 'wicked' in Shaw's and Lady Cicely's sense. The good man of Shaw cannot but be uncreative, for which lack the playwright substituted by sleight of hand (and the substitution is slick indeed) an 'objective' problem-solving mentality. What Shaw sought was the supersession of the human race by a new, innocuous species. The values of these Houynhnhnms would be fixed and universal and thus there could be no further creation. For it is pointless to fantasise about a form of creation (unmatched in all our strife-torn centuries) which shall proceed from beings who know no harm, no wretchedness and above all, no struggle for self-assertion. The dream is monstrously absurd and why even desire such conditions? The answer, as will become clearer in the next chapter, is that such future beings would neither cause nor feel hurt, and the whole Shavian enterprise was for the purpose of eliminating pain.

3   Shaw's Later Plays

Pain to Shaw seems to have been chiefly, if not exclusively, the result of a mismatch between one's own purposes and those of nature. Here, it should be said, we are coming face to face with Shaw's chief problem as an artist–legislator. To consider that problem we must bear in mind that he believed life to be essentially distinct from nature. Life was without purpose, while nature exhibited purpose in all its manifestations. He once wrote as follows to a Miss Eva Christy:

> Happiness is not the object of life, life has no object: it is an end in itself; and courage consists in the readiness to sacrifice happiness for an intenser quality of life.[1]

These brave words camouflage and rest upon a confusion. Life is merely our general term for all the activities of plants and animals, and of course 'it' has no object. Nature is a more inclusive word (indeed to the materialist an all-inclusive word) which embraces inanimate as well as living things – rocks and metals for example, in addition to vegetation and creatures. But Shaw believed that nature had purpose while life had none. He apparently thought of life as 'stronger' than nature, so that the purposeless must be guided by its weaker, purposeful affiliate, as a vacuous giant might be directed by an intelligent dwarf. Is it not a fact, however, that in time as well as in space the word 'life' simply refers to a variety of developments in nature. And, as we have remarked in an earlier chapter, the only being is the universe to whom we confidently attribute purpose is man himself.[2] It is necessary to be clear about these matters as we approach *Man and Superman* (1903).

The paradox is that *Man and Superman* is one of Shaw's outstanding half dozen works, yet 'in itself', so to speak, it appears to be nothing of consequence. A high quality is there, but exactly *where* is it? Except for Jack Tanner the characters are not

especially amusing or intricately developed and the contrapunta
plots of Violet, Octavius and Hector Malone as against Tanne
and Ann Whitefield are less engaging than the plots of many othe
Shaw plays. On the other hand, 'Don Juan in Hell' is original in
subject matter and technique. While it neatly forms part of the
third act, it may just as neatly be excised, and usually is. Bu
without the serious 'Don Juan in Hell' the comparatively flippan
bulk of *Man and Superman* still has mysterious weight. Presumably
Shaw's earnest, indeed passionate thoughts colour the drama
proper while scarcely finding expression there.

As a heroine Ann Whitefield lacks the sheer presence, the
'impasto' of Vivie Warren or Lady Cicely Waynflete or Joan o
Arc, and to tell the truth she is from one point of view mediocre.
mean that she says little that is memorable, for Shaw in creating
her set himself the awkward task of bringing forward a heroine
who was at once an incarnation of undifferentiated energy and
perforce, a unique person. It is Ann's uniqueness that is hard to
detect. Margery Morgan goes so far as to call her 'rather stupic
where anything beyond her narrow personal range is concerned',
and we must surely agree. Shaw had no opinion of her brains
talents or looks ('a well-formed creature, as far as that goes') bu
nevertheless introduced her as a 'vital genius'. (Not an 'oversexec
person', which he without justification called a 'vital defect'.
Ann's conversation is neither especially energetic nor striking in
any way, so the actress must of her own accord, without help from
the playwright, impart a sort of zest to the personality which is
physical, captivating and not inordinately sexy. On the page Ann
is little more than a husband-hunter whose amusing trick is the
attribution of her own wishes to her mother's or guardian's
advice. On stage, of course, the actress will lend her own
personality to the part, but that is none of Shaw's doing. Ann is a
heroine because of her capacity to entrap and devour. She is saic
to be more of a siren than Violet, but then Violet is exquisitely
pretty. In the way of purely human traits we can allow Ann only
her slight sense of fun.

Contrariwise, Jack Tanner is exuberant, vastly energetic and
eccentric, though it seems he is no 'vital genius'. In this curious
fashion Shaw seems to be saying that the intensest vitality is
subhuman or non-human; that even the most glittering and
bustling of human beings lacks the vitality of a beast. Is he no
implicitly keeping vitality apart from the singular shades o

ndividuality where it truly resides? Even the greatest simpleton
1as more 'life about him' than an animal, because he is more
ndividuated. Tanner, of course, has far more individuality than
Ann, though his polemics and play of fancy are but intermittently
onnected with the world around him. His intelligence is often
mpractical and he survives as comfortably as he does because
mployees such as Straker minister to his needs. But we may not
herefore suppose that Tanner is a potentially influential
philosopher, an untimely fellow whose ideas will later bear fruit.
'or his philosophy will have no outcome. In practical terms he is
lmost a dunce and an absurdly selective observer of others.

For that matter even the theoretical exposition of Tanner's
philosophy is a mixture of the acute and the silly, though Shaw's
ntentions were entirely serious. The section of 'The Revolution-
st's Handbook and Pocket Companion' entitled 'Maxims for
Revolutionists' is a quite Shavian collection of first-class and
hird-rate observations. For example, the first maxim advisedly
eminds us of the diversity of individuals: 'Do not do unto others
1s you would they should do unto you. Their tastes may not be the
ame.' Here, as so often, Shaw saw the truth but not its amoral
onnotations, for how can one allow for others' tastes yet at the
ame time insist that their tastes be moral? What if my tastes
1appen to be sadistic – and it is unwise to argue that in a tolerant,
1ccommodating society no one would be a sadist. Then, what are
ve to make of the maxim, 'Those who understand evil pardon it:
hose who resent it destroy it'? Are understanding and resentment
of evil mutually exclusive? Perhaps they are, but then why is
esentment superior? Is it not possible that to resent something
for instance, terrorism) is shoddy, however fashionable or
earfully tempting? It is certainly both unChristian and
1nphilosophical.

Despite his wonderful energies ('a sensitive, susceptible, exag-
gerative, earnest man') Tanner is principally the one who does
1ot wish to marry Ann – or anyone else. That is his prime
unction. He and Octavius Robinson are neat antitheses, the
atter relishing sentiment, the former hating it. Octavius is the one
vho thinks he wishes to marry but will make a model melancholy
pachelor (these are Edwardian times), while Tanner will enjoy
he role of reluctant husband. The important point is that Tanner
s purely a talker with little enough resolution. For all that,
ncluded in his talk is the interesting recollection, which we

noticed earlier,[4] of how in youth his 'mob of appetites' was transformed into an 'army of purposes and principles' (Act I) Therefore we are encouraged, or in fact obliged to see Tanner as Don Juanesque in Shaw's odd sense, that is as a man who aspires to 'destroy evil'. He is the enemy not of the flesh alone in the narrow sense but of matter itself. His goal is to rid himself of the matter that encumbers him: he would be a *sprite*.

Lesser members of the cast are the results of sound though unremarkable turn-of-the-century observation. Straker, the new man, technologically apt and down to earth, the servant on his way to becoming master, prefigures a type that has not worked out so well as Shaw imagined. The Malones, father and son, are sub-Henry Jamesian Americans in Europe, the father fierce and unsubtle, the son a model of innocent chivalry. Mrs Whitefield is supposed to be colourless (that is her 'distinction'), but she is anyhow amusing in her correct, unflattering judgements of her daughters. The play as a whole amounts to reconciling Hector Malone Senior with his son's bride Violet, and bringing Tanner securely into Ann's web. In short, the body of the play superficially seems to be a light-hearted work which turns on the celebrated recognition that woman rather than man is the hunter And even this perception is scarcely true so much as a distortion of the plain fact that women have historically required breadwinners and protectors.

'Don Juan in Hell', the playlet within the play, therefore remains the important and original element of *Man and Superman* This dialogue raises the whole work to its high level while itself being readily dispensable. It is as if *Hamlet* had been provided with a symposium emphasising Shakespeare's private views about the worthlessness of man. The argument of the Hell scene is both eccentric and impressive. The Devil left heaven of his own accord, finding it angelically dull. Hell is the region he created for the pleasures of such as himself, the overwhelming majority. 'It takes all sorts to make a universe' (Act III). The gulf between heaven and hell is perfectly passable but as a rule people do not transfer from one to the other any more than in life they move from the racecourse to the concert hall. It is entirely a matter of taste.

In hell our make-believe ideals, say of love or heroism, are not in the least contradicted by facts; a mere mortal's dreams here come true, and he, a 'damned' spirit, can live for eternity in a romantic world of amour, derring-do, political power, military triumph and so forth. Hell is subordinated to its inhabitants' wishes and is thus a sphere of adolescent omnipotence. Heaven is the opposite, a sphere where the good man's desires are subordinated to external nature. For that reason one might go further and say that 'desire', as human beings know it, does not exist. The heavenly ones have no egocentric wishes and the hellish ones have no such wishes that are not instantly gratified. All the world's a stage; hell's a stage where dreams are reality, and heaven has no stage and no drama, nothing but reality.

Life, says Don Juan, is an irresistible force without a brain. (It occurs to no one to make the monist assertion that the brain is just part of life.) Don Juan aspires to give life intellectual guidance, though here again nobody points out that an irresistible force can scarcely be guided by one of its trivial parts. The body is said to be insignificant, since the greatest bodies, for instance that of the icthyosaurus, are now only museum fossils.

But the Devil has good arguments. Man makes toys and regards them as grand inventions: law, morality, gentility, art and politics are all amusements and pretensions. Man's highest form of literature is the tragedy, 'a play in which everyone is murdered at the end'. Man has invented *especially* the most remarkable instruments of torture and destruction. He is an ingenious imbecile. Ah yes, says Don Juan, but do not forget that man is flattered to be called bad. He revels in the name of tyrant, pirate, bully and the like. The last thing he wants to be is good. As for women, they exist to breed children, so they view men as implanters of seed.

The ultimate purpose of nature, however, is to produce the perfect individual; omnipotent, omniscient, infallible and utterly, Hegelianly self-conscious. The being of Don Juan's vision is a contemplative who seeks to discover the 'inner will of the world'. Here again we notice the anthropomorphism: the world has an inner will; nature incessantly aspires to 'higher' organisation. What Don Juan or Shaw cannot accept for a moment is the utter inclusion of man in nature and his utter solitude as the natural creature who imagines purposes. Along with language, the sense of purpose is a pointless peculiarity of the animal man.

Indeed the Devil tells Don Juan: 'You think because you have a purpose, Nature must have one.' To this overwhelming objection Don Juan replies that since his finger has a function, namely to grasp things, nature in the large must indeed have purpose. Here is the hub on which Shaw as artist turns. If the Devil is right Shaw himself is so wrong as to shatter his whole enterprise. In fact he neither at any stage gave the Devil his due in this respect nor confidently pushed him out of mind.

From now on Shaw twists and turns about this problem. Whatever the vigour of the plays he is held in a dilemma. It is evident that man may only achieve what is materially possible. The permutations of natural forces are no doubt infinite but we can never evade those permutations and our 'highest' conceivable form of organisation would still accord with the world of nature. We have sought to escape from that world by idealist philosophy, by religion, by politics and even by science, but our only valid way forward, as Shaw recognised at the beginning of his career, is by ridding ourselves of all idealism. We must therefore stop wriggling away from nature, but Shaw failed to see that wriggling is not the cause of hardship. That simply gives the hardship a certain character, and there can be no kind of life which is at the same time painless, moral and invigorating.

So far, however, we have not focused precisely on the problem of pain in Shaw. He was concerned with suffering in general, it is true, but his worst misery came from observing moral emptiness. His own awareness grew clearer about this matter and seems to have become perfectly sharp at the time of *John Bull's Other Island* (1905).

It is eccentric to call this the best of the plays, though there are good grounds for doing so. In the first place, Shaw was uniquely well qualified to deal with differences between the English and Irish national characters. This was his forte, so that his treatment of other topics seems in comparison hazy or tendentious. And it is not the portraits of the English or the Irish as such that display Shaw at his best, but his juxtaposition of the two. No one but he can have spent so much time and energy marvelling first at the ways of Irish peasants and priests then at the equally lunatic ways of English professional men. Similarly no one else has diagnosed so accurately how the English have succeeded in lording it over the Irish. (By way of contrast, Yeats wishes to promote a positive Irish culture and Joyce's observations suffer from his own bitterness. Shaw alone was quite without prejudice in this matter.)

In this sense *John Bull's Other Island* is the Shaw play par excellence. It has what *Man and Superman* lacks: an Ibsenist gallery of apprehended individuals, each one minutely himself and *consequently* the illustration of a general principle. Further, the play has no longuers and no unlikely aphorisms, and even the few impressive passages of oratory are plausible as well as acceptably poetic. More important than these merits is the striking merit that for once Shaw presented his ideas without transparently manipulating the plot or characters to do so. It is a model play of ideas, because the ideas are in harmony with everything else.

Thomas Broadbent is the best observed Englishman, qua Englishman, in modern literature. His *automatic* bad faith, his way, both shrewd and stupid, of not letting the right side of his brain know what the left side is doing (to adopt Peter Keegan's remark in Act IV) is practised in a distinctively English style. Briefly, all principles are subordinated without scruple or even thought to the exigencies of the moment. Broadbent so insistently brays forth the principles he so promptly abandons. That is common enough the world over, but what is less common outside these shores is the monumental self-ignorance with which the trick is played. If there is anything Broadbent genuinely loathes it is a hypocrite. He is far from being a bad man for on the contrary he is decent, helpful and absolutely sincere. He means every word he says at the moment of saying it. He is unaffectedly worldly and so can remark to Keegan in the fourth act that of social evils 'some are necessary for the preservation of society and others are encouraged only when the Tories are in office.' Broadbent is successful in love and business because he is blind to the realities he manipulates. Thus, Nora Reilly, the ethereal Roscullen woman to whom he proposes about two minutes after first meeting her is a dreary, underfed creature, and his plans for the local people include lending the landowners more than their land is worth, thus permanently putting them in his power. What Shaw is once again saying is that hell is the sphere where such despiritualised persons as Broadbent (and Larry Doyle) get their own way. Thus hell and earth are one and the same.

Laurence Doyle is the Irishman in voluntary, or to be exact enthusiastic exile, Broadbent's partner in the London firm of civil engineers, who sees everything that Broadbent fails to see and callously accepts it. Yet he is not unlikeable (though Shaw regarded the role as 'very unsympathetic')[5] and the difficulty for us lies in understanding how Larry can see so clearly yet commiserate so little. He knows that 'an Irishman's heart is

nothing but his imagination' (Act I); that Irish conversation is
'eternal fouling and staining and degrading' (Act I) and that the
Englishman camouflages himself as a fool in the way that a
grasshopper camouflages itself as a leaf, and, of course, he realises
that Nora is absolutely dull and sour; indeed he has helped to
make her so by keeping her on a string for eighteen preposterous
years. How can Larry be so open-eyed yet seemingly contented,
for in fiction such things are possible but not in life, and the play as
a whole is very lifelike. The answer is that Shaw projected part of
himself into Larry, reserving a complementary part for another
character.

Shaw was also, plainly, Peter Keegan and in a moment we will
deal with Keegan at adequate length for one who is the axis and
justification of the play. At this point we should remark that *John
Bull's Other Island* sums up the condition of Ireland at the time
when Home Rule was still debated. The play as a whole is the
summary, but consider especially the political chatter at Cor-
nelius Doyle's house in the third act. Here the attitudes and
mannerisms of the senior Doyle, Father Dempsey, Barney Doran
and Matthew Haffigan are plausible to the last degree (as good as
anything of a similar nature in Ibsen), while Shaw, through
Larry, gives his own reading of the situation, namely that no
smallholder will be better off in a scheme of local autonomy. The
case against 'local government' and 'power-sharing' is well – and
cynically – argued.

For all that, the point of the play, governing the comedy and the
realism, dominating and passing judgement upon the ludicrous
sequence of events as Broadbent prepares the ground for his
business ventures, agrees to be nominated as parliamentary
candidate and gets betrothed to Nora, is Keegan's judgement
upon the all-too-worldly scene. It is here, as Alfred Turco Jr
rightly says, that 'For the first time in Shaw's work, the
apocalyptic note is struck'.[6]

Keegan then, is an aspect of Shaw. To be exact, Keegan is Shaw
at his Bunyanesque best, the standard which, I suggest, he could
not have maintained without descending into the madness with
which the locals believe Keegan to be afflicted. Keegan says,
Chestertonianly, that his 'way of joking is to tell the truth' (Act
II). But he always tell the truth, flippantly or solemnly. To
Keegan the hilarious accounts of the incident of Broadbent and
Haffigan's pig constitutes hell itself. 'Nowhere else', he says (Act

IV), 'could such a scene be a burst of happiness for the people.' He means that the savage, inane, contemptuous, schoolboy derision is the negation of holiness.

Business efficiency is as much a torment to Keegan as is its opposite, Irish slovenliness. It is the world as a whole that he loathes. 'Every dream is a prophecy; every jest is an earnest in the womb of time' (Act IV), because Shaw himself cannot contemplate a morally unimprovable society. Keegan's mad dream of a 'godhead in which all life is human and all humanity divine' (Act IV) is and will remain Shaw's dream. 'All life is human' means that life conceived as an immeasurable force, will somehow fall under the control of one of its negligible units. Man and God will not merely be reconciled (or Paradise be regained) but will wholly merge. Alternatively, God will finally be created in and through man. Shaw's implication is that Keegan is not mad but magnificently sane; yet the vision is preposterous. What saves this play is that Shaw is not effortlessly sure of himself. That is why, as Turco says, 'the apocalyptic note is struck'. For if man is not potentially divine he is nothing, a being without value.

These alternatives are too stark and the happy alternative too remote for Shaw (who cannot consistently be Keegan), so we find him immediately looking for another way of containing evils. Having announced in so many words that the only solution is for man to become God, Shaw now entertains a doctrine for man as the Lilliputian creature he is to render evil harmless, to take the malignancy out of the malign. What if evil is not evil but just our designation for presently unacceptable forms of behaviour? By now (1905, to be exact, when *Major Barbara* was first staged) Shaw has heard of *Beyond Good and Evil*, though he has not read it and indeed knows Nietzsche's work only by reputation. Shaw's understanding of this matter is a mixture of shafts of perception and false inferences. For example, he remarks in a letter of 1905 that Nietzsche apparently regarded slave morality as 'an imposition of the slaves themselves', which is correct, but this piece of accuracy is entangled with the conjecture that Nietzsche is 'academic', in the sense of ivory-towered.[7] The point is that a resemblance between the ideas of Shaw and Nietzsche was already proposed at the turn of the century, and Shaw rightly denied any such origin of his own opinions. Just the same, *Major Barbara* is a beyond-good-and-evil play. It may be regarded as a theatrical exposition of that phrase, provided we realise that

Shaw's fashion is unwittingly a parody and debasement of
Nietzsche's insights.

Major Barbara is almost as far along the road to conspicuous
artifice as *John Bull's Other Island* is along the other road to realism
(or covert artifice). The later, 'salvationist' play is of a more
perfectly Shavian kind than the earlier – which is not to say that it
is better. No matter that Adolphus Cusins was drawn from
Gilbert Murray, Barbara Undershaft from Murray's wife and
Lady Britomart from Murray's mother-in-law the Countess of
Carlisle, the play is still stagey, for good or ill.[8] Nor is it less
histrionic, needless to say, because the management techniques of
the hero Undershaft owe something to what Shaw knew of the
careers of Friedrich Krupp and Alfred Nobel. For in every
instance Shaw was concerned with the presentation of clear,
contrasting opinions on morality and power, and sheer por-
traiture took second place. Shaw too often used to be accused of
reducing his characters to arguments but in *Major Barbara* the
accusation strikes home. As a matter of fact, in most of the plays
the characters are well enough developed for comedy but in this
play the chief personalities do coincide too nicely with their
opinions. If Lady Britomart ('copied', I repeat from the Countess
of Carlisle) is an exception, she is a Wildean exception, a Lady
Bracknell figure and a pure delight. But perhaps all this is to stress
overmuch the mannered nature of the work.

However, Shaw regarded *Major Barbara* as a 'frankly religious
play in which the most effective scene is the conversion of a rough
by a Salvation girl'.[9] But is it religious? In what extraordinary
sense is it so, especially as the 'rough', Bill Walker, is converted
only to respect for Barbara? For in reaction against *John Bull's
Other Island* (or at least against Father Keegan) Shaw contrives
here to reconcile goodness with worldliness, to identify Christian
with Worldly Wiseman. I do not mean what must seem plain to a
materialist, that everything, good and bad alike, is of this world,
but that Shaw is actually offering some such maxim as 'the
worldlier the better'. He is not saying that we should make the
best of this life, but rather that we must sever the connection
between goodness and simplicity. This is one point over which
Shaw's notions differ interestingly from Nietzsche's. In *Beyond
Good and Evil* Nietzsche states that 'Wherever slave morality
becomes preponderant language tends to bring the words "good"

and "stupid" closer together.' The good man is 'good natured, easy to deceive, a little stupid perhaps, *un bonhomme*'.[10] So far Shaw would not necessarily disagree, and in *Major Barbara* he endeavours to show how goodness (or higher value of some sort) might be caused, on the contrary, to belong with cleverness and sophistication. But Nietzsche, despite his observations about the terms 'good' and 'stupid', had long been aware of the conjunction of cleverness with a hieratic sort of virtue and regarded exactly that conjunction as the deadly invention of ascetic priests and, in philosophy proper, of Socrates. Thus the philosopher and the playwright are really poles apart.

Once it was common to complain that Shaw was a paradoxical fellow and naturally *Major Barbara* was seen as an excellent and perhaps outrageous example of the tendency. More recently the chief argument of the play – to the effect that decency, prosperity and a sense of security go hand in hand – has been uncritically accepted. Yet this argument, the Undershaft thesis, is thoroughly dubious. The theatregoers of eighty years ago could see what our modern specialists miss: that Undershaft is a casuist. Undershaft's premise (or Shaw's) is that poverty is 'the worst of crimes'. He continues: 'All the other crimes are virtues beside it: all the other dishonors (sic) are chivalry itself by comparison' (Act III). Now that is nonsense, a distortion of Samuel Butler's satirical point in *Erewhon* to the effect that to eliminate poverty would be to eliminate criminal vice. Vice is independent of standards of living, or rather, it assumes different forms according to one's means. As so often, Shaw saw efficient causes where there were only antecedents and predispositions.

In the Preface, 'First Aid to Critics', Shaw maintains that Undershaft's career stands the 'Kantian test', since he realised as a young man that what faced him was 'not a choice between opulent villainy and humble virtue, but between energetic enterprise and cowardly infamy'. If everyone acted as Undershaft acts, society would be splendid; there would be 'a raising of hell to heaven and of man to God', as Barbara puts it at the end of the play. This contention too is false, for it is an argument in favour of energy masquerading as an argument in favour of morality. Undershaft is not remotely a Nietzsche (who maintained that morality has the function of weakening or misdirecting energy) but is rather a modern Machiavel. Perhaps – though one mustn't

be crude and hasty here – Shaw was anxious to reconcile his own
riches and literary success with his otherworldly Keeganesque
apprehensions.

Yet there are other, more valid arguments from Undershaft.
For instance, he declares in Act I that 'there is only one true
morality for every man'. If he had added that that one true
morality is not codifiable and must endlessly be adapted (not
perverted) to every singular situation, he would then have
anticipated a rare kind of modern awareness. Similarly, when, in
Act III, he retorts to Lady Britomart's statement, 'What does it
matter whether they [disreputable matters] are true if they are
wrong', by saying, 'What does it matter whether they are wrong if
they are true', he is at least speaking as that remarkable creature,
the lover of truth above all.

The trouble with Undershaft is that he appears to be certain of
truth and, further, that truth brings happiness. Here is Shaw's
familiar error: the conviction that misery might be and must be
banished from the earth. If Undershaft could only admit that
what he maintains is merely a different set of values, possibly a
more invigorating set, all would be different. As it is we are left
with Shaw's old confusion. This confusion is best illustrated in the
very scene that Shaw singled out as 'the most effective in the play',
the business in Act II when Bill Walker is changed from a lout
searching for his ex-girl to beat up to a merely rude fellow who
recognises the value in Barbara Undershaft. His violence is
defeated by her arguments (rather as Brassbound was defeated by
Lady Cicely) but that is not the point and Barbara's remarks are
anyway not obviously superior to Bill's physical threats. The
point is that Bill's cry of 'Wot prawce Selvytion nah?' is a proper
reflection on the absurdity of 'salvation'. The nice feature of the
episode is that Barbara is transformed before Bill's eyes from
overconfident Salvation Army girl to admirable woman. He and
she part at the close of Act II as opponents who respect each other:
he wants none of her help and she appreciates that she has no
argument left to put up against him. Barbara indeed is an
interesting portrait of an idealistic girl first disheartened by her
father's intelligent cynicism and her fiancé's apostasy (as Cusins
decides to foresake the study of Greek for the manufacture of
armaments), then coming to accept that the Salvation Army and
the munitions factory are mutually dependent. Presumably
Barbara thus grasps that 'right' and 'wrong' are intermingled and

confused. Her final assertion is to the effect that God's work must be done in the world, using every worldly means. We are meant to be bowled over by this contention – as we are certainly bowled over by Barbara herself. But the viewpoint is, once again, hopelessly flawed. For what Barbara really does at the end of the play is give up God entirely. To make money out of cannons and then *incidentally* feed the poor may be justified in some fashion, but it is not (as Barbara originally recognised) to do God's work at all. Like Shaw himself, she has seen a stark choice and converted it into a conscious-salving muddle.

No doubt, as Charles Lomax says in Act III, '. . . there is a certain amount of tosh about this notion of wickedness'. This is the anti-moralistic moral of the play. But Shaw's attitude, expressed through Lomax, is quite innocent, since this latest notion of wickedness is bound up with causation and cure and has ceased for the moment to resemble the formidably hopeless view of Peter Keegan.

At this stage of his career Shaw had evidently picked up from Gilbert Murray a concept of Dionysianism.[11] Rather he had mislearned it, unless in the portrait of Cusins he was tilting at Murray more fundamentally and more subtly than seems likely. To judge from Cusins's behaviour, especially the drum-banging at the close of Act II, Shaw thought of Dionysus as a god merely of high spirits and tame cavorting, somewhat in the manner of the music hall; the 'irrepressible' in one or other of its relatively harmless nineteenth-century manifestations. But Dionysus with his panther-drawn chariot was a god of absolute fleshly licence; his cult was often enough orgiastic, delirious, sly and cruel, though it was not confined to such qualities. In other words, the Dionysian in its proper Mediterranean form of three thousand years ago subsumed and hugely magnified much of what Shaw had recoiled from all his life. Dionysus was the 'wicked' god (though the word is anachronistic) and represented the bounty and destructiveness of vigour, the zest and pains of birth and becoming. It was those pains that Shaw felt man might – or must – overcome. The artless references to Dionysus in *Major Barbara* therefore help us to see why the attractive features of the play disguise intellectual confusion.

As in the past so in the future, Shaw periodically tackled this central problem of how to demonstrate that morality and vigour were, as he supposed, readily reconcilable. But the problem was

never superseded: in some not always clear sense it helps to
trivialise the more trivial plays and to misdirect the more serious
ones. (*Back to Methuselah* is a piece of massive and revealing
ingenuity.) For example, *Pygmalion*, though comic and high-
spirited, is a serious study of class in Britain. Maurice Valency
discriminatingly calls it 'a play of *déclassement*'.[12] Even so, certain
issues are characteristically dodged and if Shaw had not believed
in the triumph of the will he could not have conceived *Pygmalion*.
For everyone rightly assumes that Eliza Doolittle turns into a lady
by changing her accent and learning grammar. Many critics have
spoken of Cinderella, but Shaw saw no enchantment in the
process Eliza undergoes. We are given some impression of the
difficulties in her metamorphosis and certain objections are met
head on (for instance, the Hungarian phonetician Nepommuck,
at least discerns that Eliza speaks English 'too perfectly' for an
English lady, as indeed she would do). Just the same, the comic
and optimistic machinery of *Pygmalion* revolves around the
assumption that the whole personality may be assimilated to
manners. And that was very nearly Shaw's own solemn belief.

He was exceptionally aware of many of the problems a real
young woman of Eliza's class would face and what sort of person
she would be before an actual teacher began his work. Shaw's
Eliza is not the charmingly pseudo-coarse maiden of the Pygmalion film and 'My Fair Lady' but a filthy, smelling creature who
has slept in the same set of underclothes for long enough and has
bad teeth. To clean her requires Mrs Pearce's scrubbing brush as
well as mustard, bath salts and scented soap. Her Lisson Grove
accent is nearly impenetrable and her one room is a slum. She is
illegitimate and her father tries to sell her at the slightest
opportunity. It is characteristic of her to jump to the conclusion,
in Act I, that Higgins is a police spy and that he throws money at
her because he is drunk. She is distrustful, untrustworthy and
generally low in character as in social station.

If we ask whether the transformation of Eliza could take place
as Shaw describes it and if his grasp of a flower-girl's psychological, moral and hygienic condition was matched by an accurate
reckoning of her possibilities, the answer to both questions is 'no',
or a yes so heavily qualified as to be almost a no. These are not
Nell Gwynne's circumstances (mentioned by Shaw in the
'epilogue' to the play) or those of courtesans in Balzac. If
anything, Eliza is rather a prudish girl and Higgins is pretty well

he reverse of a Restoration or post-Napoleon lecher. The type of
woman who rose in English society at the turn of the century did
o by additional means to Eliza's. She is not an actress, a scholar,
a fortune-hunter or, at this early stage, a businesswoman. She
achieves her ends exclusively by learning pronunciation, grammar and etiquette and by 'dressing up'. The process is a matter of
changing or acquiring manners, and that indeed was Shaw's
whole point.

Eliza is Shaw's own dream, not, of course, of a girl he wished to
obtain, but of the relation between the individual personality and
society as a whole. Shaw's dream (marked by an awareness of
facts and a conjurer's gestures in the direction of obstacles)
concerned the superficiality of social distinctions and conventional honours. He saw advancement in society as mainly a
matter of luck, knavery, posturing, relentless self-propulsion and,
often enough, acquiring some variety of elegance. The last is
Eliza's chief or only method. Her metamorphosis is the reduction
of discord to melody. (In 'London Music' Shaw, as we observed
earlier, refers to his own youth by saying, 'I had not then tuned the
Shavian note to any sort of harmony.')[13] More appropriately we
ought to bear in mind that the exquisite shape of Galatea emerged
from a shapeless chunk of ivory.

Thus the development of Eliza rests upon Shaw's assumption
that craft or technique is almost all the battle. At least that is his
assumption in the play proper, while the biological aspect of the
case is consigned to the 'epilogue'. It is there that Eliza is caused
to marry Freddy Eynsford Hill on the convincing grounds that
Higgins is not 'biologically attractive to a degree that overwhelms
all her other instincts'. Here Shaw is right: Eliza would marry the
weak and personable Freddy, for life with Higgins would be a
wearying struggle. These are important matters and they are
omitted from the stage performance.

As I have implied, at the outset Eliza has neither a 'flower-girl
style' nor a cockney style, but no style at all. She merely makes
vernacular noises to indicate her wants and fears. Through
Higgins she acquires a style too bloodlessly correct. Yet her will
and spirit enhance her, override her unnatural perfection of
manner. Interestingly enough, what Eliza's self-determining will
wills is not in the service of the Life Force but is just a flower shop.
Shaw never suggests that the shop is only a stepping-stone to a
husband. The tests she undergoes are means to a bourgeois not a

creative evolutionary end, and a husband is more or less an afterthought. In standing up to Higgins and in winning the support of his mother she asserts that she has ends of her own for which Higgins's end are only means. But Eliza's self-definition as lady in a flower shop is commonplace and what makes her appealing is her resolve to define herself at all in such circumstances. Shaw implies that the important thing is to get people to treat you as you wish to be treated, and this Eliza achieves.

Doolittle, her father, has posted himself on the outskirts of society. His trade is that of navvy but he prefers to be a dustman because it is less tiring. Shaw pretends – or possibly really believed – that the lowest class, to which Doolittle belongs, resembles the highest in being irresponsible. That is a familar and misleading comparison. Doolittle (in the first presentation of whom there is again no softening of the usual kind, since he is a rogue who stinks of rubbish and liquor) is transmuted into a wretchedly respectable fellow when he receives an income of £3000 a year on condition that he gives up to six lectures annually on moral reform. Now he has responsibilities, dependants and sycophants. But so has an aristocrat. Presumably the middle class is the most hidebound, though each class has a system of obligations which some of its members manage to minimise. Doolittle, having evaded working-class decencies, fails to discover a technique for evading middle-class morality. Being witty and original, he is taken up by hostesses. What Shaw does here is obscure the fact that the classes are or were distinguished from one another chiefly in degrees and types of power.

The Doolittles, father and daughter, are, then, declassed. Now the Eynsford Hills have been declassed all along: they are in Shaw's family's situation, that of the hard up bourgeoisie. Freddy is a helpless fellow; Mrs Eynsford Hill with her house in Earl's Court manages on a small jointure, while Clara (and here Shaw is peripherally inventive, so that Clara's story would be interesting in itself) loses her former snobbery – the silly repetition of the word 'bloody', for example – by means of reading H. G. Wells and Galsworthy and reaches an agreeable independence of mind and spirit working in a furniture shop.

The relation of Higgins to all this is again a Shavian dream. Though Shaw produced at least as great an alteration in his own career as Higgins produces in Eliza's, the real life change was based on art. Higgins probably originated in the following manner. First there was the example of George Vandeleur Lee, singing teacher, showman and manipulator of social possibilities through cheek and personal style. We remarked in the fifth chapter that he was, or became, rather a quack, but the bent of his career was to mould people into productions of his own. A Lee production might literally be a performance given in Dublin by his Amateur Musical Society or, alternatively, a young lady perfectly turned out from his Park Lane studio with the accent of a debutante and a singing voice fit for polite musical turns. He persuaded one of his housemaids to try to pass herself off as one of his well-to-do pupils, just as Eliza plays her part at Mrs Higgins's and the Embassy reception.[14] Lee hustled through life, unabashed by his not uncommon failures. Further, in a sense he made a good deal of Bessie Shaw. It is impossible to say if he effected any change in her manner, though he quite transformed her situation from poor and discontented Dublin housewife to lady of moderate means and energetic interests in London.

Then, as Shaw makes plain in the Preface to *Pygmalion*, there was the example of Henry Sweet. There are 'touches of Sweet in the play'. Possibly Shaw found Sweet's rooms cluttered with a phonetician's paraphernalia: phonograph, laryngoscope, tuning forks, 'a life-size image of a human head' (Act II), wax cylinders, and the rest. Sweet had a keener contempt than Higgins for academics in general and when he was made a reader in phonetics at Oxford 'managed by sheer scorn to alter his personal appearance until he became a sort of walking repudiation of Oxford and all its traditions' (Preface).

More important than Lee and Sweet is Shaw himself. To offer examples, Eliza's creator could have taught an Eliza without taking the smallest sexual interest in her; would cheerfully have realised before meeting Doolittle that Doolittle was a 'blackguard' (Act II); was able to overwhelm people of all classes; had such a high regard for his mother that romantic entanglements were for long impossible for him; was unmoved by the plight of individuals, though willing to help them; might well have said that 'making life means making trouble' (Act V); would have 'treated a duchess as if she were a flower girl' (Act V), and in effect regularly contrasted the warm and violent life of the gutter with the cold life of 'Science and Literature and Classical Music and Philosophy and Art' (Act V). Shaw was the man to whom life was one thing (to be unemotionally managed) and art or the

representation and contemplation of life a soaringly higher thing –
life's justification in fact and, if we proceed rightly, its apotheosis.

Yet, like Higgins, Shaw never grasped the limitations of living
by the will. He wrote his admirable *The Quintessence of Ibsenism*
without appreciating either that there are such limitations or that
Ibsen, another man of will, was by a creative paradox so
extraordinarily aware of them as to write the only thoroughgoing
modern tragedies – that is, tragedies which are not remotely
Christian or moralistic. Even *Heartbreak House*, the one play of
Shaw to seem to cast doubt on the efficacy of the will, presents no
solution to man's condition other than to 'learn navigation'.
Captain Shotover, who utters that counsel to various guests at his
Sussex house (the drawing room of which is designed to resemble
the after part of a high-pooped ship, a navigable craft rather than
a stationary dwelling), explains himself well enough and his
meaning is at best a grimmer version of Shaw's old teaching. Will
and knowledge still count above all, precisely because the danger
of shipwreck is now so great. (Shaw started writing the play in
1913, but completed it, with difficulty, in 1916 and 1917.)

To be exact, the similitude of a ship applies to England, though
the psychology is universal. If a skipper lies abed sodden with rum
his ship will be lost. Trusting to providence is the drunken
captain's calamitous way, though, as Shotover angrily points out,
it might be the way of a sober captain too. The difference is not
between drunk and sober but between those who navigate and
those who drift. The plain advice is that we must steer towards
specific destinations. Shaw has always said something of the sort,
but just now he is more aware of currents and shoals.

The view here is certainly different from Undershaft's confident
linking of paternalism and individual liberty and it is also
different in some degree from the craving of Don Juan in *Man and
Superman* for the subordination of man's purposes to nature's. To
steer a ship is to co-operate with nature but here for once Shaw
dwells less on the way than on the difficulties. There is a
suggestion that the difficulties might be too great, while everywhere else in Shaw, leaving aside the melancholy of Peter Keegan,
that suggestion is inconceivable.

Heartbreak House is the oddest of the plays and the hardest to
digest. Perhaps, as Colin Wilson says,[15] Shaw simply failed to
master his material, but we have to take the material as it is and,
mastered or not, it is highly polished. To reverse T. S. Eliot's

celebrated remark about *Hamlet*, this play is certainly an *artistic* success.[16] I do not mean that it is exciting or persuasive, for it is neither, but that it is nicely moulded. Any intellectual or philosophical shortcomings are disguised by craftmanship. The result is that critics are apt to praise as ambivalence what is merely contradiction. For once in his career Shaw was evidently unable to utter a clear message, but why must we regard his failure as a virtue? It might be a virtue in another dramatist, but Shaw excelled before and after *Heartbreak House* at knowing his own mind and trouncing his opponents.

This is not a well made play like *Arms and the Man* and *John Bull's Other Island*, and no character joins the gallery of English literary figures in the way of Lady Cicely Waynflete, Jack Tanner, Lady Britomart, Higgins and Joan. On the other hand, Shavian dialogue, by means of which Shaw's characters define themselves rather than interact with others, is here perfected, so that this might well be the wittiest of the plays even though it is one of the least euphoric. Everything is paradoxical: the conversation sparkles yet what people are saying is usually sterile; many of the people themselves are miraculously both radiant and moribund; the author's spokesman Shotover is not wholly admirable, and the heroine Ellie Dunn at first seems duller and stupider than everyone else. In addition, apart from the arrival of the burglar in Act II nothing much of a dramatic nature happens until the bombs fall at the end. It is true that Ellie's heart breaks but Shaw is at pains to turn that event into a spiritual awakening with none of the usual theatrical manifestations. Ellie is thus exalted in the middle of Act II (the change is not remotely a dramatic climax), which means that she loses all personal concerns. The only resemblance to Chekhov (to which Shaw draws attention in the full title of the play) is the deliberate futility, but the true 'Russian manner' is made up of tone and mood, while most of Shaw's figures make pointedly pointless assertions. To be sure, the assertions are often shrewd, even penetrating, but they do not fall into a pattern of ideas. Meaning is therefore dislocated. For once in Shaw the audience carries away an impression of a malady rather than its cure.

Shaw does not seem, by the way, to have been cast down by the war. The Preface to this play gives a misleading impression here, to judge from the information in Stanley Weintraub's *Bernard Shaw 1914–1918, Journey to Heartbreak*.[17] We might judge it the best of the prefaces, containing some of Shaw's most winning prose. It is an anti-war piece, of course, written in 1919 and saturated with scorn.

> Shakespeare may have seen a Stratford cottage struck by one of Jove's thunderbolts, and have helped to extinguish the lighted thatch and clear away the bits of the broken chimney. What would he have said if he had seen Ypres as it is now, or returned to Stratford, as French peasants are returning to their homes today, to find the old familiar signpost inscribed 'To Stratford, 1 mile,' and at the end of the mile nothing but some holes in the ground and a fragment of a broken churn here and there? Would not the spectacle of the angry ape endowed with powers of destruction that Jove never pretended to, have beggared even his command of words?

That is the broad attitude of the Preface; not exactly gloom and despair, not pity and a wringing of hands, but rather a contemptuous contrast between man's supposed possibilities and his doings. Shaw was no more sad about the war than he was about anything else. Nor was he without hope of a strange sort, for – to insist once again on this fundamental point – he was confident that nature had far larger and purer purposes than man's and could well do without him.

Thus *Heartbreak House* is not a play of heartbreak in the usual fashion, and certainly not an exhibition of grief over contemporary history. In the play heartbreak is a devastation devoutly to be wished, for the pain of it is quickly followed by the inability to feel pain. And that is more or less what happens to Ellie.

She arrives at Shotover's house, having been invited by his eldest daughter, Hesione Hushabye, and, typically in this slipshod *ménage*, is left to fend for herself. She meets in turn Nurse Guinness, a forthright and at times malicious servant; Captain Shotover himself, an 88-year-old retired adventurer; Lady Utterword, Shotover's younger daughter, elegant, blonde and lovely; Hesione, dark and beautiful, a siren; Mazzini Dunn, her own father, earnest and well mannered; Hector Hushabye, Hesione's husband and a handsome flirt of fifty; Boss Mangan, a drearily self-justifying captain of industry; Randall Utterword, Lady Utterword's brother-in-law and an amiable parasite, and (in Act

I) an old, malevolent burglar who goes out of his way to get caught in all the houses he burgles.

What happens in this uneventful play is worth recalling, since we are apt to forget the plot. In Act I Ellie, having previously become engaged to Boss Mangan out of gratitude for Mangan's financially rescuing her father, discloses a romantic interest to Hesione and promptly learns that her lover is Hesione's philandering husband. As a surprising but plausible result Ellie loses all concern for herself, becoming an assured and decisive woman. In the second act she enters into a spiritual alliance with the ancient captain. Further a burglar is seized and explains that householders always give him money to save the trouble of legal proceedings ('The very burglars can't behave naturally in this house', Mangan declares). In Act III Shotover talks of navigation, and bombs fall upon a nearby rectory and the gravel pit where Mangan and the burglar have fled for safety.

What is the purpose of the play? There is certainly the point, nicely expounded by Margery Morgan, that Mangan represents the empty power of money or, more inclusively, the practical man, the entire getting-and-spending fraternity who use up the creative energies of such as Shotover.[18] In strict Marxian terms Shotover is alienated and Shaw adds his weight to the familiar presumption that a non-acquisitive society, as compared with the centuries of slavery, feudalism and capitalism, would bring forth more and richer works of the imagination.

In this way the irreconcilable opposition of Shotover and Mangan is a reversal of Shaw's thinking at the time of *Major Barbara* when he was determined to unite the man of action with the thinker. Shotover, says Margery Morgan, is 'the undifferentiated energy of life itself morally directed'.[19] I would rather say that that is the absurd 'ideal' of materiality from which Shotover naturally falls away. It is impossible for him to be undifferentiated energy and he is merely an interpreting, evaluating human being, as we all are. It is simply that Shotover regards mankind in general as either oppressive or futile (though Ellie Dunn promises to be something of an exception), while placing himself, as he supposes, at the service of natural energies. Shaw's regular assumption that energy and goodness belong together (or that morality is of a piece with nature) is never seriously challenged by any of his disputatious characters, simply because Shaw never saw it as challengeable. It was his faith, so that morality was beyond question, part of the cosmic order. Neither in writing this play nor at any other time did it occur to him that his vision thus rested entirely upon an unexamined belief and that some thoughtful modern persons (including Ibsen) took exactly the opposite view.

For that reason Shotover is bound to be glad when Mangan and the burglar are killed, since they are the despoilers. They are beyond the pale while everyone else, despite imperfections, nestles within it. The moral categories seem to be: first and lowest, Mangan and the burglar; next (leaving aside the unimportant Nurse Guinness) Shotover's daughters and their agreeable satellites, excluding Ellie Dunn; then Ellie who appears to move between Hesione and Captain Shotover, and finally the Captain himself who is head of the household as well as its moral pinnacle. Ellie is the one mobile character who makes great strides in the course of the play and utters some of the author's own observations. We should be clear about the sheer charm of nearly everyone else; indeed they are exceedingly attractive. The blonde loveliness of Ariadne, Lady Utterword, is meant to dazzle us. For that reason and because she so eloquently defends conventionality her own conventionality is distinctive. She is wittily orthodox, or gives the impression of being so, with the result that, for example, her praise of horses in Act III is almost convincing. Even Shotover thinks there is something to be said for Ariadne's opinion that society is made up of the equestrian classes who live wisely and the neurotic pedestrian majority. (At this point Lady Utterword is lauding aristocratic ways in contrast to the jostling customs of the market place.)

Her sister, Hesione Hushabye, is yet lovelier, specifically more voluptuous and bohemian, a dark bewitching woman who rules her social sphere by a combination of beauty, intelligence and aplomb. She says in Act II that she plays the siren as a means of surviving in this 'cruel, damnable world' and is thus a sorceress who is appealing as a sufferer too – Circe weeping before Ulysses.

Except for Shotover the men are put in the shade by these two women, but they also are charmers. Mazzini Dunn is an exquisitely courteous Utopian dreamer, Hector Hushabye a matinée idol, absurdly yet likeably self-absorbed, and Randall Utterword a libertine of the Shavian variety, in other words a man spellbound by female beauty.

These people then, are more than agreeable and their conversation is clear, epigrammatic and unrealistically candid. Each is a performer playing the role of himself and while that may generally be true of Shaw's figures in all the plays, histrionic effects are here marked for their own sake. The style itself, or the harmony of individual styles, draws attention to itself as part of the message: it is to that degree an *aesthetic* work.

But Shotover and Ellie are set over against the rest, making stylish remarks that surpass style and are in fact among the most memorable in the Shaw canon. 'You can't spare them' [your enemies], Shotover tells Ellie in Act I, 'until you have the power to kill them.' (In this play, let it be noted, Shaw dwells a good deal on the need to kill people.) In Act II Ellie remarks of the breaking of hearts (in short, despair): 'It is the end of happiness and beginning of peace.' (Happiness, it might further be remarked, is regarded as a bad thing, a lotus-eating condition.) 'A man's interest in the world,' Shotover famously asserts – in Act II – 'is only the overflow from his interest in himself.' In youth and age we are wrapped up in ourselves. (Is it not possible, to the contrary, that an alert child is the least self-centred of people?) Ellie says, also in Act II, 'I feel now that there is nothing I could not do because I want nothing.' Shotover replies, 'That's genius.'

Such utterances fall like precious stones among shining fakes. It is not a matter of our agreeing with them but of Shaw's meaning them. Shotover is the leader fading with age and drink while Ellie is his rising disciple, ready to take up the standard, though perhaps still apt to stumble in her own fashion. The 'Chekhovian' characters are not objectionable but fatally beautiful. Their vice or rather their life-failure is their drifting. In contrast, Shotover at least desiderates goals for the human race and Ellie Dunn, one supposes until the very end, must do the same.

But the end turns out to be a qualification or a piece of teasing. There is no sense in puzzling our heads about it, for Shaw gives us no reason why Ellie, the promising youngster, should join the compromising Hesione and Hector in hoping for another zeppelin raid. The chances are that Shaw was merely amusing himself and the finale was composed in a cheerfully sardonic frame of mind. Shaw means, in so far as he means anything clear-cut, that the war could be conducted only by people bent on self-destruction. That prospect excites his characters and he for once has nothing to say but, 'May you enjoy your footling lives until the next bombs fall.'

Heartbreak House is therefore unique among Shaw's plays because in it he recommends neither a goal nor a style of life. We should navigate, but to where? In the past specific abuses were attacked and some aspect of the regular delusion of idealism was unmasked, but here Shaw seems temporarily to have given up. The human race should not stand convicted of local errors since the entire human enterprise is liable to founder through mis-guided procedures.

Assuming *Heartbreak House* to be more than a dramatic exercise in the 'Russian manner', Shaw could logically follow such a sweeping indictment by one of only two possible courses: he could either sink into pessimism (as H. G. Wells later did) or look for some biological improvement in man. Now Shaw's career was built on a formidable degree of a familiar sort of will. His great effort was made in the early eighties when he transformed himself from an uncouth nobody into GBS; when he learned to speak so well and fashioned his unfalteringly confident, self-conquering personality. I am not suggesting that he needed repeatedly to inhibit wayward impulses, far from it, but that conquest of self and others became the norm for him, the very air he breathed. (No one who has recorded impressions of Shaw seems to have heard him speak uncertainly or to yield the smallest point in argument.) In that sense then, Shaw was a man of will and his solution to the problems of mankind necessarily depended on will.

This means in turn that the solution could not be instantaneous – no sudden, irreversible vision that the kingdom of heaven is within or that we should take no thought for the morrow – but on the contrary strenuous and cumulative. Unlike Ibsen's notion of struggle, Shaw's perforce entailed an infinite series of goals. It followed that on being confronted with alternative theories of evolution Shaw embraced neo-Lamarckianism as opposed to neo-Darwinism.

> To them [believers in creative evolution] therefore mankind is by no means played out yet. If the weight-lifter under the trivial stimulus of an athletic competition can 'put up a muscle', it seems reasonable to believe that an equally earnest and convinced philosopher could 'put up a brain'.[20]

Shaw thought of the brain as an animal's problem-solving equipment. That is a quasi-scientific attitude and indeed Shaw's related view of art and culture was to the effect that they are means of resolving man's difficulties. Thus a play was to him neither purely an entertainment nor a piece of self-subsistent beauty but an answer to a social problem. What we think of as the aesthetic features of a play were to Shaw parts of the answer, yet always modes of gilding the pill. Thus beauty was never an end – as it is, for example in G. E. Moore's *Principia Ethica* – but one of the means. It follows that a tragedy of Aeschylus, say, is a primitive and therefore unsatisfactory answer to the real-life difficulties of adultery and murder. This view used to be common enough, but few have held it so candidly and unqualifiedly as Shaw. No one else except Tolstoy has had the audacity to attack Shakespeare on the nevertheless consistent grounds that Shakespeare's plays do not even aim to clear up social and ethical problems.

It may, of course, be true that all works of culture have a didactic and self-assertive purpose; that a fairy tale or a porno-graphic thriller no less than a 'serious' novel gives a view of the world which the author wants his readers to share. Just the same, Shaw made a virtue of undisguised revolutionary didacticism, so that sooner or later he was liable to ask of himself that he expound the basis of his thought, his total world-picture. I do not think it accidental that after *Heartbreak House* he saw no need for a well-made play but a crying need for a 'metabiology', a study of man's development which should postulate ends beyond biology. The result, *Back to Methuselah*, is a series of plays which no one wants to see on the stage but large numbers ought still to want to read. The reason for that 'ought' is that the plays are at once the most thoughtful and the most barren exploration of the pos-sibilities of human progress.

Part I of *Back to Methuselah*, 'In the Beginning', reveals Shaw's assumption to be fundamentally a fantasy of omnipotence. The argument is that man may do whatever he wills and will whatever he imagines. Adam, having been frightened by the sight of a dead fawn, the only dead creature he has seen, learns first from an inner voice and later from the Serpent that he must conquer death. He must immediately counter the certainty of death by making birth. The Serpent's attitude towards every wish-fulfilling dream is 'Why not?' And this Serpent is not the tempter of the Bible, a tempter away from God, but in effect a herald of God, or of man's own divine destiny. In this way Shaw is Luciferian (as he in fact liked to suppose), though Lucifer, meaning the Serpent, is not Satan but the light-bringer. The light of knowledge thus brought to Adam and Eve is an understanding of the omnipotence of the will.

This ancient Serpent remembers Lilith herself and how Lilith in her first avatar (so to speak) overcame death by willing birth.

> She had a mighty will: she strove and strove and willed and willed for more moons than there are leaves on all the trees in the garden. Her pangs were terrible: her groans drove sleep from Eden. (Part I, Act I)

The process by which Lilith so mightily invented birth was first to imagine it, then to will what she had imagined until the miracle came to pass. The procedure, the Serpent tells Eve, is that 'You imagine what you desire; you will what you imagine, and at last you create what you will' (Part I, Act I).

These words of the Serpent are the foundation of Shaw's creed. Desire is not wicked as it is to many people; nor should one desire only the will of God. There is no God as yet, for he is the unreachable end of all our willing. Wickedness is a blocking of the road to God and therefore specifically an interference with our will. We are often intimidated and so become aggressive. Fear and submissiveness form the root of iniquity. Thus Adam fears the uncertainty of the future and is consequently quite uncreative, a simple status quo-ite moralist. Whatever is is right. In this way Shaw explains what he considers to be the psychological source of immorality. It is not a matter of breaking commandments, but of acting or failing to act out of fear. We might ask: What of supposedly fearless predators? Are they not wicked? Shaw's answer to that question is his portrait of Cain.

Cain's bravery is physical rather than moral, since he loves the excitements of the chase, of murder, of his painted and masochistic woman Lua. But what he fears is the visionary individual. For that reason he kills Abel and, like Adam, favours the status quo. Cain's picture of the future is an endless line of victims for an endless succession of warriors. In other words, Shaw thought of destruction as the true (not merely the verbal) antithesis of creation. There are three broad ways: the way of infertile stability (Adam); the way of the hunt (Cain), and the way of eternal creation (Lilith and Eve). The last is the only valid procedure and

Shaw is opposed both to the preserver Adam, and the wrecker Cain. These two both detest genuine progress.

The significant feature of the beginning of Part II, 'The Gospel of the Brothers Barnabas', is that after scores of thousands of years (the time is the early 1920s) nothing significant has happened to homo sapiens. His philosophies, religions and scientific accomplishments have left him spiritually where he was, though his terrain is now the world and a world war has just ended. This section is made up of effective political satire against Lloyd George and Asquith, into which impish motif the next stage in Shaw's argument is woven. There is an election slogan of 'Back to Methuselah', which summarises the gospel of Franklyn and Conrad Barnabas to the effect that man needs to live longer in order to live wisely. If the usual life-span were about three hundred years, politicians, for example, would be unlikely to make silly decisions.

The two politicians listening to this argument think immediately in terms of party advantage and what the electorate will swallow, but the Barnabas brothers point out that nature proceeds in jumps every twenty thousand years or so and maintain that post-Darwin poetry, philosophy and religion all converge on creative evolution. The present task is therefore to will the prolongation of human life to some three hundred years. We must plan our next evolutionary step. Paradoxically (and here is an absurdity in Shaw's own thinking) the real inner will is hidden from the individual. Somehow or other, then, people must arrange to will what they may only will unconsciously. Being aware of this contradiction, Shaw remarks (in the Preface to *Back to Methuselah*) that we shall unconsciously do what is necessary 'out of desire for self-preservation'. As a matter of fact, though, self-preservation seems to be low on man's scale of priorities.

At all events that is the Promethean plan which leads to the supposedly improved condition of man in Part III, 'The Thing Happens'. It is now AD 2170; Chinese and Negroes have ousted a good many white folk from positions of influence; various people have contrived to live for over two centuries, and new schemes are afoot for preventing accidental deaths.

In Part IV, 'Tragedy of An Elderly Gentleman', Shaw juxtaposes 'shortlivers', or persons surviving up to about three score and ten, with 'normal' persons who are hale (and profoundly

rational) for about four times as long. It is AD 3000 in the vicinity
of Galway Bay and here an elderly shortliver of about sixty-five,
having evaded his nurse–guardian, utters his prejudices to a
normal 50-year-old woman. (The normals are divided into
primaries, secondaries and tertiaries, according to their centuries
of life.) In addition to some quite agreeable and wholly justified
fun at the expense of attitudes and phraseology circa 1920, Shaw,
it seems to me, makes two interesting points in this part. First, his
normal woman, unaccountably named Zoo, has an unprecedented impulse to injure or kill in response to the shortliver's
idiocies. Here once again is Shaw's assumption that 'good' people
are driven to wickedness by 'bad' people. Why did it never occur
to him either that the bad actions of bad people might similarly be
caused by frustration or, better still, that compulsive behaviour,
whether we call it 'good' or 'bad' is simply a sort of weakness?
Secondly, the Elderly Gentleman (so called), after his disturbing
experiences among the normal people can no longer live among
his fellow shortlivers, to whom nothing is real. It seems, then, that
Shaw assumed further that our ideals, our stupidities and our
misdeeds are all consequences of a brief life-span.

(It should be emphasised that in Shaw's eyes culture and
reality were distinct from each other, the former distorting the
latter in some degree though at its best drawing attention to
culture-free moral significances. On the other hand, Ibsen
believed that at least there is no essential difference between life
and fiction, since the thoughts of real people and a storyteller's
characters are governed by the same sort of circumstances.)[21]

The fifth part of *Back to Methuselah*, entitled 'As Far as Thought
can Reach', consists of conversations taking place in AD 31 920.
The classical fashions of Shaw's figures suggest freedom from the
restraints of earlier post-classical periods. Many features of life
have come to seem pointless or just minimally necessary.
Dancing, music, poetry, sex, clothing, eating, sleeping: all these
will be seen as grotesque if we merely contemplate them. Shaw
really had that curious and, to my mind, futile detachment. The
He-Ancients and She-Ancients are barely distinguishable, both
sexes being moreover unattractive and non-individuated. Now
there is only the species and not its unique members. The human
body is a doll, and a fanatical scientist called Pygmalion has
manufactured some human creatures after the old style, in other

words people who make only reflex responses. If you flatter them they smirk; if the woman caresses the man he caresses her.

Art is now viewed as simple wish-fulfilment: it is, says the She-Ancient, a 'magic mirror you make to reflect your invisible dreams in visible pictures'. The Ancients, however, have a 'direct sense of life'. Here once more is that surely invalid distinction, as if art were at best an illustration of the moral law and at worst representation at a 'third remove from reality', as it is in Plato's Republic.[22]

Life itself is a blind force and man must aim to direct it completely. For that reason there must be 'redemption from the flesh', as Lilith finally declares. Shaw regarded the flesh as inessential as well as abhorrent. The Serpent happily prophesies that wisdom and good will come together, for is it not plain that the flesh alone keeps them apart? Above all, the 'whirlpool in pure force' that was the beginning – almost exactly the Chaos described by Hesiod – must be wholly replaced by a 'whirlpool in pure intelligence'. Thus man will be God, informing all creation, and problems will remain only as painless intellectual games.

If *Back to Methuselah* is not a Shavian metaphysics, it points to what such a metaphysics must have been. In the flesh there is no being but only becoming; man is a bridge to God, and God is the spiritual end of all things. Now we can clearly see the basis of Shavian ethics: that alone is ethically good which aids or at least prefigures man's evolutionary advance. The test of the value of an action is to ask oneself if the action will help man's ascent from flesh to spirit. We might remark in passing that other authors do not conceptualise their fundamental assumptions in this fashion and would generally expose themselves to ridicule if they did, no matter how exalted their talents.

It will be best to examine *Saint Joan* with Shaw's underlying beliefs in mind. For this play (first performed in New York in 1923 and first published in 1924) concerns the sort of historical change that makes no essential difference to human life, although the heroine, an agent of the change, lights the way by her character to a 'higher' future. We may never follow her. Joan is not an earnest of such a future but a specimen of what might conceivably be brought about. According to Shaw (and many historians hold roughly the same opinion) Joan helped to produce protestantism and European nationalism. Neither of these can be said to have been a clear advance on the Middle Ages, but Joan played her part by a sort of innocent and solemn inconclasm, the very quality that has a chance of edging mankind upwards.

Joan heeded those voices which only she could hear of St Catherine, St Margaret and the Blessed Michael rather than the counsels of the Church or the plodding wisdom of the army commanders, thus leading the French to some notable victories over the Anglo-Burgundian alliance. So she unwittingly assisted the amalgamation of the Ile de France and the duchies into the nation of France. Whether one is mad or not, Shaw argues in the Preface, depends not upon the provenance of one's ideas but upon their feasibility. Joan was sane because her Voices gave her sound advice. They told her that she could raise the seige of Orleans and crown the Dauphin, deeds improbable for anyone and far-fetched for an illiterate teenage girl. The real Joan supposed she conversed with God by means of her Voices and Shaw's Joan, when told that the Voices are imagination, replies (Scene I), 'Of course. That is how the messages of God come to us.'

Joan is not a wise simpleton, though the matter and manner of her utterances together with her artlessness about power and cruelty relate her to that fictional tradition. Rather she asks pertinent questions and looks for genuine answers without reference to the conventions. Like all Shaw's (and Ibsen's) heroes her first quality is that she stands apart from society. Shaw had in common with Ibsen a belief that the majority is always wrong; that communal notions are by definition false. The solitary individual has a chance of being right – though he might, of course, be simply mad. The signal difference between Ibsen and Shaw is that to the former the individual is destroyed by an unregenerate society and that is his glory, while to the latter the individual, destroyed or not, is society's only hope.

Shaw's Joan, then is unknowingly the herald of the Reformation and the nation-state. She is also, incidentally, a precursor of Shaw. He is 'prefigured', so to speak, in his own Joan. The historical personage helped to destroy feudalism so that after her and others of roughly her independent kind neither noble nor cleric stood between God and his servant. But that was not Joan's intention, for as Shaw portrays her she just finds herself regularly circumventing the priesthood and has no design to weaken the general authority of the Church.

Scenes I and II – there are scenes and an epilogue only, after the manner of a pageant – illustrate Joan's ready mastery of almost everyone she meets. Captain Robert de Baudricourt, his associates and servants are subdued by her unqualified self-assurance when she arrives at the castle of Vancouleurs. Later in Chinon something similar if more complicated befalls various eminent personages including the Dauphin (feeble but Dauphin nonetheless), the Lord Chamberlain and the Archbishop of Rheims. To be exact, some people at Chinon are deeply impressed by Joan while others are merely defeated, but the point is that she gets her own way and holds the centre of the stage; acts with ease and grace as a sort of principal boy around whom others revolve as satellites. This is the effect she always achieves, though she lacks every advantage of birth and education. Shaw insists in the Preface that Joan's father was a 'working farmer', but most scholars believe he was simply a labourer. To be sure, there was a flexibility of social intercourse in the Middle Ages lacking in our own theoretically classless period, but the actual Joan's agreeable freedom of manner with high and low impressed her contemporaries.

The Joan of the play is a likeable eccentric who dresses in men's clothes, stops people from swearing, forms innocent friendships with men, asks and answers the most socially inconvenient questions, is eager, serious and utterly candid and appears to lack sexual desires altogether. Nor is she good-looking but pleasantly plain. (As a matter of fact no one knows what the real Joan looked like.) Her genius – for that is what her capacities amount to – seems to be connected with her utter straightforwardness. She has no social armour and little sense of her own strangeness. Like a clever child unused to adult ways she proposes courses to which others are blinded by custom, anxiety and lust for power.

And that is presumably the way of genius – in science, the arts, warfare, every sphere indeed. The Archbishop of Rheims, who is cleverer than Joan and cleverer than the rest at the castle of Chinon, tells her that she is 'in love with religion' (Scene II). The Archbishop is something of a modern intellectual: he happily foresees a scientific age and believes that any event that creates faith must be classed as a miracle. As in the case of Joan's hallucinatory Voices the value of a happening depends not upon its intrinsic qualities but upon its effects.

Thus Shaw gives us in Joan a genius of profoundly religious temper whose intermittent contact with the 'world', the ways of society, makes her both powerful and vulnerable. The power lies in the intelligent freedom of her thought, an absolute freedom from social constraint and not that reflex defiance of constraint which is but one mode of slavery. Joan's vulnerable quality is her ignorance of the ways of men. She cannot tell how small-minded people feel, how they will long to destroy her.

All this naturally makes Joan a splendid heroine whose quality would be dimmed for us if she had sexual urges, or if she subordinated herself to them. Joan is a comrade, a 'good fellow', a keen soldier, a friendly face across a camp fire. And yet her womanliness, in other words her sexuality, is not a matter of indifference but the basis of her appeal. Like any principal boy or like any dashing fictional heroine who actually fights or defies her captors, Joan's gender is important because it is muted. The very unobtrusiveness of Joan's femaleness in her circumstances (talking to soldiers, arguing in the Bishop's court at Rouen, always the one woman among men) is an aspect of her curious appeal.

And Joan who is in love with religion is also in love with war, as Dunois tells her when, in Scene III, they talk on the banks of the Loire. She is religious in the sense in which death is not fearsome and fighting practically consists of the zest of sword-play, the smell of earth and blood, the fires, the shouts, even the screams; the sheer medley of rich sensations. The warlike Christianity of the Middle Ages was presumably connected with belief in an after life, as modern pacifist Christianity suggests an absolute and perhaps despairing attachment to this world.

The characterisation of Joan as a martial saint – a saint because of her unquestioning faith, not her works – naturally takes place in a worldly political sphere represented chiefly by Peter Cauchon, Bishop of Beauvais, and the Earl of Warwick. Both these able men recognise the danger to their sort from Joan's healthy innocence, yet we do not lack sympathy even with them.

In Scene IV, in the English camp, the Earl of Warwick talks with the Chaplain John de Stogumber and with Cauchon. This scene (which recalls *The Devil's Disciple* in that Warwick is a less charming Burgoyne and De Stogumber a more bloodthirsty Major Swindon) is generally supposed to show how Joan's downfall is arranged specifically by a politic English aristocrat and a subtler, more humane French ecclesiastic. It could equally well be argued that Warwick is the more intellectually honest of the two. It is Warwick who understands that if the people of the fiefdoms in England and their counterparts in the French provinces start to think of themselves as respectively Englishmen and Frenchmen, then it is 'goodbye to the authority of their feudal lords, and goodbye to the authority of the Church'. For him it is a simple matter of those in power, nobility and churchmen, joining forces to kill the Maid before she works the ruin of the power-structure. Patriotism in the modern sense is unheard of, since Europe is politically an aggregate of feudal loyalties and ecclesiastically the greater part of Christendom.

But for Cauchon Joan is an instrument of the Prince of Darkness whose grand target is the entire spiritual world. Only the Church stands between Satan and his prize. Joan is not a witch, as Warwick carelessly calls her, but a heretic. For a witch's tricks are all capable of natural explanation while a heretic undermines the Church itself. Cauchon loses his temper when De Stogumber points out that Joan scrupulously follows religious practices. She is monstrously proud, Cauchon says; she communes with God through His dead saints, ignoring the 'accumulated wisdom and knowledge and experience' of the Church (Scene IV).

So far as Warwick is concerned Joan's wishes that kings should reign as 'God's bailiffs' amounts to a 'cunning device to supersede the aristocracy' (Scene IV). It is Warwick who invents the term 'Protestantism' and senses its gathering force. While Cauchon sincerely wants Joan to recant and be saved, Warwick wants simply to dispose of her. All in all Warwick seems to be the clearer of the two and therefore more intellectually competent, if less refined. For Cauchon believes when he says and what he says is philosophically dubious, while Warwick as an aristocratic Machiavel actually has a better grasp of the issues involved.

The fifth scene is shortish but necessary because it shows Joan's increasing isolation. Her friends warn her of the effects of her 'pride', which quality she rightly calls common sense. The Archbishop of Rheims insists that if she sets herself above her spiritual directors the Church will disown her. Ought we not to suppose that Shaw was again thinking of his own protestant self? As we have amply seen, he was never a 'freethinker' because he was bound by a moral vision, but he bypassed every sort of authority and every piece of collective wisdom. Joan does the same: her 'pride' is a higher common sense which must inevitably be overthrown by the lower common sense of prudence, expe-

diency and the impulse towards solidarity. The majority sincerely
regards the Joans of this world (there are many lesser Joans) as
mischievous wretches or else lunatics. Clinging together is
unaffectedly seen as a virtue (loyalty, fellow-feeling) and 'heresy'
of some sort is even today, and perhaps for ever, the one
unforgiveable sin.

So the ground is prepared for the trial scene, possibly not the
cleverest thing in Shaw but the best judged piece of theatre. What
should be noticed especially here, in addition to the obvious
features – the scrupulosity of the judges, Joan's ingenuousness,
the Chaplain's shattered nerves when he sees her burning – is that
the Inquisitor's celebrated speech (a highlight of the whole
Shavian oeuvre) is a disguised hymn to power. I cannot guess how
far Shaw himself realised that fact or if he intended the
Inquisitor's premises to be 'hysterical' – as Louis Crompton
rightly calls them.[23] Purposely or not, the speech makes plain to us
that at all times those who have come to serve a system based on
power (democratically perhaps, well meaningly as a rule) will use
every ounce of intelligence and every refinement of cruelty to
sustain the system. The Inquisitor is an honourable man who only
wants Joan to return to the arms of the Church. Being mortal, he
is in a prison, the world is God's prison and the priests are God's
jailers, so how can she stay free? The Inquisitor will not tolerate
Joan's remaining at large and is therefore, I suggest, in a valid
sense of the word 'lunatic', despite or because of his measured
arguments. But his is a shared lunacy as opposed to the isolated
lunacy of a technically mad person. Joan is utterly alone. The
judges pronounce their imbecilities: she is 'infected with the
leprosy of heresy', a 'member of Satan'. Warwick alone is shrewd
enough to doubt that they have heard the last of her.

The point of the Epilogue is not to soften an otherwise tragic
effect, but to maintain that the essential pattern of Joan's isolation
and defeat must be repeated in future generations and possibly in
all the generations of the race. When Joan's apparition, having
frightened away the living and the dead who have gathered in
King Charles's bedchamber by asking if she should return to life,
finally declares, 'O God that madest this beautiful earth, when
will it be ready to receive Thy saints?' Shaw presumably implies
that some day the earth will be ready. That is the usual
interpretation. But there is no certainty and Joan's wistful tones
might echo for generations in a moral void, then die away. Did

Shaw himself wonder if the time would never be ripe? If he did, then even the evolutionism of *Back to Methuselah* was overthrown and Shaw was at last, after thirty years of authorship, contemplating the very possibility with which Ibsen, in *Catiline*, started out. Even then Shaw's progress would have been anything but futile, since no other author has charted the possibilities of progressionism (pretty well the only modern creed) so enthusiastically, so thoroughly, and towards the end with such an honourable lack of conviction.

Epilogue: Tragedy and Comedy

Tragedy tends to ennoble the spectators, comedy to vulgarise them: that is the distinction which a score of qualifications should not be allowed to blur. A tragedy makes each member of an audience feel more distinguished than usual, while a comedy encourages people to feel cheerfully mediocre. The first attitude may be described as a 'pathos of separation' of oneself from others and the second as a 'pathos of union'. The individual who is temporarily elevated by tragedy senses a kinship between himself and the natural order, while the individual influenced by the comic senses a kinship between himself and society.

Perhaps the two conditions are merely dissimilar but it is hard not to grasp them as antithetical. The responsive spectator of a tragedy suffers along with the tragic hero and by that means is raised up, not cast down. For tragic personages are 'better', as Aristotle puts it, 'than the ordinary man', meaning that they are more impressive or remarkable.[1] The spectator empathises with the hero and thus loses his usual pettiness. Nor does he scorn the continuing pettiness of those around him but simply notes the distinction between himself and them. He certainly does not wish to belong with them, though as likely as not his habitual desire is to be one of the crowd. Now he belongs with, say, Oedipus, whose sufferings have removed him from the generality of men. Perhaps it would be better to say that the spectator is on a par with Oedipus, saluting him across the barren plains of the commonplace.

On the other hand, comedy places the individual spectator back in the crowd, or keeps him there. He is verified as a bumbler or a comic rogue, a being of low value. Everyone else is the same, more or less. The person who would be a hero in a tragedy is unheroic now; Antigone is just a perverse girl. In a comedy we are all poorish specimens and our decency lies in modestly recognising the fact. Note that both tragedy and comedy enable the individual to surpass himself, but the first takes him towards universal nature and the second towards society.

Perhaps George Steiner had this difference in mind when in *The Death of Tragedy* he mentioned the latter-day 'prevailing nervousness, or falling away of the imaginative'.[2] For the nervousness in question causes people to cling together in the absence of religion, as if any price might be paid in order to belong to some group or other. No amount of conflict between nations or groups and no amount of talk about personal uniqueness can cloak the absence today of the specifically tragic hero, the complete recusant whose deeds are awesome. The reason he doesn't exist is not that western society is now tolerant enough to permit almost any attitude, but that no one has the confidence to 'think beyond' mankind. Thus Hamlet thinks beyond mankind and so does Ibsen's Brand. A tragic hero in the 1980s would have to soar above the seeming safety of society. The imagination of his creator, which as Steiner says has 'fallen away', would need to transpose the hero to a larger sphere. Such a creator must think in terms of 'whatsoever is grave and constant in human sufferings', as Joyce's Stephen Dedalus puts it,[3] rather than in terms of local circumstances.

Contrariwise, comedy keeps us in the realm of social reality and for practical purposes assumes that no other reality exists. Therefore no standard may be applied to the characters other than a social standard, which must inevitably lean towards the 'democratic'. In the comic sphere we see with Rosencrantz and Guildenstern not Hamlet, and Hamlet's splendour becomes a pose or at most a reputation. It is not a 'real' quality. Now we cannot understand why anyone ever thought much of Hamlet, who is after all, vacillating, unfriendly, possibly mad and certainly murderous. He is obviously no more virtuous than we are, since we have never killed anyone or forced our fiancées to suicide. The fact that Hamlet is measuring us – mankind as a whole – by grander criteria never occurs to us. In any event such a grand way would simply be *his* way, his peculiarity, of no more value than our own idiosyncrasies.

In *The Birth of Tragedy* Nietzsche writes that to the tragic poets before Euripides 'everything existing was deified, whether good or bad'.[4] It seems then that even the silver bath in which Clytemnestra kills Agamemnon is somehow 'godlike', since it belongs as much as the human characters to a world enhanced by the visiting gods. It is easier for us to grasp that Clytemnestra herself, a natural creature, is deified, despite being an adulteress and a murderer, and that the same is true of her unattractive victim. There is no moral question here since the gods are not moral and in Aeschylean society there is only a morality of custom together with certain magnanimous values. Nevertheless, one god is higher than another, and the highest person is not the purest but the most astounding.

In the late twentieth century the exact opposite is true: nothing is deified. Consequently tragedy has gone, for we do not believe that anyone has spiritual value. Not only is the bath no longer deified, but neither is the killer. Stabbing someone in a bath is now a subject of comedy rather than tragedy: it is a sickening deed, but also farcical, confused, absurd. A murder is simply a social event, a crime but not an impiety, for there is nothing to be pious about.

To a far greater extent than we the Greeks lived in states of terror and joy. Since such words are used loosely today it might be as well to mention that by 'terror' I mean something approaching panic and by 'joy' I mean rapture. In 458 the spectators at the *Oresteia* bolted when the Erinyes appeared.[5] According to Nietzsche the terror of daily Greek life led to beauty, 'as roses break forth from thorny bushes'.[6] That is an insight rather than a documented historical fact, but Greek drama alone bears it out. Only an extremity of horror needs to be controlled in so rigid a form as Greek tragedy, and if today we would stage, for instance, Medea's killing of her children it is because we are less stricken by the deed. The susceptibility to horror in the Greek audience reflected the emotionality of their daily lives and presumably led, as Nietzsche remarked, to the beauty of the tragedies, for example to the beauty of Euripides *Medea*. Now we fancy we understand Medea, that we can 'cure' her, so she is less monstrous. But she is also less monstrously beautiful.

When Aristotle speaks of pity and terror we can be sure that he refers to an intensity and clarity of feelings seldom experienced by adults today – though they are still experienced by imaginative children. The terror was wilder than anything felt by modern audiences and the pity more vehement; really self-pity in fact, rather than commiseration from on high. The celebrated catharsis of emotions really was a quieting of the turbulent soul for a while after living through the performance of tragedy. For we must remember that Greek emotions were never alternatively weakened either by explanation of their workings (the psychology of the emotions) or by promise of better times ahead.

Though it is something of a departure from my argument, it is interesting also to note that in the opinion of Elder Olson, the Greek catharsis could be achieved only by means of an *imitated* world.[7] It could not happen 'in real life', so to speak. For the important aspect was that the emotions should be real while the events inspiring the emotions were unreal and artistically regulated. One was terrified by the masked and heightened actor playing Medea as if he were actually the murderous witch from Colchis, yet only in this mimesis of an action could one's fears be suitably laid to rest. Presumably a Greek did not make our distinction between fiction and reality, since the same emotions were aroused by both, but only through a *properly constructed* fiction could his emotions be both aroused and discharged.

Comedy as a form began with the satyr play following the tragic trilogy: in effect it was a mockery of the splendidly hideous events the spectators had just witnessed. Therefore comedy was from the start derivative, secondary and purposively ignoble.

The ridiculous character in a comedy, says Olson, 'is always inferior . . . he is not merely bad, but bad in a way which renders him worthless or of no account even as bad'.[8] How accurate that is, and how often overlooked. The chief attraction of a comedy for the audience is the opportunity to look down on most of the dramatis personae. If someone on the stage is witty then someone else in the play or far afield is the butt of his wit. As a rule we are taken up not so much with the skill of the epigram as with the inferiority of the victim. Our laughter is a wounding, even a negating of the victim.

Not only that, but comedy removes our cares by making us assume that nothing in the world – not sickness or death or dreadful crime – is actually serious. Ugliness is funny, accidents are funny, every sort of sorrow is a joke. The very people we find formidable in life (bosses, dictators, bullies of all sorts, even torturers) are, it seems, ridiculous. Everything is absurd, so that all our fears and constraints flow away. There is nothing to be afraid of – but, at the same time, there is nothing to respect. In romantic comedy even the serious lovers are scarcely worthy of respect, for everyone is part of the comic totality.

In other words, we too, the audience, having lost fear have lost

self-respect as well. Laughing at the dictator is a way of fending
him off but it scarcely leaves us with a high opinion of ourselves.
We cannot stand outside the comic sphere, remaining honourable
and upright. Naturally we partake of the absurdity and our
fearlessness is also a shamelessness. So in robbing others of worth
we have robbed ourselves as well.

   The comic situation is not essentially different from the tragic,
and the people likewise may be similar in character. The spirit of a
play resides in the perspective from which we view the action.
King Lear, for instance, contains the most potentially ludicrous
happenings and Lear himself might be a clown. I do not mean
that he is more foolish than the Fool, though of course he is, but
that he is potentially more laughable. For the Fool's jokes are not
funny and Lear's deeds are quite ridiculous. Of the predators of
the play Edmund might be excused for taking his bastardy so
seriously but Goneril and Regan could be presented as comically
bad tempered and greedy. Alternatively, of course, we might be
persuaded to regard them as the only sensible persons in the story.
The point is simply that a fresh perspective changes the meaning
of the work: we might then laugh at Lear and share, say, Goneril's
vision of the same events.

   Comedy, says Olson, takes a 'lighthearted view ... by
establishing causes *contrary* to those that would produce a grave or
serious view'.[9] I doubt if it is a question of causes, for it is rather a
question of our valuation of a cause. The causes of everyone's
actions in *King Lear* could remain exactly the same – the king
might yearn for flattery, Goneril and Regan be circumspect and
Cordelia proud – yet all these matters, *together with their consequences*, be topics for amusement. Every piece of psychology in
the play could stay substantially as it is and we would laugh if a
new dramatist wanted us to laugh. Nothing is either solemn or
funny but thinking makes it so.

   For that reason tragedy and comedy are not about different
kinds of happenings or people, but about different values. The
same happening may be tragical–heroic or comical–pedestrian.
The writer of tragedies, Ibsen for example, has one set of values
and such a comic writer as Shaw has another set. There is a
tendency for modern critics to contend that tragedy proper
petered out after Racine, though George Steiner calls *Woyzek* 'the
first real tragedy of low life'[10] and finds a 'conception of tragedy as
waste' in Brecht.[11] My contention is that the classification

'tragedy', has better not contain works so diverse in spirit as the *Oresteia*, *King Lear*, *Mother Courage* and, for the sake of argument, *The Glass Menagerie*. Aeschylus and Sophocles were not protesting about anything because they never imagined that man's intellect could finally 'solve' problems created by his passions. And, of course, they did not remotely conceive a beneficent God and a compensatory heaven. Therefore the lamentation in their plays is genuine lamentation, not protest. For a protest, however despairing in tone, is always founded on a belief that someone, some lord or deity or other powerful force, might eventually come to the protestor's aid.

Ibsen alone in modern times has something of the pre-Christian and pre-Socratic spirit. We misconstrue him and do so symptomatically or *morbidly* if we see him as a writer of social drama with a reformist message. Society in Ibsen is governed by nature; that is the vision of Anne Berg and Johannes Birk as early as *St John's Night* and of Rubek and Irene at the end. It is we not Ibsen who assume that identifiable contemporary causes produce the passions of the characters rather than functioning just as the occasions of those passions. Likewise it is we who suppose the causes and the passions to be in principle remediable.

I have earlier made observations of this sort about Ibsen but I think it worth briefly saying once more that the thrust of Ibsen's feelings was against ordinary hopes and for that matter against the parade of hopelessness which is itself a style of pleading. In *The Greeks* H. D. F. Kitto declares,

> The tragic note which we hear in the *Iliad* and in most of Greek literature was produced by the tension between those two forces, passionate delight in life, and clear apprehension of its unalterable framework.[12]

Ibsen is properly apprehended as one who yearned to share that original Greek vision. He scarcely had a passionate delight in life in Kitto's sense but he wished he had and knew (as we can tell from those of his plays that celebrate vigour) that the post-Renaissance desire for change in society had weakened delight to the level of dreary pleasure. A similar accusation is levelled at Christianity in *Emperor and Galilean*.

At the other extreme Shaw believed altering society to be a source of delight in two senses: first, a revolutionist's occupation might well be pleasurable in itself, and secondly, a new society should by definition contain fewer obstacles to happiness. More than that, Shaw's comedies aimed ultimately at changing not society alone but the biological foundations of human life. He assumed that natural conditions, as experienced by us, depend upon our opinions. Opinion is the basis of every experience, for experiences, after earliest infancy, are always value-laden. Opinion is also the root from which God will develop, since we have the ability to create God ultimately out of our own convictions. Many people implicitly think the same, though they might be disturbed to see their assumption baldly stated.

Shaw's procedure was therefore to use comedy to change opinions. But he was such a dialectician that whenever he saw a faulty notion he assumed that its opposite must be correct. The opposite of a fallacy is not merely a verity but *the* verity, so far as the dialectical mind can discern at any given moment. Thus, if longing for revenge is a psychological straitjacket imposed by romantic fiction, as it is in *Captain Brassbound's Conversion*, then all one has to do is stop seeking revenge. But we might contend that whether one is an avenger or a wiper of the slate is a personal matter: why should there be a general rule and a moralistic prescription for happiness?

The Shavian comic position was that the human will alone can undo the errors of the intellect, *which are errors of defeated will.* Perhaps they are, but Shaw never even glimpsed the true tragic position to the effect that the will must always be exercised and fairly regularly defeated. In this, far from being alone among comic authors, he was continuing the age-old comic tradition which conceives of defeat as humiliation. Next time, or at any rate some day, things will be different.

One of the plainest expositions of the beginnings of comedy seems to be this by Robert Flacelière:

> Like tragedy . . . comedy was born from the cult of Dionysus. It developed out of the wild tumult of the *komos* (from which the word *komoedia* is derived), a burlesque procession in honour of the god of wine, in which cheerful and half-drunk revellers, after a copious feast, roamed about, shouting out coarse jokes at the passers-by.[13]

Such revellers were often enough reacting against a tragic trilogy which they and many others in the crowd had just witnessed, and, in a general way, against life's hardships. So comedy was from the start a reaction. It proclaimed that such dreadful matters as had recently been imitated were not necessarily dreadful; that is, the dread could always be driven away. The wildness of those pioneer 'comedians' was presumably a measure of their horror at the tragedies.

A symptom of comedy, says Bergson, is the 'absence of feeling which usually accompanies laughter'.[14] The feelings of pity and terror proper to tragedy are thus defeated, or held at bay, though as we can tell from the origins in drunken hilarity, such triumph is also an admission of baseness. Bergson's thesis is to the effect that comic action reduces the fully human to a social mode of being. Bergson does not add, would not have wished to add, that human worth is therefore verified by the tragic experience which comedy aims to deny.

I am not concerned with the history of comedy but with its forms since Shaw. As a rule Shaw himself seems anything but helpless. His comedy is a knocking down of the old in order to build the new. He is denying tragedy – in the case of Ibsen by taking the tragedy to be satire. Shaw too, like the Dorian revellers, renders tragic action absurd and so turns pain into pleasure. Instead of seeing the natural joy in the pains of tragedy he finds only misery, masked by idealism.

After the First World War it was apparently impossible for newcomers to write comedy of the hopeful Shavian sort. To the extent that later comedy has been of a new kind it has seemed to be precisely hopeless. Perhaps the most revealing instance of this fresh tendency is the forerunner of all the rest; not a play but a story published as early as 1915, namely Kafka's *The Metamorphosis*. Gregor Samsa, having become a bug overnight, is comic because of the inadequacy of his response to his fate. In terms of values *The Metamorphosis* is at the furthest point from heroic poetry and tragedy. It also exhibits the one constant feature of later comic developments.

For notable comedy has become almost exclusively 'absurdist', which is as much as to say, derived from Kafka. It is important to grasp the metaphysical implications of such works, or rather, the absence of metaphysics which the authors are comically lamenting. Absurd drama is not a set of techniques but a fretting, an anger, a harsh mockery about the vanity of our lives. But we have brought about the vanity by abandoning divine values yet not replacing them with personal judgements of the same hierarchical and discriminatory kind. To put the matter another way, in the eyes of the Church all are equally loved but not all are equally good. Some deeds are certainly worthier than others. The new secular attitude is to the effect that no deed is necessarily worthier than another, except, of course, that discrimination itself is deplorable.

In *Waiting for Godot* Vladimir and Estragon can do almost nothing but wait. They cannot imagine Godot except as the one who may conceivably come. He has no qualities, for if he had, those qualities would form the basis for the values which the tramps manifestly lack. The pair of them may not arrive at their own values. Neither has the confidence to say, 'To me this is admirable, that deplorable.'

When Hugh Kenner calls *Waiting for Godot* a 'comedy of incapacity'[15] he refers to the inability of mind to impinge upon the non-mental universe. However, what matters is that we and Beckett seem unable to live with nothing more than a sense of our own self-made value in the world as it appears to us. It goes without saying that following one's own route is at the opposite pole from the safe and sterile caprices of the present day. That is why Vladimir and Estragon, our representatives, wait for an authoritative voice. Such is the 'absurdist' writer's dilemma, an articulation of the universal dilemma, and we could find illustrations of it in a good proportion of the best writing of the last thirty years.

Harold Pinter said in an interview, 'The thing is not necessarily either true or false; it can be both true and false.'[16] Put another way, it may be neither, for Pinter is here recognising that truth and falsehood are often no more than notions. The important difference, as a matter of fact, is not between true and false, but between admirable and contemptible. And we must draw that distinction without aid or sanction. Something cannot be true because we say it is true, but it is always admirable when we esteem it so.

That is what tragedy anciently declared and Ibsen defiantly rediscovered. Shaw refuted exactly that assertion, aiming at all costs to rid the world of inequality of esteem. Now it seems that if we abolish inequality of esteem we abolish esteem itself and go sneering and giggling into a void. The emptiness will be filled only when we are again sure enough of our own personal values for tragedy to return.

Notes and References

Preface

1. *Shaw and Ibsen: Bernard Shaw's 'The Quintessence of Ibsenism' and Related Writings* ed. and intro. J. L. Wisenthal (Toronto, Buffalo, London: University of Toronto Press, 1979).

1 Stoic Leanings

1. Ibsen's fragment of autobiography was first published in the biography by Henrik Jaeger, *Henrik Ibsen: et livsbillede* (Christiania, 1888). For modern translations see Michael Meyer, *Henrik Ibsen*, Vol. I, *The Making of a Dramatist 1828–1864* (Rupert Hart-Davies, 1967), pp. 22ff and *Ibsen Letters and Speeches*, Evert Sprinchorn, (Macgibbon & Kay, the Colonial Press, Clinton, Massachusetts, 1965), pp. 1ff.
2. See Meyer, p. 20.
3. Ibid., p. 36.
4. Ibid., p. 28.
5. *Peer Gynt*, Act One, The Oxford *Ibsen*, Vol. III, ed. James Walter McFarlane, trans. James Kirkup and Christopher Fry (Oxford University Press, 1972). All quotations from Ibsen's plays are taken from the Oxford editions.
6. The Oxford *Ibsen*, Vol. IV, *The League of Youth*, Act One, ed. and trans. James Walter McFarlane and Graham Orton (Oxford University Press, 1963).
7. The Oxford *Ibsen*, Vol. VI, *The Wild Duck*, Act One, ed. and trans. James Walter McFarlane (Oxford University Press, 1960).
8. Meyer, p. 30.
9. Hans Heiberg, *Ibsen: A Portrait of the Artist*, trans. Joan Tate (George Allen & Unwin, 1969), p. 28.
10. See Heiberg, pp. 28 f.
11. See The Oxford *Ibsen*, Vol. VI, pp. 446f.
12. Ibsen once said in a speech to students at Christiania that 'to write is essentially to see'. *Henrik Ibsen: A Critical Anthology*, ed. James Walter McFarlane (Harmondsworth, Penguin Books, 1970), p. 85.
13. Albert Camus, *The Myth of Sisyphus*, trans. Justin O'Brien (Hamish Hamilton, 1955), p. 27. Originally *Les Mythe de Sisyphe*, (Paris, Gallimard 1942).
14. *Ibsen: Letters and Speeches*. Letter of 9 December 1867 to Bjørnson.
15. Ibid., pp. 9f.

16. Michael Meyer (p. 60) considers it likely that Ibsen was influenced by Shakespeare's *Julius Caesar*. I think he might well have been influenced by *Antony and Cleopatra*.
17. Bergliot Ibsen, the writer's daughter-in-law, so reproduced a description of Suzannah as a young woman. 'But what was most deep-rooted in her nature was, and remained, her sense of the epic in life, her feeling for everything that was intense and powerful like herself, her understanding of the monumental and the tragic.' Meyer, p. 146.

2 The Poet–Dramatist: 'Catiline' to 'Peer Gynt'

1. *The Oxford Ibsen*, Vol. I, *Early Plays*, ed. and trans. James Walter McFarlane and Graham Orton (Oxford University Press, 1970), p. 1.
2. See above, Chapter 1, p. 11.
3. See Chapter III, Book IV of Aristotle's *Ethics* and below p. 72.
4. *Early Plays*, *Catiline*, Act Three, p. 106.
5. *Early Plays*, p. 151. This translation is of the first version of *The Burial Mound*. The second version is translated p. 183 as follows:
    The North shall also rise from out the tomb to purer deeds of spirit on seas of thought.
6. Ibsen at twenty-two told his sister that he wanted fulfilment 'in greatness and in love' and afterwards to die. See below p. 98.
7. Meyer, p. 114ff.
8. It was Henrik Jaeger in his biography, *Henrik Ibsen et livsbillede*, who first pointed out the historical inaccuracies. Harold Clurman in his *Ibsen* Macmillan, 1977) illustrates the modern tendency. He refers to *Lady Inger* as 'an appeal to public patriotism, an effort characteristic of the Norwegian intelligentsia in the 1850s to renew their pride in their national identity and to arouse the people's former vitality' (p. 38). This seems to me to describe Ibsen's subsidiary motive rather than his main one.
9. George Steiner, *The Death of Tragedy* (Faber & Faber, 1961).
10. Georg Brandes, *Henrik Ibsen: A Critical Study*, trans. Jessie Muir (New York, Benjamin Blom, 1964), p. 95 (first published by Macmillan, 1899).
11. Ronald Gray, *Ibsen: A Dissenting View* (Cambridge University Press, 1977).
12. La Rouchefoucauld, *Maxims*, trans. and intro. Leonard Tancock (Harmondsworth, Penguin Books, 1959), p. 119.
13. *Early Plays*, Appendix VII, p. 700.
14. *See Early Plays*, p. 372.
15. Brandes, p. 28.
16. For a discussion of this possibility see *Shaw and Ibsen*. Note also that Ibsen may have taken the basic theme of *Love's Comedy* from a passage in Kierkegaard's *Either-or* and/or from Camilla Collett's novel, *The Sheriff's Daughter*. See Meyer, p. 225 and Brandes, pp. 74f.
17. See above p. 14.
18. For a discussion of the 'schizoid character' see Charles Rycroft's *Anxiety and Neurosis* (Allen Lane, The Penguin Press, 1961), pp. 53f.
19. See above, p. 20.
20. Brandes, p. 24.

21. Harold Clurman, *Ibsen* (Macmillan, New York, 1977, London, 1978), p. 86.
22. The remarks in this paragraph are abbreviations of information given in the following places: The Oxford *Ibsen*, Vol. III, p. 21; F. L. Lucas, *Ibsen and Strindberg*, p. 95; Brandes, p. 34, and Meyer, *Henrik Ibsen*, Vol. 2, *The Farewell to Poetry* 1864–1882 (1971), p. 67.
23. The Oxford *Ibsen*, Vol. III, p. 21. Letter of 28 October 1870.
24. This phrase is often quoted. See The Oxford *Ibsen*, Vol. VI, pp. 446f and below p. 72.

3 'The League of Youth' to 'The Wild Duck'

1. For a fuller account of Ibsen's mood and purposes see the Introduction to The Oxford *Ibsen*, Vol. IV, ed. and trans. James Walter McFarlane and Graham Orton (Oxford University Press, 1963), pp. 2f. Note especially the letter to Bjørnson: 'If I am not a poet, I have nothing to lose. I shall try my hand as a photographer.'
2. The Oxford *Ibsen*, Vol. IV. All translations are from this edition.
3. The Oxford *Ibsen*, Vol. IV. Translations are from this edition.
4. Brandes, p. 74.
5. See The Oxford *Ibsen*, Vol. V, pp. 127–57 and 423–34, where these are reproduced by the editor James Walter McFarlane.
6. For details see Meyer, Vol. I, pp. 46f.
7. Heiberg, p. 43.
8. Meyer, p. 476.
9. For clear expressions of this pervasive view in Lawrence see especially Chapter XV of *The Rainbow* and the essay 'Reflections on the Death of a Porcupine'.
10. This and similar remarks are reproduced in Meyer, Vol. II, p. 263.
11. For a convincing argument that Oswald's illness would now be diagnosed as schizophrenia see Derek Russell Davis's 'A Reappraisal of Ibsen's *Ghosts*', *Family Process*, Volume No. I, 1963.
12. The Oxford *Ibsen*, Vol. V, p. 477. Letter to Sophie Adlersparre, 24 June 1882.
13. Daniel Dervin, *Bernard Shaw: A Psychological Study* (Cranbury, New Jersey, Lewisburg Bucknell University Press, Associated University Presses, 1975), pp. 190f.
14. The Oxford *Ibsen*, Vol. V, p. 468.
15. See above, p. 42.
16. Karl Marx and Frederick Engels, *Collected Works*, Vol. 3, 'On the Jewish Question', (Moscow, Progress Publishers, 1975 and London Laurence and Wishart, 1975), pp. 146ff.
17. For further details see The Oxford *Ibsen*, Vol. VI, trans. and ed. James Walter McFarlane, p. 3.
18. F. I. Lucas, *The Drama of Ibsen and Strindberg* (Cassell, 1962), pp. 179f.
19. M. C. Bradbrook, *Ibsen the Norwegian* (Chatto & Windus, New Edition, 1966), p. 103 (first published, 1946).
20. See Lucas, p. 184.

21. See the 'Notes and Jottings' relevant to *The Wild Duck* in Appendix II of The Oxford *Ibsen*, Vol. VI, pp. 492ff.
22. Ibid., p. 437.
23. Clurman, p. 136.
24. See above, p. 10.
25. The Oxford *Ibsen*, Vol. VI, p. 9.

4 'Rosmersholm' to 'When We Dead Awaken'

1. The Oxford *Ibsen*, Vol. VI, pp. 446f.
2. F. Nietzsche, *Beyond Good and Evil*, Part 9, and *The Ethics of Aristotle*, trans. J. A. K. Thomson, Book 4, Chapter III, (George Allen & Unwin, 1953), pp. 103ff.
3. S. Freud, 'Some Character-Types Met with in Psycho-Analytical Work', *The Complete Psychological Works of Sigmund Freud*, Vol. 14, ed. James Strachey (The Hogarth Press, 1953).
4. The Oxford *Ibsen*, Vol. VII, ed. James Walter McFarlane, trans. Jens Arup, 1966.
5. The Oxford *Ibsen*, p. 449.
6. Ibid., p. 450.
7. See Meyer, Vol. I, p. 130.
8. Quotations are from The Oxford *Ibsen*, Vol. VII.
9. See Heiberg, p. 255.
10. The Oxford *Ibsen*, Vol. VII, p. 482.
11. See above, p. 33.
12. Michael Meyer, *Henrik Ibsen*, Vol. 3, *The Top of a Cold Mountain* 1881–1906 (1971), p. 216n.
13. Quotations are from The Oxford *Ibsen*, Vol. VII.
14. Meyer, Vol. II, p. 305.
15. Meyer, Vol. III, p. 334.
16. Quoted by Heiberg, p. 261.
17. See Meyer, Vol. III, p. 127. Helene Raff was a German painter whom Ibsen met in September 1891 at the time he was so friendly with Emilie Bardach. Both girls were staying at Gossensass. In the autumn Ibsen and Helene renewed their acquaintance in Munich.
18. An extract from this letter is quoted in *Henrick Ibsen: A Critical Anthology* ed. James McFarlane, (Harmondsworth, Penguin Books, 1970), p. 171.
19. In various biographical comments concerned with this play there are references to Ibsen's parents, his sister Hedvig, his brother Nikolai (injured by being dropped on the floor as an infant) and his son Sigurd. But nothing positively resembling a *Little Eyolf* theme has emerged.
20. Quotations are from The Oxford *Ibsen*, Vol. VIII.
21. The Oxford *Ibsen*, Vol. VIII, p. 216.
22. Heiburg, p. 272.
23. Quotations are from The Oxford *Ibsen*, Vol. VIII.
24. Meyer, Vol. III, p. 268.
25. See above, p. 8.
26. Meyer, Vol. I, p. 69.

27. Quotations are from The Oxford *Ibsen*, Vol. VIII.

5 Lilith's Champion

1. Bernard Shaw, *Immaturity*, (Constable, Standard Edition, 1931), p. xi. The novel was written, but not published, in 1879 and the preface was added in 1921.
2. Ibid., p. xxiii.
3. Ibid., p. xiii.
4. 'Who I am and what I think', *Sixteen Self Sketches* (Standard Edition, Constable, 1949), p. 48.
5. Shaw's mother too, for all her strength of character, was not domineering. 'Both my parents, as it happened, were utterly uncoercive,' Shaw remarks in 'My Mother and Her Relations', *Sixteen Self Sketches* (Constable, 1949), p. 10.
6. Shaw in fact said, 'It was to me what the blacking warehouse was to Dickens.' See 'Shame and Wounded Snobbery', *Sixteen Self Sketches*, p. 20.
7. John O'Donovan, 'The First Twenty Years', *The Genius of Shaw* ed. Michael Holroyd (Hodder & Stoughton, 1979), pp. 16ff.
8. 'My Mother and her Relatives', *Sixteen Self Sketches*, p. 12.
9. *Immaturity*, p. xxii.
10. George Bernard Shaw, *London Music in 1888–89* (Constable, 1937), pp. 11f.
11. Ibid., p. 10.
12. Ibid., p. 15.
13. See Preface, *London Music 1888–89*, p. 24.
14. Hesketh Pearson, *Bernard Shaw: His Life and Personality*, (Methuen, 1961), p. 57 (first published by Collins in 1942).
15. See Colin Wilson, *Bernard Shaw: A Reassessment* (Hutchinson, 1969), p. 127.
16. 'My Mother and her Relatives', *Sixteen Self Sketches*, p. 14.
17. *Sixteen Self Sketches*, p. 12.
18. *Back to Methuselah*, Part V, 'As Far As Thought Can Reach'.
19. Preface to *Immaturity*., p. xliii.

6 Shaw's Quintessence

1. Daniel Dervin, *Bernard Shaw: A Psychological Study* (Lewisburg, Bucknell University Press, Associated University Presses, Cranbury, New Jersey, 1975), p. 236.
2. *Shaw and Ibsen*, ed. J. L. Wisenthal (University of Toronto Press, 1979), p. 3.
3. Ibid, p. 42.
4. Bernard Shaw, *Major Critical Essays* (Constable, Standard Edition, 1932), p. 12.
5. Ibid.
6. Ibid., p. 6.
7. Ibid., p. 3.
8. Ibid., p. 19.
9. Ibid., p. 24.
10. Ibid., p. 125.

1. As soon as *The Quintessence of Ibsenism* was published William Archer said that Shaw had 'reduced the poet's intentions and the motives of his characters to a diagrammatic definiteness'. But he added, in my view wrongly, that Shaw's procedure entailed 'a drawback inseparable from expository criticism.' It is not quite inseparable. *Shaw and Ibsen*, p. 17.
2. *Major Critical Essays*, p. 44.
3. See above Chapter 2, p. 42.
4. *Major Critical Essays*, p. 44.
5. Ibid., p. 66.
6. Ibid., p. 73.
7. Ibid., p. 78.
8. *Shaw and Ibsen*, p. 33.
9. *Major Critical Essays*, p. 97.
20. For Ibsen's doubts about Rita Allmers see p. 94.
21. *Majore Critical Essays*, p. 106.
22. Ibid., p. 115.
23. Wilson, p. 45.
24. Ibid., p. 57.
25. *The Pilgrim's Progress*, 'The Author's Apology for His Book'.
26. Ibid.
27. It might be said that this idea had already been implanted by Dickens in his post-1850 novels, but Shaw's exposition of it was plainer and harder to misrepresent.
28. *Back to Methuselah*, Part V.
29. Margery M. Morgan, *The Shavian Playground* (Methuen, 1972), p. 332.
30. Preface to *Immaturity*, p. xx.
31. *Man and Superman*, Act I.
32. Dervin, p. 121.
33. Stanley Weintraub, *Bernard Shaw 1914–1918, Journey to Heartbreak* (Routledge & Kegan Paul, 1973), p. 217.
34. Ibid.
35. Ibid., p. 218.
36. Dervin, p. 298.
37. Morgan, p. 344.

7 Shaw's Plays of the Nineties

1. See *Bernard Shaw: Collected Letters 1874–1897*, ed. Dan H. Laurence (Max Reinhardt, 1965), p. 384.
2. See *Collected Letters*, p. 870.
3. Alan S. Downer, 'Shaw's First Play', *Shaw: Seven Critical Essays*, ed. Norman Rosenblood (Toronto and Buffalo, University of Toronto Press, 1971), p. 9.
4. Blanche's violence with the maid Shaw took from a scene he once witnessed in Wigmore Street. See *Shaw: An Autobiography 1856–1898*, selected by Stanley Weintraub (Max Reinhardt, 1970), p. 26.
5. For mention of Mrs Patterson's nature see *Collected Letters 1874–1897*, p. 151.
6. Maurice Valency, *The Cart and the Trumpet* (New York, Oxford University Press, 1973), p. 106.

7. 'The Quintessence of Ibsenism', *Major Critical Essays*, p. 24.
8. Morgan, p. 81.
9. Valency, p. 127.
10. See Valency, p. 134.
11. Louis Crompton, *Shaw the Dramatist* (University of Nebraska Press, 1969; George Allen & Unwin, 1971), p. 54.
12. See the Preface to *Three Plays for Puritans* (Standard Edition, Constable, 1931), p. xxvi.
13. Ibid., p. xxiv.
14. See above, Chapter 2, p. 20.
15. See 'Notes to Caesar and Cleopatra' in *Three Plays for Puritans* (Constable, 1931), p. 195.
16. Ibid., p. 202.
17. Ibid.

8 Shaw's Later Plays

1. *Collected Letters* 1898–1910, ed. Dan H. Laurence (Max Reinhardt, 1972), p. 20.
2. Chapter 6, p. 129.
3. Morgan, p. 107.
4. Chapter 6, p. 131.
5. *Collected Letters* 1898–1910, p. 444. Letter of 24 August 1904 to Harley Granville Barker.
6. Alfred Turco, Jr, *Shaw's Moral Vision The Self and Salvation* (Cornell University Press, Ithaca and London, 1976), p. 191.
7. *Collected Letters* 1898–1910, pp. 553f. Letter of 5 September 1905 to Archibald Henderson.
8. Ibid., p. 565. See the editor's comment upon the letter of 7 October 1905 to Gilbert Murray.
9. Ibid., p. 582. Letter of 25 November 1905 to Ellen Terry.
10. F. Nietzsche, *Beyond Good and Evil: Prelude to a Philosophy of the Future*, trans. with a commentary by Walter Kaufmann (New York, Vintage Books, Random House, 1966), p. 207.
11. It was in 1902 that the Court Theatre began to stage Murray's translations of Euripides.
12. Valency, p. 313.
13. See above, Chapter 5, p. 112.
14. See Wilson, p. 9.
15. Wilson, pp. 232f.
16. T. S. Eliot, 'Hamlet', *Collected Essays* (Faber & Faber, 1932). 'So far from being Shakespeare's masterpiece, the play is most certainly an artistic failure.'
17. Weintraub, see especially chapter 7.
18. Morgan, pp. 203f.
19. Ibid.
20. Preface to *Back to Methuselah*. 'Creature Evolution'.
21. Thus in *Emperor and Galilean* (Part I, Act 2) Ibsen has Julian speak for him.

'Aren't the mind and will in fiction subject to the same conditions as those in real life?'

22. Plato *The Republic*, trans. and intro. Desmond Lee (Harmondsworth, Penguin Books 1951), Part X, p. 425.
23. Crompton, p. 211.

Epilogue: Tragedy and Comedy

1. Aristotle, *On the Art of Poetry*, trans. Ingram Bywater, preface by Gilbert Murray (Oxford University Press, 1954), p. 57 (first published, 1920).
2. George Steiner, *The Death of Tragedy* (Faber & Faber, 1961), p. 121.
3. James Joyce, *A Portrait of the Artist as a Young man* (Jonathan Cape, 1960), p. 209 (first published, 1916).
4. F. Nietzsche, *The Birth of Tragedy or Hellenism and Pessimism* trans. Wm A. Haussmann, Ph.D. (London, George Allen & Unwin; New York, The Macmillan Company, 1909), p. 33.
5. This is well known but see Robert Flacelière's *A Literary History of Greece*, trans. Douglas Garman (Elek Books, 1964), p. 111. Originally published by Librairie Arthème Fayard, Paris 1962.
6. Nietzsche, p. 35.
7. Elder Olson, *The Theory of Comedy* (Bloomington, Indiana University Press, 1968), p. 35.
8. Ibid., p. 20.
9. Ibid., p. 58.
10. Steiner, p. 274.
11. Ibid., p. 341.
12. H. D. F. Kitto, *The Greeks* (Harmondsworth, Penguin Books, 1977), p. 61 (first published, 1951).
13. Flacelière, pp. 170f.
14. Henri Bergson, *Comedy*, intro. Wylie Sypher (New York, Doubleday, 1956), p. 63.
15. Hugh Kenner, *Flaubert, Joyce and Beckett: The Stoic Comedians* (W. H. Allen, 1964), p. 106.
16. Quoted in Martin Esslin's *Pinter: A Study of His Plays* (Eyre Methuen, 1973), p. 40.

Bibliography

The place of publication is London unless otherwise stated.

Aristotle, *On the Art of Poetry*, trans. Ingram Bywater, pref. Gilbert Murray (Oxford University Press, 1954). First published 1920.

——, *The Ethics of Aristotle*, trans. J. A. K. Thomson (Allen & Unwin, 1953).

Bergson, Henri, 'Laughter', *Comedy*, intro. Wylie Sypher (New York: Doubleday Anchor Books, Doubleday, 1956).

Beyer, Edward, *Ibsen: The Man and his Work*, trans. Marie Weles (A Condor Book, Souvenir Press, E. & A., 1978).

Bradbrook, M. C., *Ibsen The Norwegian: A Revaluation* (Chatto & Windus, 1946).

Brandes, Georg, *Henrik Ibsen: A Critical Study*, trans. Jessie Muir (New York: Benjamin Blom, 1964). First published Macmillan, 1899.

Bunyan, John, *The Pilgrim's Progress* (Faber & Faber, 1947).

Camus, Albert, *The Myth of Sisyphus*, trans. Justin O'Brien (Hamish Hamilton, 1955). *Le Mythe de Sisyphe*, (Paris: Gallimard, 1942).

Clurman, Harold, *Ibsen* (Macmillan: New York, 1977; London, 1978).

Crompton, Louis, *Shaw the Dramatist* (University of Nebraska Press, 1969; London: Allen & Unwin, 1971).

Davis, Derek Russell, 'A Reappraisal of Ibsen's *Ghosts*, 'Family Process', Vol. 2, No. 1, 1963.

Dervin, Daniel, *Bernard Shaw: A Psychological Study* (Lewisburg Bucknell University Press, Associated University Presses, Cranbury, New Jersey, 1975).

Downs, Brian W., *A Study of Six Plays by Ibsen* (Cambridge University Press, 1950).

Egan, Michael (ed.) *Ibsen: The Critical Heritage* (Routledge & Kegan Paul, 1972).

Eliot, T. S., *Collected Essays* (Faber & Faber, 1932).

Esslin, Martin, *Pinter: A Study of His Plays* (Eyre Methuen, 1970 and 1973).

Flacelière, Robert, *A Literary History of Greece*, trans. Douglas Garman (Elek Books, 1964). (Originally published by Librairie Arthème Fayard, Paris, 1962).

Freud, Sigmund, *The Standard Edition of the Complete Psychological Works of Sigmund Freud*, ed. James Strachey, Vol. 14 (The Hogarth Press, 1953).

Heiburg, Hans, *Ibsen: A Portrait of the Artist*, trans. Joan Tate (Allen & Unwin, 1969). First published, Oslo, 1967.

Holroyd, Michael (ed.), *The Genius of Shaw* (Hodder & Stoughton, 1979).

Ibsen, Henrik, *Ibsen*, Vol. 1, *Early Plays*, ed. James Walter McFarlane and Graham Orton (Oxford University Press, 1970).

——, *Ibsen*, Vol. 2, *The Vikings at Helgeland*, *Love's Comedy*, *The Pretenders*, ed. James

Walter McFarlane, trans. Jens Arup, J. W. McFarlane, Evelyn Ramsden, Glynne Wickham (Oxford University Press, 1962).

——, *Ibsen*, Vol. 3, *Brand, Peer Gynt*, ed. James Walter McFarlane, trans. J. Kirkup and C. Fry (Oxford University Press).

——, *Ibsen*, Vol. IV, *The League of Youth, Emperor and Galilean*, ed. and trans. James Walter McFarlane and Graham Orton (Oxford University Press, 1963).

——, *Ibsen*, Vol. V, *Pillars of Society, A Doll's House, Ghosts*, trans. and ed. James Walter McFarlane (Oxford University Press, 1961).

——, *Ibsen*, Vol. VI, *An Enemy of the People, Rosmersholm*, ed. and trans. James Walter McFarlane (Oxford University Press, 1960).

——, *Ibsen*, Vol. VII, *The Lady from the Sea, Hedda Gabler, The Master Builder*, ed. James Walter McFarlane, trans. Jens Arup and J. W. McFarlane (Oxford University Press, 1966).

——, *Ibsen*, Vol. VIII, *Little Eyolf, John Gabriel Borkman, When We Dead Awaken*, ed. and trans. James Walter McFarlane. (OUP, 1977).

——, *Henrik Ibsen: A Critical Anthology*, ed. James Walter McFarlane (Harmondsworth: Penguin Books, 1970).

——, *Ibsen: Letters and Speeches*, ed. Evert Sprinchorn (MacGibbon & Key, The Colonial Press, Clinton, Massachusetts, 1965).

Jaeger, Henrik, *Henrik Ibsen: et livsbillede* (Christiania, 1888).

Jones, John, *On Aristotle and Greek Tragedy* (Chatto & Windus, 1962).

Joyce, James, *A Portrait of the Artist as a Young Man*, (Jonathan Cape, 1960). First published, 1916.

Kenner, Hugh, *Flaubert, Joyce and Beckett: The Stoic Comedians* (W. H. Allen, 1964).

Kitto, H. D. F., *The Greeks* (Harmondsworth: Penguin Books, 1977). First published 1951.

La Rochefoucauld, *Maxims*, trans. and intro. Leonard Tancock (Harmondsworth: Penguin Books, 1959).

Lucas, F. L., *Ibsen and Strindberg* (Cassell, 1962).

Marx, Karl and Engels, Frederick, *Collected Works*, Vol. 3 (Moscow: Progress Publishers, 1975; London: Lawrence Wishart, 1975).

Meyer, Michael, *Henrik Ibsen*, Vol. 1 *The Making of a Dramatist 1828–1864* (Rupert Hart-Davis, 1967).

——, *Henrik Ibsen*, Vol. 2 *The Farewell to Poetry 1864–1882* (Rupert Hart-Davis, 1971).

——, *Henrik Ibsen*, Vol. 3 *The Top of a Cold Mountain 1881–1906* (Rupert Hart-Davis, 1971).

Morgan, Margery M., *The Shavian Playground* (Methuen, 1972).

Nietzsche, F., *Beyond Good and Evil*, trans. with commentary by Walter Kaufmann (New York: Vintage Books, Random House, 1966).

——, *The Birth of Tragedy* or *Hellenism and Pessimism*, trans. Wm A. Haussmann, Ph.D. (London: George Allen & Unwin; New York: The Macmillan Company, 1923). First published in English 1909.

Olson, Elder, *The Theory of Comedy* (Bloomington, Indiana and London: Indiana University Press, 1968).

Pearson, Hesketh, *Bernard Shaw: His Life and Personality* (Collins, 1942; Methuen, 1961).

Plato, *The Republic*, trans. and intro. Desmond Lee (Harmondsworth: Penguin Books, 1974).

Rosenblood, Norman, *Shaw: Seven Critical Essays* (Toronto and Buffalo: University of Toronto Press, 1971).

Rycroft, Charles, *Anxiety and Neurosis* (Allen Lane, The Penguin Press, 1961).

Shaw, Bernard
   The Standard Edition of Shaw's plays, published by Constable, and the Bodley Head edition are the sources for quotations and references in this book. The following is an alphabetical list of the plays discussed, together with dates when the plays were completed.

Arms and the Man 1894
Back to Methuselah 1920
Caesar and Cleopatra 1898
Candida 1895
Captain Brassbound's Conversion 1899
The Devil's Disciple 1897
Heartbreak House 1917
John Bull's Other Island 1904
Major Barbara 1905
The Man of Destiny 1895
Man and Superman 1903
Mrs Warren's Profession 1894
The Philanderer 1893
Pygmalion 1913
Saint Joan 1923
You Never Can Tell 1896
Widowers' Houses 1892

Immaturity (Standard Edition, Constable, 1931).
London Music in 1888–89 As heard by Corno Di Bassetto (Standard Edition, Constable, 1937).
Major Critical Essays (Standard Edition, Constable, 1932).
Sixteen Self Sketches (Standard Edition, Constable, 1949).
Collected Letters 1874–1897, ed. Dan H. Laurence (Max Reinhardt, 1965).
Collected Letters 1898–1910, ed. Dan H. Laurence (Max Reinhardt, 1972).
The Complete Prefaces of Bernard Shaw (Paul Hamlyn, 1965).

Steiner, George, *The Death of Tragedy* (Faber & Faber, 1961).

Turco, Alfred, Jr, *Shaw's Moral Vision* (Ithaca and London: Cornell University Press, 1976).

Valency, Maurice, *The Cart and the Trumpet: The Plays of Bernard Shaw* (New York: Oxford University Press, 1973).

Weintraub, Stanley, *Bernard Shaw 1914–1918, Journey to Heartbreak* (Routledge & Kegan Paul, 1973).

——, *Shaw: An Autobiography 1856–1898*, selected by Stanley Weintraub (Max Reinhardt, 1969).

Wilson, Colin, *Bernard Shaw: A Reassessment* (Hutchinson, 1969).

Wisenthal, J. L. (ed.) *Shaw and Ibsen: Bernard Shaw's 'The Quintessence of Ibsenism' and Related Writings* (Toronto, Buffalo, London: University of Toronto Press, 1979).

Index